The New American Regionalism

To my wife Gabriele

The New American Regionalism

Heinz G. Preusse

Eberhard-Karls University
Tuebingen, Germany

Edward Elgar
Cheltenham, UK • Northampton, MA, USA

Published by
Edward Elgar Publishing Limited
Glensanda House
Montpellier Parade
Cheltenham
Glos GL50 1UA
UK

Edward Elgar Publishing, Inc.
136 West Street
Suite 202
Northampton
Massachusetts 01060
USA

A catalogue record for this book
is available from the British Library

Library of Congress Cataloguing in Publication Data
Preusse, Heinz Gert.
    The new American regionalism / Heinz G. Preusse.
        p. cm.
    Includes bibliographical references and index.
    1. America—Economic integration. 2. Regionalism—America. 3. Free trade—America. 4. Canada. Treaties, etc. 1992 Oct. 7. 5. MERCOSUR (Organization) 6. Free Trade Area of the Americas (Organization) 7. America—Foreign economic relations. I. Title.
    HC94.P74 2004
    337.1'7—dc22
                                                                            2003064349

ISBN 1 84376 612 4

Printed and bound in Great Britain by MPG Books Ltd, Bodmin, Cornwall

Contents

Figures

Tables

Foreword

Sidney Weintraub

The trade policy models used in the Americas changed in about the mid-1980s. The United States, which until then had generally shunned bilateral agreements, entered into a Free Trade Agreement (FTA) with Canada, its largest trading partner.[1] Canada, which until then had resisted earlier proposals, generated either internally or from the United States, for free trade with the United States, took the initiative in this endeavor. Professor Preusse deals with the motivations that prompted these changes in the two high-income countries of the Americas. For Canada, the principal objective was to assure access in the face of what it feared was incipient protectionism in the United States; and, for the United States, the change was designed not only to cement relations with Canada, but also to prod the member states of the General Agreement on Tariffs and Trade (GATT) into some action in global negotiations. Neither side fully achieved what it then sought, but their FTA was significant in that no two countries trade as much with each other as the United States and Canada, then or subsequently.

Professor Preusse is quite eloquent in his comments on the combined political and economic motivations of regional integration agreements. Entering into bilateral free trade with the United States was seen as a major political issue in Canada. Indeed, after the agreement was negotiated, the parliamentary election of 1988 was fought primarily over the proposed FTA. The leader of the Liberal Party opposed it on the ground that the agreement would infringe on Canada's political sovereignty. In the event, the Conservatives won the election and the agreement went into effect on 1 January 1989.

A few years later, Mexican President Carlos Salinas de Gortari made his own proposal for an FTA with the United States. President Salinas had hoped to attract much investment from Europe, but discovered that the Europeans at that moment were much too engaged with what was happening in Eastern Europe after the Berlin Wall came down in 1989. He then turned to the United States, cautiously at first, suggesting some sectoral agreements, but when these attracted little interest, he proposed a full-fledged FTA. President

George H.W. Bush (the father of the current US president) probably found it impossible to reject this proposal, even if that was the inclination of his main trade advisors. What Salinas was offering, in essence, was a dramatic alteration of Mexico's basic foreign policy of keeping its distance from the United States and instead embracing the opportunity to export to the large potential market next door. Salinas had also concluded that if significant direct investment was not to come from Europe, it would come from the United States under an FTA. Salinas was offering a dramatic transformation in political relations and it would have been folly for the United States not to embrace this.

Salinas was able to suggest an FTA because Mexico had earlier discarded its extreme form of import substitution when the economy collapsed at the end of 1982. Mexico engaged in considerable unilateral shedding of its import barriers, joined the GATT in 1986, a step it had shunned a few years earlier, and concluded that its future development should be export driven rather than export pessimistic. Salinas had concluded, also, that many of Mexico's promising exports competed with those of Canada, particularly in the automotive sector, and this required removing the favored treatment Canada enjoyed from its 1965 auto pact with the United States and the FTA. Professor Preusse explains why Canada felt constrained to enter into trilateral free trade negotiations rather than allow a hub-and-spoke arrangement to emerge under which only the United States had preferential access to its two neighbors. The result was the North American Free Trade Agreement, which went into effect on 1 January 1994.

The rest of the hemisphere – the countries in South America, Central America and the Caribbean – were undergoing their own transformations. The debt crisis was triggered by Mexico's incipient default at the end of 1982 and then reverberated throughout most of Latin America and the Caribbean. The 1980s were horrible years economically in most of these countries, and the hardships led to the paradigm shift in the development model. Chile came first – it had changed its development model earlier under the Pinochet dictatorship – but the others followed, to a greater or lesser degree, after that. By now, some 15 to 20 years later, there is some fatigue with the liberal economic model adopted in most of the hemisphere because the development results have been modest in most countries. There is much discussion of what should follow, but nothing definitive has emerged.[2] There can be no return to the earlier import substitution model and most of the countries are still groping to find the new content.

The 'lost decade' of the 1980s in Latin America refers to the lack of economic growth; indeed, per capita incomes fell in most countries during that decade. Politically, however, the decade was one of considerable progress. Military and dictatorial regimes were discarded in Argentina,

Brazil, Chile and Central America. What emerged instead were fragile democracies, a situation that exists to this day. The authoritarian regime in Mexico did not disappear until the election of 2000, but the foundation for this transformation was laid in the 1980s and subsequently. Indeed, when it seemed that a *golpe* (overthrow of an elected regime) was imminent in Paraguay, the other countries of MERCOSUR intervened to prevent this.

One element of the current model that is unlikely to change is the push for exports and the desire to attract foreign investment, especially direct investment. The example of NAFTA was influential, but so were other developments in the region and in Europe. The form this took, apart from liberal policies lowering import barriers (although, in some cases, these barriers remain relatively high), was the conclusion of subregional integration agreements. Professor Preusse deals with these extensively. His description of the scores of bilateral and plurilateral agreements that have been concluded is 'spaghetti'.[3] The hemisphere is now replete with overlapping bilateral, plurilateral and subregional preferential economic integration agreements, plus combinations of these. Canada's decision to join the NAFTA negotiations was based on its aversion to becoming a spoke in a network of US FTAs, but Canada itself became a hub when it concluded an FTA with Chile. (This hub status for Canada was eliminated when the United States and Chile concluded their own FTA in 2003.) The champion hub countries in the Americas, however, are Mexico and Chile. The United States is playing catchup, as exemplified by the Chile agreement and the intention to conclude an FTA with the Central American Common Market countries. Professor Preusse makes the relevant point that a Free Trade Area of the Americas (FTAA), if concluded, could simplify the spaghetti pattern and replace much of this with a single, hemisphere-wide agreement, with its own rules of origin, dispute settlement arrangement, and perhaps even some regulatory uniformity.

The heart of Professor Preusse's book deals with the two main integration agreements in the Americas, NAFTA and MERCOSUR (the common market of the south comprised of Argentina, Brazil, Paraguay and Uruguay), and the incipient FTAA. The handling of these three cases is masterful, replete with description, data, theoretical analysis and opinion. He calls the current agreements – particularly NAFTA and MERCOSUR –'New Regionalism'. By this he means that the current economic integration agreements are generally 'open' and, in theory at least, devised to expand trade with the outside world and not just internally. These new agreements contrast with the earlier, failed agreements in Latin America designed primarily to expand import substitution by integrating many countries behind high protective barriers.

NAFTA is an FTA and MERCOSUR is set up as a customs union (CU), with aspirations to become a common market. Of the two, NAFTA is not only more important in terms of the trade involved, but it has been far more successful in achieving its objectives.

I will make only a few points about these agreements because the book that follows provides much specificity. NAFTA, as noted above and as Professor Preusse states, began life largely as a political agreement. The members were two developed democracies, one a superpower, and the third, Mexico, an authoritarian developing country. The gamble that was taken was greatest for Mexico in that it had to undertake most of the adaptation. In practice, in its roughly ten years of existence, Mexico has experienced substantial increases in trade, both exports and imports, such that it is now an important trader in value terms. Its trade, however, despite the many FTAs Mexico has concluded, is overwhelmingly with the United States. The value of foreign direct investment (FDI) moving into Mexico, increased once NAFTA was on the table. Professor Preusse concludes that the increase of US FDI in Mexico was more or less in line with increases in US FDI elsewhere. I accept this analysis, but my judgment is that absent the legal contract that was NAFTA, this would not have been accomplished.

Mexico has become a democracy since NAFTA was concluded. Did NAFTA contribute to this? My view is yes, although I can't say how large the contribution was. The end of the state driven model of development epitomized by NAFTA, plus the enormity of two-way trade with the United States amounting to $650 million a day in 2002, made the earlier heavy-handed dirigiste model of running Mexico obsolete. The contacts between Mexico and the United States have multiplied across the board, not just in business relations, but among non-governmental organizations, labor unions, universities and between government officials. 'Distant' neighbors, to use the title of Alan Riding's book, became simply neighbors, without the adjective.

A word about Canada. The big issue when the agreement was under consideration was Canada's fear of sovereignty loss. This issue has disappeared.[4] The Liberal Party, which opposed NAFTA at its birth, has since adopted not just that agreement, but advocates expanding free trade agreements generally in the hemisphere, viz., with Chile and the FTAA.

NAFTA is not necessarily overwhelmingly popular in any of the three countries. In Mexico, the expectation at the outset was that the agreement would be a panacea and cure most of Mexico's ills. It was sold that way, and that hyperbole was a mistake. The agreement has benefited largely northern and central Mexico, but has done little to increase incomes in the poor states of southern Mexico. While most trade moves freely, there have been lapses, such as the failure of the United States to live up to the trucking provisions (discussed by Professor Preusse), and disagreement about what was agreed on sugar. A similar situation exists in Canada in that most trade with the United States moves freely, but there are sectoral problems, such as US restrictions on softwood lumber imports. The main US labor confederation, the American Federation of Labor-Congress of Industrial Organizations (AFL-CIO) has trashed the agreement from day one. Because NAFTA involved free trade with a developing country, with low wages, the cry of the protectionists in the United States when opposing any new agreement is 'No new NAFTAs'.

Having said this, there is little sentiment in any of the three countries to terminate NAFTA. What exists, instead, is a desire for 'NAFTA plus' from Mexico, for a 'big' idea beyond the FTA to strengthen Canada's relations with the United States, and a strong effort by the US government for the near equivalent of NAFTA, i.e., the FTAA, throughout the hemisphere.

The progress of MERCOSUR almost 13 years after it came into existence under the Treaty of Asunción is far more mixed. Some of Professor Preusse's subheadings in his chapter on MERCOSUR reflect this sentiment: 'From integration to disintegration'; 'causes of the weak MERCOSUR performance'. The two leading countries of MERCOSUR, Brazil and Argentina, did not always carry out commitments made, acted independently to impose restrictions on their imports from other MERCOSUR countries, and pursued inconsistent exchange rate regimes, which were costly after Brazil was forced to devalue its currency, the real, in early 1999. The current presidents of these two countries, Luis Inácio 'Lula' da Silva of Brazil and Néstor Kirchner of Argentina, have each stated that their priority is to strengthen MERCOSUR and better coordinate their macroeconomic policies. The commitment to keep MERCOSUR alive, and ostensibly to make it thrive economically, has political as well as economic motives in the desire to keep relations between the two countries close.

Professor Preusse's analysis of the *intra*-industry production and trade strategy used by Brazil and Argentina as the sole basis for augmenting an economic interaction between them, rather than as a complement to *inter*-industrial restructuring, merits careful reading. Intra-industry trade growth as a unique strategy, he says, rests on the existence of sophisticated high income markets in order to flourish. This was the situation in NAFTA, but not in MERCOSUR. As he puts it: '[intra-industry] strategy is thought to be a means to avoid too much inter-industrial restructuring, which is commonly held to be particularly costly'. Because of this, he says, one would hesitate to treat MERCOSUR as a good example of the New Regionalism.

The FTAA, as Professor Preusse makes clear, is a complex project. It seeks to join 34 disparate countries (all the hemispheric countries other than Cuba), some high-income others desperately poor, some tiny and others immense, some major traders and others insignificant in this respect, some with highly educated populations and others with considerable functional illiteracy, and – perhaps most important – countries with different political and cultural heritages. Their structures of protection differ, largely tariff-based in Latin America and the Caribbean, and occult non-tariff-based in the United States. The differences in outlook between the United States, a global hegemon, and Brazil, a regional hegemon, complicate the ability of the two countries to reach agreement.

The FTAA discussions are reaching some moments of truth as the negotiators approach the scheduled deadline for completion, the end of 2004. It is becoming quite clear that the end result – assuming that the FTAA does come into existence, more or less on schedule – will be less comprehensive than originally contemplated. The United States has taken both farm subsidies and trade safeguards (anti-dumping duty procedures) off the table for the FTAA, deferring these issues to the World Trade Organization negotiations. Brazil has indicated it wishes to take intellectual property disciplines off the table in the FTAA. Other countries are wary of investment discussions, or of dealing meaningfully with opening government procurement to external competition, or even of opening too comprehensively issues of trade in a variety of services.

Hemispheric trade issues have changed substantially over the past two decades. The countries of the hemisphere are generally much more open to imports than they were previously, but protectionist sentiment is rising due to disappointment with the results of liberal economic policies. Just about every country seeks to foster its own trade position by means of preferential arrangements and, in a sense, we are witnessing a revival of beggar-thy-neighbor practices, even if in a context different from the 1930s. The United States is picking and choosing its partners in the hemisphere for special treatment, and then seeks to mitigate this bilateralism through the FTAA initiative. All this is taking place in an environment of slow economic growth in most countries of the hemisphere. If growth rates rise, this may ease the protectionist tendencies.

This is the backdrop to Professor Preusse's excellent book. His book is a most worthwhile and stimulating read, certainly for those interested in Western Hemisphere developments.

4 August 2003
Washington, DC

NOTES

1. A Free Trade Agreement had been concluded earlier with Israel in 1985, but this was seen as largely political and with only moderate trade content from the US vantage. The United

States had entered earlier into bilateral agreements with state trading countries of Eastern Europe designed to overcome the general irrelevance of tariffs in influencing imports of those countries. These agreements had trade targets. For the rest, however, the multilateral most-favored-nation principle of the General Agreement on Tariffs and Trade prevailed in trade policy.

2. A book that has attracted much attention in this respect is Pedro-Pablo Kuczynski and John Williamson (2003) (eds), *After the Washington Consensus: Restoring Growth and Reform in Latin America* (Washington, DC: Institute for International Economics).

3. I'm not sure who first used this description. The literature ascribes it to Jagdish Bhagwati, but I first heard the word in the Latin American trade context from Julius Katz, then a senior US trade negotiator.

4. See Denis Stairs (1996), 'The Canadian Dilemma in North America', in Joyce Hoebing, Sidney Weintraub and M. Delal Baer (eds), *NAFTA and Sovereignty: Trade-Offs for Canada, Mexico, and the United States* (Washington, DC: Center for Strategic and International Studies), 1-38.

Acknowledgements

This book is part of a research project that was born in the late 1990s. Apart from expert circles, the regional integration projects in the Americas had not found much attention outside the region at that time. In particular, in a more eastward oriented Europe there was little interest in the broader political, economic and social changes that have shaped the Western Hemisphere throughout this decade. Starting from this observation, I felt the need to study the American process of regional integration more deeply and from a broader perspective than the traditional economic literature on regionalism. I also held that this undertaking would gain in substance by investigating this topic from within the region and by drawing on first-hand information from local strategists, executives and analysts.

Quite a number of persons and institutions have supported this idea. In the first place I would like to emphasize the generous support of the Fritz-Thyssen-Foundation, which financed my extensive travels throughout the hemisphere. Without this support the study could certainly not have been undertaken.

This claim also applies to the German political institutions abroad, which offered me their own valuable knowledge and took care of a lot of organizational work in order to get me in contact with a great number of local professionals. In particular, I would like to emphasize the perfect management of my concerns by:

- the German Embassies in Argentina, Brazil, Canada, Chile, Colombia, Guatemala, Mexico, Peru and Venezuela;
- the offices of the Konrad-Adenauer-Foundation in Argentina, Brazil, Chile, Colombia, Guatemala, Mexico, Peru, Venezuela and the USA (Washington, DC);
- the offices of the Friedrich-Ebert-Foundation in Chile, Colombia, Guatemala, Mexico, Peru, Venezuela and the USA (New York);
- the office of the Friedrich-Naumann-Foundation in Chile and Bolivia.

It is not possible in this context to mention all the helping hands within these institutions personally. However, I especially appreciate the activities of Ambassador Georg Boomgarden (at that time director in charge of the

Latin America policies of the German Government), Dr Wilhelm Hofmeister and Dr Werner Böhler (Konrad-Adenauer-Foundation), and Peter Hengstenberg (Friedrich-Ebert-Foundation).

Last but not least I would like to emphasize the invaluable insights that I obtained from the many government officials, politicians, representatives of trade unions, and academic researchers from 12 countries, who gave me the chance to ask them my questions and to listen to their particular views of American Regionalism. They helped to shape my thinking on the New American Regionalism and greatly improved my understanding of the particular problems of the different regions. One result of this 'brain storming' has been the recognition that the New Regionalism in the Americas is indeed a quite complex new phenomenon that renders traditional economic theories on regionalism, at least partly, obsolete. Instead, it demands an interdisciplinary approach that incorporates both political and economic aspects of regional integration. This study builds on this insight and elaborates on some of the critical points of such a broader approach.

In order to proceed with an investigation like this a qualified crew at home is indispensable. Given my English skills, the highly qualified linguistic assistance of Patrick Avato was of utmost importance for this study to mature. David Bailer and Sebastian Tonn prepared the graphs and tables quite professionally and handled much of the unnamed but important side issues.

Finally, a competent organizational talent, a skillful typist, and a never-frustrated emergency manager are the guarantors of a successful team. Fortunately, Gisela Icks perfectly unites all three talents in one person, thereby constituting the focal point of the whole crew.

Without the strong engagement of all of these people it would have been hard to come up with the results of this project successfully and on time. I warmly appreciate their attention, dedication and patience.

Introduction

In the early 1980s, most of the post World War II preferential trade agreements (PTAs) had failed or stagnated. In Europe, the European Economic Community (EEC) had not much advanced beyond the status of a Customs Union (CU), when Jacques Delors, in his inaugural speech as President of the European Commission, felt urged to launch his vision of 'the Single European Market'. In Asia, only one formal agreement (ASEAN) existed, which, due to the region's intensive reliance on North–South trade, was virtually insignificant. At that time, regionalism did not find many advocates and remained a minor exception to multilateralism.

Just one decade later, the situation had changed substantially. Not only had the idea of European political and economic integration gained momentum again (the 'Single European Market Act' had been realized in 1993, and the creation of a single European currency, the Euro, was about to follow some years later), but, with the formation of the North American Free Trade Agreement (NAFTA) and the Mercado Común del Sur/do Sul (MERCOSUR/SUL) in particular, it had become an important new element of the organization of international relations in the Americas. In the Western Hemisphere, the new wave of regionalism spread most visibly and, because of the involvement of the USA and Canada, it gained much reputation. In fact, this new wave of regionalism not only changed the regional economic relations on this continent, but the relative importance of regionalism on a world scale as well.[1] The New American Regionalism and the ongoing regional integration process worldwide have also changed the deployed concepts of regional integration qualitatively. While traditionally, regional integration agreements had mostly been restricted to the formation of Free Trade Agreements (FTAs) and CUs, thereby testifying their character as basically economic ventures,[2] the modern integration concepts of the 1990s, even when formally pretending a simple FTA, are most often targeted to become 'areas of deeper integration' (Lawrence, 1996). As such they involve a much higher political content than former agreements. In fact, one might argue that the New Regionalism is both political *and* economic. This is also particularly true for the American Regionalism, be it in the North (NAFTA), the South (MERCOSUR, the Andean Community, the Central American Common Market [CACM], CARICOM), or the entire Western Hemisphere, as envisaged in the Free Trade Area of the Americas (FTAA). Last but not least, in as much as Anglo and Latin American countries are involved, the specific cultural dimension of the New American Regionalism should not be ignored.

This volume, though focused on the still important economic aspects of the New Regionalism, follows a broad approach, including some important political and cultural dimensions of the New American Regionalism into the discussion. Chapters One, Two and Three set the theoretical framework. As will be argued in Chapter One, it is important to note that regionalism can be interpreted as evolving out of an interdependent decision-making calculus involving political and economic parameters. Following this thesis, policy-makers will have to decide simultaneously on political and economic costs of regional integration. The outcome of the procedure reflects both, the impact of the relevant local conditions (e.g. the expected changes of the levels of security and economic development and their perception in the public) and the external environment, such as the end of the Cold War and the changing international economic situation. The latter point calls for special attention, since the globalization of the world economy has changed the international relations substantially, thereby altering the external conditions for regionalism.

In fact, the evolving global economy is central to the analysis of the New Regionalism from at least three different standpoints:

1. It forms the external environment, in which the New Regionalism may or may not succeed.
2. It is an important benchmark for the discussion of the welfare effects of regionalism.
3. It may itself become an important cause of the New Regionalism.[3]

Under these conditions it is essential to discuss the New Regionalism with due consideration of the global environment. This will be done in Chapter Two by briefly elaborating on an analytical framework of the internationalization of production and trade. This presentation will be based on the transaction cost approach to the multinational enterprise (MNE) as developed by Buckley and Casson (1976), Dunning (1981), and Caves (1982) among others. I will argue that, given the institutional setting and technical capabilities, the process of economic globalization is a result of rational decisions of national and multinational enterprises. These firms expand in international markets in order to exploit specific and comparative advantages, thereby intensifying trade in goods and services. The trade structures that are evolving out of these activities can easily be traced to the conventional theories of international trade (Ricardo, Heckscher–Ohlin, and intra-industry trade). Following this observation, it will be argued that globalization gives rise to virtually the same benefits from trade, which have been discussed extensively in this literature. Under the specific conditions of the present world economy (internationalization of production), these gains are, in fact, much larger than in a world economy that is strictly confined to trade in goods, because capital arbitrage and technology transfer add to the conventional benefits. Finally, another element of beneficial international arbitrage is (could become) international migration.

In order to better understand the fierce public dispute on globalization, given these benefits, it is necessary to weigh them against the (perceived and real) costs of the expanding international activities. Four groups of costs are prominent in this debate:

1. Increasing international trade and production, by fostering specialization and upgrading of production, causes a more speedy change of economic structures and stands for growing interdependencies between the national economies. While the former puts pressure on capital and labor to adjust, the latter may challenge political sovereignty.
2. International trade and production, by fostering worldwide economic growth and the exchange of goods and services over large distances, draws on scarce natural resources. This observation gives rise to fears that globalization may contribute to increasing environmental degradation.
3. International migration, though clearly beneficial economically may have a number of negative side-effects. Analytically, these effects are close to the adjustment issue, though they are mainly non-economic.
4. Globalization has freed international capital markets and raised capital mobility. This development has given rise to high volatilities of the international financial system and has substantially increased the risk of currency and banking crises (especially in the emerging markets).

It will be argued that these challenges of globalization, though their costs may become quite substantial, are not sufficiently serious to lead to a rejection of the whole concept. On the contrary, on balance, the main problem of globalization is not the costs, which have to be borne by its participants. Rather, the real problem is the performance of those not joining the international community of globalizers. Thus, globalization is not the problem for those who are currently being left behind, but the solution.

Chapter Three discusses the New Regionalism in the light of the global international system. Drawing on the benefit–cost approach the basic question is, whether the (New) Regionalism is appropriate to improve the balance between benefits and costs of the international division of labor as compared to the multilateral system. This question has been extensively discussed from the economic point of view under the 'stepping stone–stumbling block' metaphor. Here the political notion of the New Regionalism as a permanent *third option* between multilateralism and (relatively closed) regional blocks will be introduced and analyzed. I shall argue that the viability of the concept of the New Regionalism will critically depend on its ability to generate economic growth permanently and at a sufficiently high rate. In the theoretical literature on this subject there is currently open dissent concerning the capacity of the New Regionalism to generate sustained growth. Proponents and critics alike offer an array of arguments to either underpin or reject the growth enhancing power of the New Regionalism. Under these conditions, a key to solving the puzzle is empirical evidence. That is, more emphasis will have to be put on asking how the modern regional agreements are actually performing.

Chapters Four, Five and Six will concentrate on exactly this task. They will analyze three distinct regional projects, which are the centerpieces of the New American Regionalism: NAFTA, MERCOSUR and the envisaged FTAA. These three regional agreements are the most important integration projects in the Western Hemisphere and they will most likely shape the future of the Americas – both politically and economically, not to mention the cultural dimension. A more complete analysis of the New American Regionalism would of course have to extend the scope of this book con-siderably to include the Andean Community, the Central American Common Market, CARICOM and others. Even without being able to do this in the given context, I believe that this limited approach, by concentrating on the three core regions, is still able to capture some of the more important facets of the issue.

Chapter Four discusses the case of NAFTA. NAFTA qualifies for the New Regionalism, because it goes beyond a typical FTA in several respects and follows the philosophy of open regionalism. Thus, it is important to know whether the outcome of this regional integration project fits with the expectations on a successful exercise in the New Regionalism. Intra-regionally this would mean that economic growth would have to perform well and that the economic interconnectedness of the three economies would have to increase. Furthermore, distinct new patterns of specialization should be observed.

These theses are analyzed by means of some relatively simple indicators. In order to test for structural change the investigation extends to include three sector studies (apparel, automobiles and parts, and the Maquiladora industries). By and large, one can conclude from this exercise that NAFTA has been a clear economic success. Not only has the internal liberalization process been put forward ahead of the schedule, and tariff protection is at a historically low level now, but it can also be shown that the expected responses of the economic actors to the new structure of incentives are really taking place.

However, there is one caveat to this positive picture. This is the observation of lagging FDI inflows to Mexico in recent years. FDI had been predicted to become the most important growth enhancing factor of NAFTA for Mexico. Thus, if FDI does not pick up again, this might cause distress concerning the future role of this country in the NAFTA.

Externally, the New Regionalism claims openness and WTO compatibility. The treaty does indeed take care of these issues, and NAFTA qualifies as an open regional agreement in a politically meaningful sense. This observation should not obscure the fact that all three countries are far from being 'perfect' free traders.

However, concerns arise from some less visible background developments. These are, first, the apparently changing perceptions of globalization in the American public opinion and the distinct changes of the treatment of trade policy issues in Congress (and, possibly, also in the administration) in the years following the formation of NAFTA. Second, following the de facto standstill of foreign economic policies in the USA in the second half of the 1990s, Canada and Mexico have built up a web of bilateral treaties outside NAFTA that has contributed to the development of highly opaque regional economic relations. Though it is difficult at the moment to give hard proof of a causal link between these developments and the foundation of NAFTA, both are definitely not compatible with the New Regionalism and might, in fact, be a first indication of non-viability of this concept in the longer run.

Chapter Five discusses MERCOSUR. This venture by four developing countries is an ambitious project from different points of view. First, MERCOSUR is thought to become a fully integrated common market (CM), which implies a more demanding integration effort compared to NAFTA. Second, it has also signed up to the concept of open regionalism. Third, implementing openness in MERCOSUR is a much more difficult task compared to NAFTA because the MERCOSUR countries still carry the legacy of the failed import substitution strategy. In fact, integrating and at the same time changing the economic paradigm does not only mean a bold liberalization process, but, perhaps even more importantly, it provokes a complete transformation of the political and economic structures and the correspondent patterns of behavior.

In fact, MERCOSUR already has an upsetting history. After some successful years at the beginning, it was shaken by external and internal crisis and, at the time of writing, was at the brink of disruption. Consequently, the New Regionalism does not find a reliable advocate in the performance of this region. Nevertheless, given the particular situation in the region, it would be premature to take these difficulties as a proof of the opposite. Rather, due to the exceptionally difficult political and economic circumstances in the region, the New Regionalism never really had a chance to work. As will be argued, specific strategic failures such as the so-called intra-industry strategy and the still fragile macroeconomic regimes are pointing to inherent deficits of the opening-up strategies as major explanatory factors of the present crisis of MERCOSUR.

Chapter Six is on the planned FTAA. The very nature of this future oriented chapter implies that the analyst neither has any firm facts on the issue, nor on the definite institutional structure of the treaty, nor on the functioning of the integration process. Under these conditions, any statement on the FTAA is necessarily speculative. In order to deliver some useful information on the state of the affairs and the prospective effects on the FTAA I will elaborate on the character of the envisaged project and identify some critical aspects of the project itself and the particular difficulties of the negotiation process.

It is important to note that the FTAA appears to be as much a political project as an economic one. In fact, the economic task to create an FTA is embedded in an ambitious regional program that neatly resembles the Doha Round agenda of multilateral trade talks – transferred to the regional level. What may be even more important, however, is the political approach on which the economic agenda rests. This political approach aims at a close cooperation on basic political and economic issues, which can be subsumed under two headings:

1. the creation of a sound development concept for the South;
2. the implementation of closer integrated management systems for the so-called spillovers of globalization (drugs traffic, migration, and terrorism in particular).

Both areas of cooperation are highly political (regarding hegemonic and security issues) and, at the same time, touch upon fundamental questions of the economic organization of the national economies. That way, the analytical structure of the FTAA negotiation process resembles the basic model of Chapter One. The fact that this process will most certainly be shaped by the North (the USA) brings in an important cultural dimension: what is at stake, in essence, is the question whether and to what extent the Anglo-protestant social model of the North is prepared to coexist with its Ibero-catholic counterpart of the South.

Following these considerations, I will discuss the cultural, the political and the economic dimension of the prospective FTAA. From this analysis it will be concluded that the FTAA project incorporates a multitude of stumbling blocks so that the present negotiations cannot at all be predicted. There is some hope that the negotiating parties are willing to create a treaty that follows the ideas of the New Regionalism closely. Such a treaty, though not necessarily superior to the multilateral solution, may at least lend support to the positive forces of the New Regionalism and counterweigh the present situation of 'spaghetti bowl regionalism' in the Americas. Unfortunately, a much less desirable outcome is not unlikely. That is, the parties are unable to agree on a sound regional concept and regress to an inherently ambiguous and incomplete FTA, that cannot constitute a reliable basis for a prospering Western Hemisphere. In that case the FTAA threatens to define just another level of sophistication of the existing regional web of bi- and plurilateralisms. The New Regionalism in the Americas, then, would probably not only damage the region but the world economy as a whole.

NOTES

1. At the end of the 1990s, almost every trading nation has been at least a member of one PTA and about 42 percent of world trade took place under preferential and not under most-favoured-nation conditions (Hauser/Zimmermann, 2001, 4).
2. Note, however, that the European integration was aimed at the formation of a political union from early on. The FTA (1957) and the CU (1968) were only meant to be transitional stages on the way to the final goal.
3. It has been argued, for example, that the New Regionalism is essentially a response of the nation state to globalization (Hurrell, 1997, 56, Schirm, 1999, 22).

1. Regionalism between Politics and Economics

Regionalism, though often described in economic terms (Free Trade Agreement etc.) is a phenomenon that goes well beyond economics. It has important links to politics, geography, culture and history. Constructivists, in particular, have stressed 'natural' conditions to be an important though inherently imprecise element of regionalism (Wallace, 1990; Hurrell, 1997, 41). These 'natural' conditions evolve out of geographical, cultural and historical proximity and may provide the 'humus' for regional integration. That is, shared values, intense social communication and similar organizational structures are believed to facilitate the development of common aspirations and mutual identification. These, in turn, make it more likely that a common political culture and consensus about political and economic objectives evolve (Mace/Bélanger, 1999b, 53).

The impact of proximity on the development of 'natural regions' also has empirical relevance. Anderson/Norheim (1993), for example, have demonstrated for the case of Europe that between 1830–1990 the decline of 'imperial trade preferences' following the decolonization has – within a scenario of increasing intra- and extra-regional 'propensity to trade' – contributed to the increase of intra-European trade. Thus, when artificially erected political barriers are removed 'natural' regions begin to recover. In the case of Canada, too, the 'natural' partners hypothesis appears to have intuitive appeal, and in the case of Mexico even historical and cultural differences have been unable to block the development of particularly intensive trade relations with the United States even before the formation of NAFTA.

Political scientists as well as economists tend to accept the relevance of 'proximity' in region building, and this topic is particularly relevant in the context of a future Free Trade Area of the Americas agreement (FTAA) and NAFTA, where at least two such 'natural' areas are planning to unite. This common perception notwithstanding, both politicians and economists point to the preponderance of political and/or economic factors of regionalism respectively and downgrade the natural partners hypothesis from the status of an important independent cause of regionalism to one of a merely stimulating factor. In other words, for regional integration to be initiated a sufficiently high political and/or economic propensity to integrate must exist in advance. Only if this propensity leads to political action, favorable natural conditions may then become a stimulating factor.[1]

1.1   REGIONALISM IN POLITICS

Traditional political (realist) theory has perceived the international system as anarchical in the sense that between sovereign states no commonly agreed enforceable rules exist. Under these conditions and common interests among sovereign states being absent, self-interested politicians (governments) are engaged in rigorous powerpolitical competition – military threat and action included.

Regions, from this point of view, are an anomaly in international politics and will evolve only 'in response to external challenges' (Hurrell, 1997, 47). Increasing economic welfare through successful economic integration, which is the core argument of economic reasoning in favor of regionalism, has no role to play in this concept. Economics, instead, is instrumental to politics and based on mercantilist ideas. That is, the economy is a means of improving the material basis for power politics, and itself follows a power political philosophy. In this concept there is no scope for the discussion and implementation of institutions that are prepared to organize common interests, and harvest its beneficial effects. Consequently, realists interpret European integration, for example, as the outcome of specific international political conditions after World War II, such as the beginning of the Cold War, the decline of political influence of the old colonial powers Great Britain and France, and the preponderant impact of US (hegemonic) pressures to cooperate (in exchange for the supply of military security) (see for example Wallace, 1990).

Likewise, the new wave of regional integration of the 1990s in the Americas is explained by the declining hegemonic power and economic competitiveness of the USA and the changing international structure of power relations after the end of the Cold War.[2] Thus, while the declining hegemon employs regionalism as a tool to strengthen its international position and as a bargaining chip in multilateral negotiations (Uruguay Round), regionalism in Latin America is perceived as a reaction of small (developing) countries to the end of the Cold War (and the disappearing option for less developed countries [LDCs] to bargain between the blocs) and to 'Third Worldism'.

While the systemic perspective of the realist approach (outside in) is useful in identifying a number of important political parameters of the process of regional integration it is clearly insufficient for designing a comprehensive framework for the discussion of the topic. The reasons for these deficiencies are many-sided and cannot be discussed in detail in this context (see for example Hurrell, 1997, 53 ff.). However, one crucial point has to be emphasized. This is the rudimentary role of economics in realist thinking. Indeed (traditional) realists treat international economics not only as simply instrumental to (foreign) politics, but they discuss its impact on welfare predominantly in the light of obscure mercantilist ideas. This deficit has long since been recognized by modern political theorists who explicitly consider the rising economic and political interdependencies in the global international economy as a development that renders naive realist power political views increasingly obsolete (Morse, 1976; Keohane/Nye, 1977; Keohane, 1984).

One strand of this literature, the so-called 'neo-functionalism', has adopted some kind of a counter-position to realism, and attaches extreme importance to the dynamic and self-enforcing effects of economic integration. According to this view, economic integration inevitably leads to policy externalities, which call for collective action. Furthermore, integration provides incentives for the reduction of transaction costs and for the exploitation of intra-regional linkages. All together, the interplay of these forces, which are generated by the initial formation of more open regional markets, exerts pressure on the creation of new and tighter formal and informal inter-state cooperative institutions. These arguments, which have initially been developed by authors who analyzed the European integration process,[3] are presently used to characterize North American regionalism. NAFTA too, according to these ideas, has not been born out of the necessity to move closer to each other (economic links with Canada and Mexico have been very high before). The crucial point is 'rather whether the management of the increasingly complex and dense economic, environmental and societal interdependencies that had emerged over the past forty years should be formalized and institutionalized or left to an ad hoc political bargaining' (Hurrell, 1997, 63). Consequently, the most important deficiency of NAFTA from this point of view is the discontented state of (institutionalized) cooperation beyond the Free Trade Agreement (Weintraub, 1994, 56 ff.; Pastor, 2001).

The main critics of the institutionalist approach argue that it may go too far in its concentration on the economic aspect of integration and be blind on the power political implications of region building. Inspired by these critics, the so-called neo-liberal institutionalists suggest an 'in between' approach that allows for mutual consideration of power political and economic aspects of (regional) integration.[4]

According to this approach changes in the interdependent international economic system (now frequently called global system) that arise as a consequence of technical progress and economic development stimulate mutually reinforcing, ongoing changes of economic and political competition. In that way a dynamic, interdependent political–economic system evolves. Within this framework, governments are dedicated to the realization of two fundamental objectives: first, the pursuit of power as a means to establish security and peace for its people, and, second, the pursuit of economic development as the principle source of wealth. Both objectives are highly interlinked and, therefore, 'in the real world of international relations, most significant issues are simultaneously political and economic' (Keohane, 1984, 22). Both objectives appear to be complementary, too, at a first glance, since security and peace are an essential precondition for economic growth while economic growth is essential for the provision of the material resources to secure peace (see Viner, 1948, 10; Nau, 1995). However, this harmony in objectives does not necessarily hold in the short and medium run, if particular interests of individuals and groups or short-term (short-sighted?) interests of society force governments to drop the 'optimal' long-term strategy in order to serve specific interests.

In fact, according to Keohane, this is a crucial point of political economy: 'The key trade-offs for the US in the 1980s ... as in the late 1940s are not between power and wealth but between long-term power/wealth interests of the state and partial ... or short-term interests ...' (Keohane, 1984, 23). And he adds that 'the US is not the only country that has been unable to formulate long-term goals without making concessions to partial economic interests' (ibid.).

By identifying this potential trade-off between long- and short-term interests, the modern political economy points to a fundamental problem of the political management of modern (democratic) societies but it does not give any precise instruction about how to handle this trade-off. This is because there is no commonly accepted approach to quantifying the costs and benefits of particular strategies nor is there any consensus about the relative importance of power and wealth in the utility function of individuals (and governments), apart from the occasional recognition that the relative impact of economics might have increased with globalization (Hesse/Keppler/ Preusse, 1985; Cooper, 1986).[5]

It does not come as a surprise, therefore, that the discussion of the impact of the increasing (global) interdependencies on regionalism currently is no more than a shopping list, consisting of different scenarios and factors favoring or discarding regionalism (see for example, Hurrell, 1997, 55 ff.). This statement gains even more substance when the discussion of the so-called 'New Regionalism' is considered.

1.2 IS THERE A 'NEW REGIONALISM'?

While globalization has changed the international economic environment for regionalism, regionalism itself may have changed qualitatively. It has been claimed, for example, that recent developments in regional integration in America are so much different from the experience of the 1960s that the term 'New Regionalism' is appropriate in order to differentiate it from the 'Old Regionalism' (Mittelman, 1996; Fawcett, 1997; Mistry, 1999).

One important aspect of this New Regionalism is politics itself, which has found a new and more complex meaning during the 1990s. In order to defend this argument a substantial list of 'new' political developments has been proposed. This list should prove the changing character of regionalism. Hettne for example presents a five-point scenario of differences between the 'old' and the 'new' regionalism (Hettne, 1999, 7 ff.):

1. ... the old regionalism was formed and shaped in a bipolar cold-war context, the new ... in a multipolar world order ... without a clear hegemon.
2. ... the new is a more spontaneous process from within the region and also from below ...
3. The new is open ...
4. The new is a more comprehensive, multi-dimensional process.
5. The new is emerging within a system in which non-state actors are active.

This prescription opens a wide field for the discussion of regionalism. However, it is neither clear whether such a wide definition has any sufficient explanatory power nor is it obvious whether all of these points are really new and relevant to regionalism. Points (2) and (5), for example, may indicate particular aspects of the changing political environment in some of the advanced industrial nations but their direct relevance for the claim of a qualitatively changing New Regionalism is not obvious.[6] Also, for analytical convenience, point (1), the changing bipolar world order may better be treated as an exogenous event, which gave rise to the foundation of new regional agreements rather than as a factor causing regionalism per se to change qualitatively.[7] Finally, the claim that the New Regionalism is an open regionalism is correct, but it is not sufficient to constitute something qualitatively new. Neither the EC nor ASEAN, both dating back to the 'old days' of regionalism, have ever followed a 'closed' economy concept. Nevertheless, openness remains an important point in the discussion, because it becomes increasingly clear that only open regional areas are viable in the longer term (Langhammer, 2003). This point is also particularly important in the context of the new regional experiences in Latin America.

What remains as a genuinely new quality of the New Regionalism is the comprehensiveness and multidimensionality of many of the new agreements. Comprehensiveness and multidimensionality in this context means that the New Regionalism does incorporate such important new aspects as the formation of common markets and even political unions (EU), social and environmental policies and aspects of changing political culture (democracy, human rights). Following this interpretation, the New Regionalism is in fact a synonym for the term 'deeper integration' (see Lawrence, 1996).

MERCOSUR and the Andean Community follow the objective to establish a common market and to promote regional activities beyond trade liberalization. They would, therefore, qualify for this New (deep) Regionalism. And even NAFTA, which is officially no more than a simple Free Trade Agreement (FTA), would have to be included because it contains a number of important political provisions that go beyond the traditional 'preferential trade agreement'(PTA) (Pastor, 2001). A distinct property of the New Regionalism in the Americas, in particular, is that NAFTA and the envisaged Free Trade Area of the Americas (FTAA) embrace both highly developed industrial and economically less developed countries.

Based on these considerations the New Regionalism will be defined as 'a comprehensive multidimensional process including new political and economic objectives beyond trade and investment issues'. These new objectives derive from growing interdependencies, which develop in globalizing markets and from changing aspirations of national policies. The New Regionalism is open in the sense that it is designed as a complement rather than a substitute for multilateralism. In the Americas it ventures to bring together countries of quite different stages of economic development.

In order to incorporate these aspects into an extended analytical framework of regionalism some qualifications of the basic concept of the Old Regionalism are necessary. First, a comprehensive analysis of the New Regionalism must take those fields of national policy into consideration that are not part of conventional trade policy but might shape the contours of regional integration. Figure 1.1 reflects this point by extending the two-tiered framework of foreign policy and international economic policy to incorporate national policies as a third pillar. National policies are classified as those aimed at economic growth (corresponding to the basic objective of international economic policy) and those concerned with the equilibration of societal aspirations (Hettne, 1999). The latter policies may be broken down further into the subcategories 'redistribution,' 'regional and sector policies' and 'other' (embracing environmental policies, migration and human rights).

Next consider foreign policy. In order to catch the essence of the New Regionalism, the initial realist concept of 'security' will have to be broadened

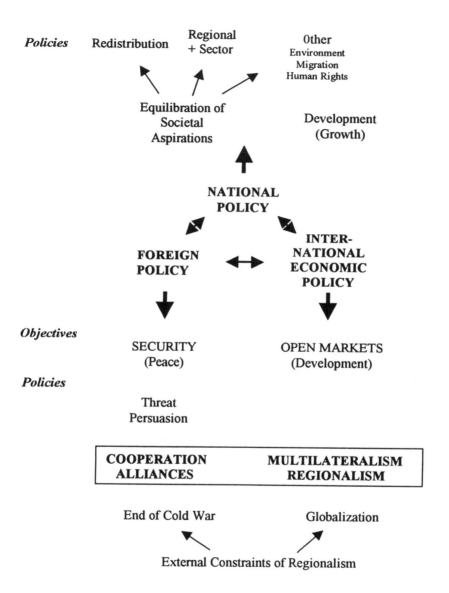

Figure 1.1   The contours of the New Regionalism

to include international political cooperation (Keohane, 1984, Part II, Chapter 4). In this concept, neither anarchy, which provides virtually no incentive for cooperation, nor harmony (classical economic model), which requires no cooperation at all, are adequate prescriptions of the political economic conditions of the international political economy. Rather, in the presence of mutual gains from trade and strong international interdependencies, there will be scope for collective action in order to reap the benefits arising from the exploitation of common interests. As long as there is no realistic chance for the formation of a world government,[8] which would have the power to control and impose internationally binding rules, and enforce them (and hegemonic leadership being absent) international regimes are suggested as a promising alternative to traditional foreign policy. International regimes are defined as 'sets of implicit or explicit principles, rules, norms and decision making procedures' (Ruggie, 1975, 570; Krasner, 1983, 2), which are appropriate to introduce behavioral constraints on (sovereign) nation states 'around which actors' expectations converge' (Krasner, 1983), thereby increasing transparency, reducing uncertainty about the range of expected behavior, and relaxing incentives for moral hazard (Keohane, 1984, 97).

In as much as politicians take the perceived advantages of international regimes into consideration the objective of foreign policy (security) can be tackled not only by using threat and persuasion but also by actively incorporating international cooperation.

While Keohane elaborated his original argument in favor of international cooperation on the basis of the regime theory, which rests on the assumption of sovereign states, it is but one step to incorporate the notion of alliances. Alliances may be defined as specific forms of international cooperation among nation states involving agreements on sovereignty sharing. Regionalism, then, can be understood as a distinct type of alliance. This distinct type is motivated by political and/or economic incentives to cooperate beyond the scope delineated by the non-binding nature of the international regime. In this concept, cooperation and the formation of alliances add to the traditional means of foreign policy. One particular form of alliance is regional (economic) integration.

In order to come to a profound conclusion about regionalism, given any political motivation, the economic benefits of regionalism must be evaluated relatively to the multilateral option. Implicit to this task is the crucial question whether (economic) multilateralism and regionalism are able to coexist and create mutually enhancing benefits or whether they are contradictory, welfare diminishing approaches. The linkages between the political and economic means to secure distinct (international) political objectives are delineated in the lower part of Figure 1.1.

Last but not least, the interplay of political–economic strategies will be constrained by the external environment. There appear to be three elements of the external environment that are crucial for the discussion of present day regionalism: the political changes brought about by the end of the Cold War, globalization, and the growing concern about the ecology. The end of the Cold War has most certainly brought (and is about to bring) a major restructuring in world politics and may in fact dramatically change power political strategies (especially after 11 September). However, the potential repercussions on regionalism are not yet clear and will not be treated in this volume.

Globalization, in turn, is central to the discussion of the New Regionalism. It is in fact the result of the prudent political decision after World War II to accept the superiority of free (open) markets over protectionism. This decision has found its manifestation in the concept of multilateralism and stands for the unprecedented period of economic prosperity (and peace) during about half a century.

To sum up, Figure 1.1 sketches an interdependent system of objectives and means of national and international policies. Within this system the decision against (or in favor of) regionalism is derived from an interdependent calculus. A prominent role is played by the relative advantages of cooperation and alliances in the fields of foreign and international economic policies. The latter have to decide on the benefits of economic multilateralism relative to regionalism, the former on the degree of political cooperation. This 'inner' decision-making procedure will be influenced by two groups of external constraints. First, it is constrained by the international (political and economic) situation, and second, by national political aspirations. Globalization is central to this calculus, because it is a distinct perception of the modern world economy based on multilateralism. Multilateralism, in turn, stands in some contrast to regionalism. In order to cover adequately the potentially tense situation that characterizes globalization in the presence of increasing regionalism, both will be discussed separately in Chapters Two and Three.

1.3 INTEGRATING POLITICS AND ECONOMICS – A BASIC MODEL

In this section a simple political–economic model will be constructed. In this model the government faces two targets: one is political (security) and the other one economic (development). For the matter of simplicity development is taken as equivalent to economic growth. Both objectives might be in conflict under certain conditions, so that the government will have to decide on some combination of means that is appropriate to optimize the combined level of attainment of these objectives (welfare). The model will be outlined in purely qualitative terms and is thought to highlight two basic points of the interdisciplinary decision-making procedure. First, it will be shown that the relative importance of both objectives determines the optimal political strategy. In order to identify this strategy it is essential for the government to have sufficient information on the benefits and costs involved in the implementation of each of these objectives. Second, the model is suitable to unveil the principle advantages and difficulties that arise from such an interdisciplinary decision-making procedure. This model will then be extended to reconsider the regional integration issue.

In order to elaborate the basic argument one might return to the brief discussion of the traditional views on politics and economics in the international system. In this scenario, foreign policy has to manage security (and peace) while international economic policy is applied in order to increase the contribution of international trade to (national) economic growth. From the point of view of realist theory these objectives are pursued by power political concepts that create a winner–loser situation. That is, in general, the political concepts of larger states involve strategies that are thought to improve their own security and growth position, but – as a matter of rule – at the expense of weaker states. The international economic strategy, in this concept, is the mercantilist strategy.

Now suppose that governments get convinced of the merits of mutual gains from a liberal, multilateral international regime, but still maintain the traditional concept of foreign policy. This will create a new situation as far as the potential benefits from foreign policy and international economic policy are concerned. While foreign policy still provides 'security' based on power politics the introduction of the liberal economic model in the field of economics allows a turn to a win–win situation in international trade for all participating countries.[9]

Under these conditions the regionalization–globalization issue must be decided on the basis of an interdependent decision-making procedure. The crucial point in this calculus is the potential trade-off between foreign policy and international economic policy. This trade-off becomes relevant if the merits of multilateralism are judged to be different from the political and the economic point of view. In this case, and if 'high politics' is not given absolute priority over 'low politics',[10] a rational decision-making process must be based on the correct evaluation of the political and economic benefits and costs of multilateralism. Thus, for example, if political intervention in international economics is believed to generate short-run economic benefits (mercantilist strategy), and these benefits are overestimated relative to the long-run gains from non-discriminatory international relations, then ignorance concerning the international preconditions for long-run growth (in the global economy) will bias the calculus of the overall political strategy in favor of intervention and at the expense of economic welfare. Likewise, security issues might dominate economic issues, just because the scope for welfare improvements from the implementation of a cooperative international system is underrated. In this case the opportunity costs of not executing the economic option will be perceived to be too low and the relative benefits of security too high.

The following model may be used to demonstrate the logic of these arguments more clearly. Assume that the government provides security by means of power political intervention (PPI). These interventions may either be purely political (diplomacy, cooperation or threat) or economic (export restrictions in high tech products, rationing of strategic inputs, entire bans of distinct trading operations etc.). For the matter of simplicity it will also be assumed that there is a strictly positive linear relationship between PPI and the level of security. Figure 1.2 outlines this security–PPI relation (POL).

Now suppose that economic development (growth) relies on the provision of an adequate institutional framework that includes an open multilateral (non-discriminatory) trading system (WTO). Such a framework may have been agreed on internationally in order to provide the collective good 'multilateral free trade'. The idea is, that free trade pushes international specialization and exchange and (by providing mutual gains from trade, increasing technology transfer etc.) this has a positive impact on economic growth for all participating countries. Of course, this multilateral approach obliges each single partner country to stay away from any regional, sector or otherwise discriminatory intervention in foreign economic relations (including those that are part of national politics but may have negative repercussions on international competitors).

In this scenario, PPI motivated by security considerations will have a negative impact on economic growth in as much as international economic relations are hindered. This may happen directly by imposing trade restrictions but also indirectly by violating internationally agreed rules, which may provoke retaliatory action from the trading partners. The relation between PPI and economic growth (ECO) will also be supposed to be linear, but it is strictly negative.

Now consider the following cases. First we assume that security considerations have absolute priority because the world is characterized by severe tensions that might even include military threat. Under these conditions a high level of PPI is considered to be indispensable even at the expense of economic growth. That is, security considerations will not be negotiated against economic objectives and economic growth will be sacrificed due to the high level of PPI. This scenario corresponds to case 1 in

SECURITY
GROWTH

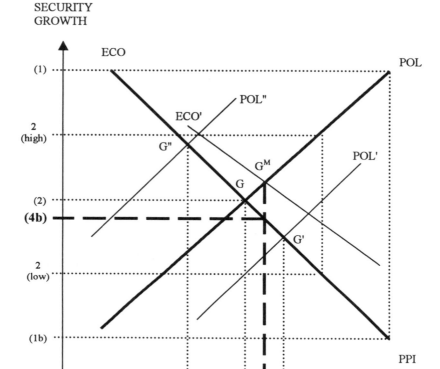

PPI = Level of Power Political Intervention

ECO = Economic Performance

POL = Political Performance

Figure 1.2 Security, economic growth and power political intervention

Figure 1.2. The (non-negotiable) SEC level (1) is achieved at an extremely high level of PPI (1a), which hinders international economic relations. The result is a relatively low level of economic growth (1b).

Now consider a world in which a medium level of political tension forces governments to pay attention to security, but the security issue is not a high priority item. That is, the government may be willing to accept a certain range of security levels between 2 (high) and 2 (low). It is also assumed that the country is able to grade the 'value' of each level of security according to the POL function. In this case, the security level chosen will depend on the opportunity cost of the damage that additional interventions bring into the economic system. This opportunity cost is equal to the loss of economic performance that will be caused by any additional PPI into the economic system. Thus, in Figure 1.2, the government may start at security 2 (high), which allows for economic performance 2 (low). Obviously this country could improve upon its overall welfare performance by lowering the security level (decreasing PPI). Turning left to a less interventionist position would lower the security level along the POL curve (but still satisfy a sufficient security standard) and at the same time increase economic performance along the ECO curve. To the left of G, any security–growth combination still increases economic performance but its benefits would not any more match the costs that arise due to the rising security deficit. G, therefore, is the equilibrium point.

Now consider a changing international security situation. For example, worldwide political tensions are rising so much that the attainment of any given security level must be provided by the allocation of more resources to PPI. This would imply that the POL function shifts to the right (POL') and the new equilibrium is G'. G' indicates a higher lever of intervention at a lower level of both security and economic growth. Likewise, relaxation in international tensions would shift the curve to the left (POL"), thereby allowing for an equilibrium point such as G". At that point a higher security level and improved economic performance go hand in hand, because the need to apply PPI to prepare for political risk decreases.

Now suppose that the position of the POL function is not shifted to the right because of increasing political turmoil, but because incomplete information or bounded rationality make a particular government believe that international threat is increasing. In this case the government would try to realize G' and sacrifice economic growth because of a wrong perception of the international situation. The result would be lower economic growth and an unnecessarily high level of intervention caused by the wrong evaluation of the security situation.

Equally devastating effects will be caused by a wrong perception of the effects of PPI on economic performance. Suppose the original ECO function correctly specifies the relation between PPI and economic performance. Now let there be a government that believes in the virtues of old-fashioned mercantilist ideas. The (perceived) ECO function of such a government would shift to the right and become flatter because the adverse effect of international economic intervention is downgraded.[11] The government then would follow a more interventionist strategy aimed at the perceived equilibrium point G^M. However, if mercantilism turns out to be a strategy that is inferior to free trade, then the true function (ECO) is still relevant (the country's assumption of ECO' is flawed). Consequently, the equilibrium point is still G and not G^M. At the PPI level (4a), then, economic performance drops to (4b).

It is important to emphasize that the model does not present a complete outline of the political–economic decision-making process. In fact, there are quite a number of conceptual challenges for the formulation of an operational in-depth interdisciplinary model of that kind, and these are touching on rather fundamental issues:

1. It is extremely difficult to measure the political and economic benefits and costs on a common scale, because security and economic growth are quite different categories of human well-being. Given the apparent impossibility of defining a meaningful social welfare function even within the narrow economic context a quantification of political issues such as 'security' in terms of economic costs and benefits will probably remain controversial.

2. The criteria for the legitimization of political and economic decisions are different. Individual voting power in (democratic) states stands against the purchasing power of the individual consumer in economics. Also, both follow different weighting procedures ('one man–one vote' in politics versus 'one unit of purchasing power–one vote' in economics) and the organization of majorities follows a different rationale (majority in economic voting can principally be organized by only a limited number of persons accumulating wealth, while in democracies it always needs the majority of the people to be able to exercise political power).

3. The differences of the voting systems in both areas reflect different concepts of distributional justice. Therefore, the relative distribution of political and economic power will influence the definition of economic and political objectives in as much as distributional interests are concerned. When political and economic voting power are changing, so do these objectives.

4. Both majority finding mechanisms are part of a common system of checks and balances. In this system, politics can employ political power in order to discipline economic voting power (competition and

redistribution policies) while purchasing power might be used to influence political power. To complicate things, political and economic coalitions may change the relative importance of economic and political voting power in favor of particular groups of interest. This latter point has particular importance when international economic relations have to be discussed.

Under these conditions, it is not surprising that the integrated political–economic decision-making process threatens to become skewed by ad hoc evaluations, derived from selective information. Mistry qualifies this statement and argues that, within this calculus, a systematic policy bias prevails: 'while economic analysis relies on quantifiable models which may offer "strong" results concerning the gains and costs of regionalism, the same type of rigorous mathematical analysis cannot be undertaken to evaluate other benefits that might flow from investment, policy-coordination, or from security of political arrangements under RIAs [Regional Integration Agreements]' (Mistry, 1999, 145). This argument, though not convincing as far as investment and economic policy coordination are concerned (general equilibrium models have been successfully employed in economics to catch these kind of effects), points to a critical aspect of political decision-making: 'For obvious reasons, the latter [the qualitative-judgmental analysis in political science] is often perceived as being based more on emotion than on reason and placing a premium on rhetorical articulation than on analytical incisiveness' (Mistry 1999). The model presented above is not capable of curing these deficiencies. But it may well be used to improve on the transparency of the decision-making calculus. Also, it may help to discuss the conceptual issues, and to formulate some qualitative statements.

As far as the conceptual issues are concerned it must once again be emphasized that in the long run there is no trade-off between security and economic development. But in the short run such a trade-off may exist, if security and economic development do call for different strategies. The model discusses this latter situation.

Under these conditions the determination of the sensitivities to PPI of both the realization of the political and economic objectives are crucial. And these sensitivities can only be estimated on the basis of a rigorous theoretical (and empirically well founded) analysis of the respective decision-making problem. Thus, for example, Mistry's 'premium on rhetorical articulation' suggests that a given security issue might be abused to overemphasize (or downgrade) the dangers that a nation's security position really faces. An overly high (low) security level will then be scheduled at the expense (in favor) of economic growth.

Likewise, in order to determine the ECO function it is necessary to have a clear vision of the effects of international economic policy on the benefits from trade (globalization). This, in turn, would imply that these benefits can be identified correctly (that is, based on an adequate theoretical concept). As will be argued in this book, the adequate views of the economic effects of globalization derive from the liberal approach to the international division of labor.[12]

From this point of view, the benefits of globalization are relatively high and their realization depends on an open non-discriminatory trade (and investment) regime. The ECO function, therefore, would start at a relatively high level of economic development (growth) when PPI is low, and its slope would be negative and relatively steep. This would be in contrast to the mercantilist approach, which would neither attribute high benefits to international economics nor accept that non-intervention may be much conducive to growth. Consequently, given the security situation, mercantilists would always tend to establish a higher degree of PPI than the liberal calculus would be ready to concede.

This point is important insofar as a bias in the short-run decision on the security–growth trade-off will have an impact on the long-run performance. Consider the case that a realist political regime with clearly mercantilist views on international economic policy realizes a degree of PPI that depresses the economy relative to the growth potential that could have been realized under a more open regime. In the long run such a state would not be able to keep pace economically with the competing countries that use this option. Eventually, the mercantilist strategy would even run out of the resources that have to be employed for (vital) security issues. This scenario is, of course, close to the recent experience of the communist regimes of Eastern Europe and some of the (Latin American) import substituting developing countries.

A bias in decision-making may also emerge, if the political decision-making capacity of a country is deficient so that changes in the international system that would enable more attention to low politics (economics) are not registered or the necessary adjustments are blocked. Suppose, for example, economic openness, which, by causing growing interdependencies, helps to develop common interests in favor of a well functioning international system. Common interests, in turn, provide a safety net against military action (states that trade among each other are not going to war). Likewise, there appears to be a robust 'link' between democracy and peace (Cohen, 1994). Thus when economic openness and democratic governments gain importance on a worldwide scale the most pressing security problems will be downgraded, and this provides scope for a new equilibrium point, which allows for even more openness. Those countries that are able to realize developments of this kind quickly and react to the new opportunities will be able to reap additional economic benefits.

1.4   THE REGIONAL OPTION IN THE WORLD ECONOMY

At this point it is convenient to introduce the option of regional integration. Regionalism may change the political as well as the economic function and it may become an alternative to multilateralism or just be a complementary strategy. Some of the possible consequences of regionalism can be discussed in terms of the basic model.

Regionalism is an inherently discriminatory strategy (see Chapter Three). Therefore, superimposing regional integration agreements upon a multilateral system or even substituting multilateralism for regionalism will inevitably increase the degree of political intervention. Consider this property of regionalism within the boundaries of the above model (Figure 1.3). Starting from the POL_M and ECO_M functions, which define the original relationships of Figure 1.2, we obtain equilibrium point G with the PPI–welfare combination (1,1). Regionalism is assumed to increase the level of PPI from (1) to (2). Ceteris paribus this causes a disequilibrium between political and economic aspirations (G'; G"). If this is all that regionalism can provide it is clearly an inferior strategy that will (should) sooner or later be dismissed. A rationally acting government will then return to multilateralism.

However, there are a number of arguments that do lend support to the thesis that the functional relationships themselves will change due to regionalism, so that a completely new equilibrium point will be obtained. Consider first the case that regional integration is neutral to economic growth. Taking the regional option, then, will provide the same economic benefits as multilateralism but at a higher level of intervention. Under these conditions, the ECO curve will shift to the right ($ECO_M \rightarrow ECO_{R1}$), and a new equilibrium point will be found at G^R. At this point, a higher level of both economic growth and security will be attained at a (slightly) higher level of PPI.

Second, consider the political argument that regional integration will also create a new security situation, because common political activities and institutional provisions do support a common position on security issues and increase the relative strength of all participating countries. This would allow the members of the community to release some PPI without sacrificing security. Under these circumstances the political function will shift to the left (POL_R) and the new equilibrium point will be at T. The level of intervention has further decreased while the political and economic aspirations can be

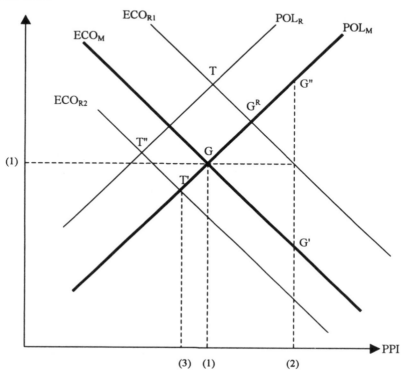

PPI = Level of Power Political Intervention

ECO = Economic Performance

POL = Political Performance

Figure 1.3   Regionalism, multilateralism and power political intervention

served more efficiently than before. This is of course a situation that would make regionalism a particularly appreciable option.

Consider, third, that there is no positive political effect of regionalism, but economically it is inferior to multilateralism. In that case, again, POL_M applies, but the ECO function shifts to the left (ECO_{R2}), so that less economic growth will be generated at any given level of PPI. Now, bear in mind that an additional set of PPI is inherent to regionalism. For the sake of simplicity, this set may be fixed. Then, in order to reach a new equilibrium point T', PPI elsewhere must be lowered to secure the level of intervention at (3). At this PPI level both the overall level of security and the economy would be worse off.

Finally, regional integration might be unfavorable in economic terms but politically desirable. This configuration could be described by a mutual shift of the two curves to the left (POL_R; ECO_{R2}). In this case, two countervailing effects are at work and the eventual result may be a new equilibrium at T''. At this point, the inefficiency of economic regionalism will be compensated by the improvement of security and both the political and the economic objective may be satisfied.

Even without a further discussion of this model it becomes clear that the mutual analysis of two objectives, one political and one economic, complicates the analysis of regionalism considerably. Adding the distinct features of the New Regionalism (Figure 1.1) to this basic framework surely multiplies these difficulties. It is advisable, therefore, to discuss these additional parameters separately, even though they are interdependent in reality. One central point in this context is the global international environment, because regionalism has to prove its viability in competition with multilateralism. Globalization and the New Regionalism will be discussed in more detail in the following chapters.

NOTES

1. It should be added that the forces of proximity are not necessarily conducive to integration, if common history and culture have led to long lived hostility (for example, one important idea behind European integration has indeed been the reconciliation of France and Germany after centuries of hostility). Nor does regional proximity necessarily comprise cultural similarity as the case of former Yugoslavia has demonstrated.

2. Note, however, that the beginning of the decline of hegemonic power of the United States dates back to the 1960s (Keohane, 1984, Chapter 8) and the roots of the New American Regionalism are to be found in the early 1980s (Krueger, 1999, 105 ff.) long before the Soviet Union broke down.

3. Walter Hallstein has been reported to have declared that 'the cunning of the idea' of European integration holds that economic integration is the motor of political integration. Behind this argument lie the dynamic forces that institutionalist ideas build on.

4. In fact, the neo-liberal institutionalist approach is not a 'regional' but a systemic theory that has implications for the analysis of regionalism.
5. I will come back to this point later.
6. The increasing significance of multinational enterprises as non-state actors notwithstanding. MNEs will be better discussed within the framework of globalization (see below).
7. For a discussion of the common factors behind the New Regionalism see Wyatt-Walter, 1997, 74 ff.
8. It is, in fact, doubtful whether such a global government is desirable at all.
9. Applying the liberal-institutional approach to politics would also allow the imposition of a kind of 'positive sum' gain to foreign policy, that is, reaping the benefits of cooperation and the exploitation of common interests (Keohane, 1984). I shall come back to this point later.
10. This case is realistic only under the condition of severe tensions in world politics, but not necessarily in times of peace (see Keohane, 1984).
11. The curve will in fact become infinitely elastic if the government does not recognize any negative effect of PPI on economic performance.
12. I shall elaborate on this concept in the next chapter.

2. Globalization and Multilateralism

Globalization has become a standard term for the characterization of the highly interdependent (multilateral) international economic system that has evolved since the 1970s. Since then this term has mutated to a 'catchword' that needs explanation. The main task of the following paragraphs is to give a brief description of the meaning of globalization in this context, and to provide the theoretical foundations for the discussion of regionalism in a globalized world. This will be done, in a first step, by elaborating on a framework of international production and trade that captures the benefits of global specialization. Afterwards, some major costs of globalization will be briefly discussed.

Globalization is the process of increasing international trade in goods and services complemented by an even more dynamic evolution of international capital flows. More precisely, trade in goods and services has grown at a higher rate than world GDP over the last 50 years. As a consequence, economic openness measured as the relation of exports + imports to GDP has increased. During this process the structure of international trade relations has changed dramatically from trade in primary to trade in manufactured products, from trade in manufactures to trade in services and from final to intermediate products (not to mention intra-firm trade).

Growing openness of international trade has been outpaced by international capital flows. After World War II private capital flows had been close to zero, and it was the primary goal of the International Monetary Fund to provide liquidity for the financing of trade. At the beginning of this century the volume of international transactions in international currencies was about 50 times that of trade in goods and services. Even taking into account that these gross figures overemphasize the true economic impact of capital flows, net international private financial transactions are still a multiple of trade in goods and services in the global economy (Siebert, 1998, 43). In order to gain some more insight into this phenomenon 'portfolio capital' and 'foreign direct investment' (FDI) should be distinguished. While portfolio capital crosses international borders in search of high yield, FDI defines capital flows that are motivated by direct entrepreneurial activities, that is, they include a transfer of technologies, capabilities and management, and they come along with the objective of enforcing the capital owners' business ideas (and bearing its inherent risk). FDI, therefore, is a core indicator of the activities of multinational enterprises (MNEs) and its evolution demonstrates the growing importance of international production. In fact, over the last 35 years, we observe the following hierarchy of the rates of growth (g) of FDI, trade and GDP:

$$g_{FDI} > g_{trade} > g_{GDP} .$$

This hierarchy of rates of growth gave rise to the claim that the internationalization of production has become the backbone of globalization (UNCTC, 1988, Part 1).

2.1   THE BENEFITS OF GLOBALIZATION

Altogether, the shifting patterns of trade and production have brought to life a new and more complex view of the international division of labor. As far as trade is concerned attention has shifted from the mainly inter-industrial division of labor based on so-called Ricardo and Heckscher–Ohlin goods (Hirsch, 1977) to intra-industry trade relations embracing goods and services. These intra-industry trade flows are mainly the result of economies of scale and product differentiation driven by increasingly sophisticated technologies rather than relative differences in factor endowments. Also intra-industry trade tends to induce a converging rather than diverging structure of production between traders (Greenaway/Hine, 1991).

The recognition of the role of technical progress for the creation of new technologies and products has led to the important insight that comparative advantage is no longer given and limited to the simple capital labor dichotomy. Rather it can be created by innovating firms that combine complex sets of factors and technological knowledge in order to gain a competitive edge (Hesse, 1974; Bhagwati, 1982).

Technological progress and its growing importance on a worldwide scale is also a core explanatory factor of internationalization of production. Because of its high and growing significance for both the explanation of trade *and* capital flows it may indeed be interpreted as the missing link in the explanation of the process of globalization. That is, technical progress is the ultimate stimulus of the mutual expansion of international trade and production within a relatively open, multilateral economic environment. Technological progress, in this context, is not confined to the intra-firm innovation of products and production processes. It is also effective in economizing on complementary inputs such as transport costs and costs of information and communication. Last but not least it is a source of efficient organizational and management techniques (Porter, 1991).

In order to incorporate this missing link into a consistent explanation of globalization it is appropriate to reverse the traditional concept of the international division of labor (which usually starts from the discussion of different kinds of trade flows between countries and then considers capital flows as an entirely new phenomenon). Instead, we will ask for the determinants of international production (the decision-making calculus of the MNE) and proceed to the discussion of trade. The starting point will be the transaction cost approach to the MNE as it has been elaborated by Vernon (1971), Buckley/Casson (1976), Dunning (1981), and Caves (1982) among others, and which builds on Steven Hymer's original contribution to the theory of the multinational enterprise (Hymer, 1960 [1976]).

According to this approach MNEs are operating within an environment of innovational competition. They develop innovations (products, process technologies, administrative, logistic and sales capacities etc.) based on exclusive knowledge and/or property rights (patents, licenses). The crucial point is the 'specificity' of the new knowledge that will be generated and employed in the modern enterprise. This knowledge forms the basis for the implementation of strategies aimed at the segmentation of markets and the realization of monopolistic rents. Specific advantages, therefore, are owner-ship advantages (Dunning, 1981), and innovating firms, MNEs in particular, are simply the owners of (teams of) specific advantages (Caves, 1982). On the international market they use their competitive strength to overcome higher transaction costs in foreign markets.

The motivation of innovating firms to operate in foreign markets derives from the fact that specific knowledge has a distinct property of public goods. That is, once this knowledge (a blueprint for example) is publicly known, no one can be excluded from its use. Consequently, once the competitors come to know about it and learn to copy the original technology, in a competitive market the market price will drop to marginal costs and the rent disappears. Thus, a profit maximizing innovating firm must try to recruit as many new consumers as possible within the time period during which the exceptional competitive situation holds. One strategy to maximize sales within a given time schedule is to intensify marketing in order to find as many consumers as possible within a given market, the other one is to broaden the relevant market by internationalization.[1]

According to Hymer's views on the nature and scope of the specific advantages on which MNEs build their competitive lead, these enterprises are fierce monopolists which exploit their dominant position on the international market aggressively and at the expense of less developed countries – a judgment that reflects many traditional concerns about MNEs, especially in

LDCs. At that point the transaction cost approach steps in and investigates more profoundly on the properties of transaction costs in foreign markets. As a result of this analysis a substantially different perception emerges of the competitive situation in which MNEs are operating. In fact, its proponents conclude that transaction costs in foreign markets are rising according to economic, spatial and cultural distance, so that the scope of the MNE to expand its monopolistic strategy in foreign markets is limited. Put differently, in a functioning market, increasing marginal costs will drive firms to expand up to the point where marginal costs meet the price line, that is, they will have to behave like any firm in a competitive market. MNEs, under these conditions, are by no means the fierce monopolists of Hymer's world that abuse unlimited power to conquer markets and which are even ready to threaten sovereign nation states.

The crucial question is, whether markets are indeed functioning sufficiently well to force MNEs to market conformity. Proponents of the transaction cost approach take this for certain. They assure that within the globalizing markets MNEs in manufacturing and services industries, each one equipped with high quality (but differentiated) sets of specific factors, are engaged in fierce competition among each other (a situation quite different from the one that primary producers might have faced occasionally in former times). This competitive situation effectively limits power by cutting any innovational lead within a short period of time.[2] Consequently, a monopoly position resulting from successful innovation will always be transitory and limited to the particular market segment, and it can only be defended by repeated efforts to upgrade and innovate. Thus, both increasing transaction costs in foreign markets and innovating and imitating international competitors with quite similar qualifications are working as a disciplinary force that might effectively limit market power of MNEs.[3] It goes without saying, that a transitory monopolist with its economic power limited to a small market segment, is in a fundamentally different position to the textbook monopolist in static price theory.

From this perspective, even the often proclaimed powerpolitical dominance of MNEs, relative to weak governments in small LDCs needs to be reconsidered. Moran, in his 'theory of obsolescing bargaining' for example, argues that the strength of market power of MNEs relative to the political power of the host country government is changing over time (Moran, 1985). Before an MNE enters the market it is in a relatively comfortable situation and may indeed dictate the entry conditions to its own advantage. However, once the MNE has started to operate from the host country market, sunk costs make a threat to leave the market almost unthinkable and the host country government may use this weakness to improve the balance between benefits and costs from its own point of view.

Still another aspect of the discussion of internationalization of production is that MNEs also operate in foreign markets in order to take advantage of local conditions such as cheap labor, low taxes and specific (low) environmental provisions etc. While early analyses of this option have been based on the framework of the product cycle,[4] a discussion in terms of the transaction cost approach is again more fruitful. In order to explain international production caused by (production) cost considerations it has to be recognized that MNEs may create a competitive advantage from the internalization of particular parts of the value-added chain. That is, rather than buying intermediate products from independent customers, these intermediates are produced and traded within the firm. The implicit economic rationale for this strategy of vertical integration is that, in imperfect markets and under certain firm specific conditions, internal organization and control of a particular activity rather than reliance on the market can be the optimal solution for the firm.[5] In a provoking formulation this is equal to saying that vertically integrated MNEs are substituting inefficient markets for efficient (in firm) planning. Firms that take this option are confronted with the question of how to allocate their activities along the value-added chain internationally in order to maximize profits. To this end they will investigate the relative competitive (locational) advantages offered by different countries and for different activities along the value-added chain. On this basis the international allocation of activities will be decided upon and vertically integrated MNEs are the result of this exercise. Ideally, they spread single productive activities (production of intermediates and parts) according to differences in comparative advantage (and other favorable locational conditions) among national markets. In doing this they are contributing to an efficient allocation of capital in the global economy.

In many cases, MNEs diversify both horizontally and vertically. That way they form so-called conglomerate MNEs, which operate by worldwide production and distribution (sales) webs, monitor and develop technological trends and consumption patterns, and react quickly to changes in the global markets. The interplay of horizontally and vertically integrated and conglomerate MNEs in (relatively) open international markets represents most visibly the phenomenon of globalization.

It goes without saying, that these firm-specific internalization strategies are particularly complicated and by no means free of pitfalls. Only those enterprises that can build on advanced skills for the management of complex production, information and transportation technologies, and its logistics will succeed in this global competitive environment. 'Internalization advantages', the capabilities needed in order to fulfill this task, are working in a similar way to the 'ownership advantages'. Without going into detail it is obvious that horizontal integration based on ownership advantages and vertical integration based on internalization advantages are distinct but complementary strategies for the establishment of international networks of production.

To sum up, the transaction cost theory applies a specific benefit–cost analysis to explain the situation and behavior of MNEs in international markets. The benefits (profits) accrue from the exploitation of the specific advantages that are developed (mainly) endogenously. These profits, which are different from traditional, monopoly profits in static welfare analysis,[6] are threatened by imitators and competing innovators, but can also be defended if the original innovator succeeds in developing new technologies in due time (Schumpeterian race for innovation).

The costs arising for MNEs from the operation in foreign markets are perceived to be increasing in distance[7] and limit the potential for expansion in foreign markets at any given point of time and level of information. However, they will decrease over time due to dynamic economies of scale, thus providing an incentive for further expansion into more distant markets.

Whatever the motive of international production may be in an individual case, it remains an open question up to this point why a local enterprise decides to enter the international market by allocating production abroad rather than producing and exporting from the home market or exploiting the economic value of a specific advantage through licensing or similar agreements.

In fact, each of these (and an extended number of other) options can be observed on the global market, and it would be helpful to have a sound explanation for these different firm specific solutions to the common task of global profit maximization. One such explanation is Dunning's ingenious OLI paradigm. The OLI paradigm is an eclectic theory that builds on the transaction cost theory but incorporates both traditional trade theories and the diversity of locational factors that can be found in the literature on imperfect markets. Consider the following matrix:

	O Ownership advantage	I Internalization advantage	L Location advantage
Licensing	X		
Exporting	X	X	
FDI	X	X	X

'Ownership advantages' (O) are equal to the specific advantages created by innovations as discussed in the transaction cost theory. 'Internalization advantages' (I) have been discussed together with vertical integration. Here, internalization advantage means that a firm is particularly well equipped with the essential means to transform a given innovation into a market-going product. 'Location advantages' (L) embrace comparative advantage and, in the case of imperfect markets, a set of additional factors, which determine the competitive strength of a country with respect to the firm's actual situation. Altogether these factors determine the relative competitive position of all firms operating from one country relative to those operating from other countries.

First, consider the case that O and I advantages are in the hands of different actors. An ingenious scholar, for example, may have invented a revolutionary machine tool and possesses a patent on it. Now suppose that the production of this machine and its distribution in a new market (markets for innovative products have to be developed as a matter of rule) needs a certain amount of capital, a skilled staff of technicians and workers, an experienced marketing team etc., which the inventor does not dispose of. He also may not be an experienced manager and (or) capital markets are imperfect. Under these conditions, the ownership advantage (intellectual property right) is in the hand of the inventor but internalization advantages are with an experienced enterprise somewhere in the machinery industries.

Now consider the case of this inventor. He obviously does not possess the means to exploit his own invention in the machinery market. In order to save at least part of the perceived economic value of his invention he is obliged to sell his patent or give the license to a firm that has the capacities to transform it into a marketable innovation. This is case 1 of the matrix.

Now assume that the machinery firm has itself invented the technology on which the new product builds. In this case, O and I advantages are unified in one hand – that of the producer. Still there would exist the possibility that licensing is the profit maximizing strategy for this producer (for example if the new machine does not match the overall strategy of the firm), but in many cases, problems of asymmetric information would make licensing an unattractive option. Then, the inventor will decide to exploit the patent by himself and also elect the place where to produce the new product. If the competitive advantage is on the home market, production will be located at home because specific and location advantages can readily be exploited from there (case 2).

Next assume that the competitive advantage exists in a foreign country. In this case the firm could still produce profitably from the home market if the economic value of the specific advantage (patent) is strong enough to compensate for the competitive disadvantage of home production. But home would nevertheless be an inefficient location for this producer. A profit maximizing strategy would force the firm out of the home country and into the market where the competitive advantage exists. Therefore, with the location advantage abroad, a rational manager will deploy the FDI approach (case 3). More generally, we can conclude that FDI will be the best strategy, when O and I advantages are in one hand and the location advantage is in the foreign market. In turn, exports (and production at home) are the efficient solution when the O + I advantages come along with a competitive advantage on the home market.

Without going into details of firm-specific decision-making it should be clear that, under these conditions, the costs of unskilled labor or of environmental provisions alone will rarely determine the decision on the optimal location of production.[8]

For the explanation of the process of globalization the OLI paradigma can easily be extended to sketch a transparent conceptual framework of international production and trade (Figure 2.1). This framework is useful to trace the seemingly chaotic and contradictory global developments in trade and production back to some well established traditional structures. In the center of this framework the MNE is located.[9]

Start considering the case of MNE (home). MNE (home) has to decide whether to produce at home and serve international markets via exports or to produce abroad and export from the foreign market. This decision will be based on the analysis of the set of determinants of the firm's decision-making calculus as outlined above. If 'home' will be identified as the optimal location this decision will imply exports from home that will cause trade structures depending on the kind of product (production process) involved. Thus, for example, if favorable factor endowments are the reason for production at home then conventional comparative advantage causes trade along the lines suggested by the Ricardo or Heckscher–Ohlin theorems (inter-industry trade). However, if comparative advantage plays no role (as among the advanced industrial countries) but economies of scale and product differentiation in heterogeneous markets are important, intra-industry trade is likely to prevail.

Now consider that MNE (home) takes the FDI option and produces abroad. This decision may either be market driven (rapid exploitation of specific advantages) or cost driven (using comparative advantage in foreign markets). In the latter case, FDI will tend to be placed in an emerging market. In the former, it will tend to flow to another advanced economy.[10]

Trade flows will change considerably in this case as compared to production at home. First, trade reversal takes place in both cases, and this will again be of an inter- or intra-industrial nature according to the type of production involved. Second, we will find simply trade destruction if foreign production displaces exports from the home market. And third, we have trade extension if the subsidiary needs investment goods and components from the home country and exports components that have not been traded before.

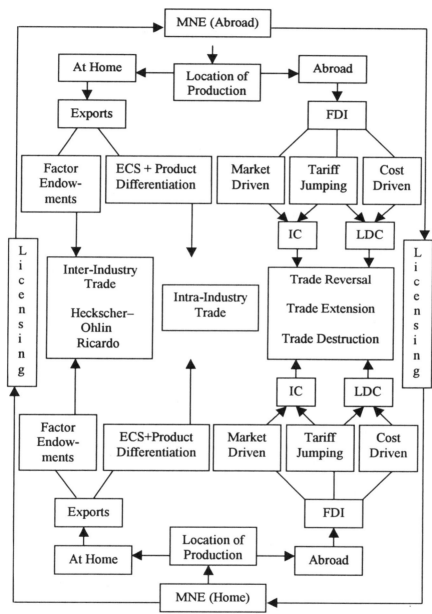

Notes: IC = Industrialized Country
        LDC = Less Developed Country

Figure 2.1 International production and trade

Much of this trade in intermediate products is intra-industry trade (at least formally) and takes place within the firm.

Still another strategy is 'tariff jumping'. In this case, a protectionist trade policy abroad hinders the penetration of the foreign market by exports. Under these conditions, production within the boundaries of this particular economy is the only way to supply this market.

Now remember that within the environment of international innovational competition MNEs from other advanced economies are competing with the home MNE on the world market. Due to similar levels of competence (skills) these firms operate along similar decision-making strategies. Therefore, we can trace a mirror-like trade and investment structure following the locational decisions of MNEs abroad. As a result we have an interdependent structure of trade and investment flows that still follow the conventional rules.

Now consider licensing. In its most simple version licensing transfers the right to produce a particular product to another (competing) company. In the case of international licensing this means that a foreign company will enter into production. This company in turn will try to identify the profit maximizing locational structure from the point of view of its own home country and again mirror-like structures will emerge.

Broadening this simple framework to a multicountry multifirm level dramatically expands the diversity of the firms' strategies of trade and international production.[11] As a result we would find the type of dense interdependent economic system that many critics of globalization take as a proof for intransparency and even chaos in the open (liberal) international markets. This impression, in turn, contributes to misinterpretations and feeds on poorly founded fears about globalization.

The preceding analysis reduces this complexity and it shows that the perceived chaos of international economic relations can be broken down relatively easily to uncover the working of some well established theories of international trade and production. These theories (namely the Heckscher–Ohlin theorem, the theories of intra-industry trade and the capital arbitrage theories) are based on the liberal economic approach and demonstrate the superiority of (non-discriminatory) free trade theoretically and on a high level of abstraction.

Since the 1970s these theories have also become subject to concise dynamic enlargements and to more and more sophisticated empirical tests. By and large, this new research demonstrates the empirical validity of the claim that free trade (open markets) provide a real chance to improve economic welfare (and political stability) for all participating countries. This claim rests not so much on the so-called static gains from trade that have been discussed in early theoretical models. Far more important are the dynamic effects that derive from an intensified international transfer of knowledge (in its widest sense), the exploitation of economies of scale and scope, and increasing international competition. These effects, it is also suggested, translate into permanent changes of the rate of economic growth.[12] The result of this dynamic interplay of growth enhancing efforts is that globalization, pushed forward by these dynamic factors, has a far more positive effect than traditional static trade theories have claimed.

The economic message from the abundant research on this topic is clear: the liberalization of trade and capital flows along the principles of multilateralism that took place after World War II has led to globalization and, thereby, stimulated economic welfare *for those who played by its rules* (WTO, 1998, Chapter II; Dollar/Kraay, 2002; The World Bank, 2002a).

This latter qualification is crucial in view of the discussion of the much debated effects of globalization on the distribution of income. Those countries that denied their participation in this market driven process of international specialization based on the principles of multilateral free trade and capital flows also did not – as a matter of rule – manage to participate in its welfare effects. Put differently, the average rate of economic growth of those belonging to the international community of 'open' trading nations[13] has been significantly higher than those staying aside. Namely, this is the case of most of the so-called least developed countries (LLDCs) which are concentrated in Africa, of many Latin American countries and India (up to the early 1990s) and, starting from an entirely different economic system, of the countries of the former Soviet bloc and the People's Republic of China under the Maoist regime.[14]

But there are also some countries out of the league of the advanced 'open' traders that have to be addressed in this context. These are those countries of Western Europe, in particular, which have downgraded or even neglected the dramatic changes in international economic relations since the 1970s and stuck to outdated political concepts. These countries, too, had to suffer from a decline of their relative economic (and political) position within the international community. It is not possible in this context to discuss any individual reason for these setbacks in detail. However, some remarks are appropriate in order to put the benefits of globalization in perspective. These critical comments on globalization usually come along under the heading: 'challenges of globalization' or, in economic terms, 'costs of globalization'.

2.2 CHALLENGES (COSTS) OF GLOBALIZATION

2.2.1 Increasing Interdependencies

Increasing interdependencies are a consequence of globalization. Since the 1970s, when Keohane/Nye (1977), and Cooper (1980), among others, have drawn attention to this phenomenon, the global economy has changed qualitatively:

- by increasing the sensitivity of national economies to changes on the world market;
- by making national economic policies more dependent on international policy standards;
- and by linking the management of the public good 'international economic order' more narrowly to national economic policies (Hesse/ Keppler/Preusse 1985).

Globalization causes an increasing sensitivity of national economies concerning international events, because of the increasing relative (and absolute) importance that international trade (exports + imports) and investment (FDI and portfolio) flows gain on national demand and supply, and vice versa (rising mutual openness). Increasing openness also implies that national economic policies, by changing the national framework of action, have a more significant and direct effect on the relative position of national and international competitors.

These interdependencies are most visible in macroeconomics, where the performance of national politics is watched permanently by international financial markets. These markets react (over)sensitively to changes in national fiscal and monetary policies, which are thought to change the expected relative (risk adjusted) yield of capital. For national (economic) policies this means that its consistency, continuity and credibility are becoming scrutinized by external actors who are prepared to punish policy failure much more quickly and rigorously than in former times.

Increasing interdependencies in the area of trade and investment, though less visible and less subject to public attention, are no less influencing the scope of national policy-making. This becomes obvious from the new developments in the GATT since the early 1980s (the Tokyo Round, for the first time, broadened the negotiating agenda to include the so-called 'new' topics such as non-tariff barriers [NTBs], subsidies, trade in services, intellectual property rights etc.). The inclusion of these new topics in the trade agenda reflects the fact that, due to increasing interdependencies, there is a growing impact of international transactions other than trade on the economies of the trading partners. Consequently, the evolving international trade order contains more and more regulations and provisions that are 'trade related' and that have a direct impact on national legislation. With the foundation of the WTO in 1995, these developments have become internationally accepted standards. In fact, the WTO, based on an improved legal foundation compared to the former GATT, requires individual country law to be brought into correspondence with the WTO codex. Since a number of these new issues had formerly been subject to national law, the WTO cuts evermore into national sovereignty (Dymond, 2001; Hoekman/Kostecki, 2001).

Altogether, increasing interdependencies are promoting a growing demand for policy coordination and call for a more complex framework for the management of the global economy. By extending the traditional framework of trade to include international investment in the context of innovation competition (intellectual property rights!) and by recognizing the diverse (potentially discriminatory) effects of non-trade policies (subsidies, administrative regulations etc.) the new WTO legislation has changed the international order profoundly. Under the conditions of globalization, national policies have to act much more closely in line with international economic conditions and political obligations. By and large, this means that globalization has a limiting effect on the sovereignty of the nation state, posing a challenge for national politics and causing tensions between national aspirations and international obligations. This is the more so, as international regimes such as the WTO are unable to install legally binding and enforceable rules.

2.2.2 Globalization and Change

Traditional trade theory (Heckscher–Ohlin theorem) concludes that countries (firms) that are operating in a world without artificial barriers to trade will specialize according to comparative advantage. If, in this world, capital and labor are the only factors of production this leads to the well known specialization of capital rich (industrialized) countries on capital intensive and labor rich (developing) countries on labor intensive products (processes). Subsequent research has shown that in a multicountry multiproduct world with still two factors of production a 'chain of comparative advantages' emerges along which countries with different factor endowments may find their optimal specialization (Deardorff, 1982). Another improvement of this approach is the redefinition of capital to include 'human capital'. This so-called 'neo-factor proportion' theorem (NFP theorem) was not only appropriate to resolve the Leontieff paradoxon but also provided a better prescription of an economic world in which human knowledge plays an

increasingly important role. These trade theories gave rise to abundant
econometric work that eventually led to the formulation of the so-called
'continuum of dynamic comparative advantages' according to which the
relative positions of countries on a 'ladder' of comparative advantages are no
longer fixed. Rather they may change according to a country's success in
promoting economic growth (which, in turn, changes factor endowments).
For a stylized presentation of this relationship consider Figure 2.2.[15]

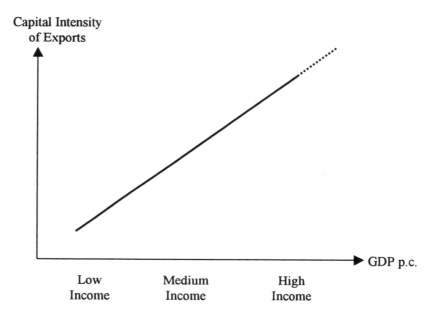

Figure 2.2   The continuum of dynamic comparative advantages

On the horizontal axis we depict the bundle of trading nations that are
classified according to income per capita as a proxy for the level of
development and the structure of factor endowments.[16] On the vertical axis
exporting industries are depicted according to capital intensity of export
production.[17] Petro-chemicals, for example, is a highly capital intensive
industry and ranks high while apparel and shoe production are relatively
labor intensive and have a low ranking.[18] Now the position of each country
with respect to the average capital intensity of its exports will be marked in
the diagram (not shown). If the continuum of comparative advantages (the
multicountry multiproduct version of the NFP theory) holds, this set of
country–industry combinations would approximate a positively sloped curve

as shown in Figure 2.2. The empirical evidence indeed exhibits such a relationship.

The essence of the extensions of the traditional trade model and its economic proof is that specialization according to the Heckscher–Ohlin theorem really takes place in North–South trade.[19] Implicit to this specialization is the relocation of the factors of production between and within the participating countries. More precisely, in a well functioning economy, capital and labor must move permanently (between regions, sectors and industries) in response to changing economic conditions.

In intra-industry trade, too, specialization is central to international trade, though the challenge of adjustment is different. Relative factor endowments do not play any important role by definition in intra-industry trade but a more sophisticated kind of specialization takes place within industries (product differentiation + economies of scale). Sometimes, analysts have concluded that the adjustment procedures are less demanding in intra-industry trade because large sectoral (or regional) reallocation can be avoided. However, it must be borne in mind that a large part of intra-industry trade takes place under particularly severe pressure of technological upgrading within a typical environment of innovational competition (see above). Thus, the need to adjust (to upgrade) is crucial in intra-industry trade, and this task may become quite critical for some groups of the labor force.

Last but not least, the international mobility of capital, by allocating capital according to its relative international scarcity, is a means to speed up the changes of comparative advantages and the specialization procedures in intra-industry trade, thereby contributing to even more pressure on the factors of production to adjust.

From these observations concerning the effect of (global) international trade and investment on the international allocation of resources it can be derived that the essence of globalization is change! Changes of the structures of production provoked by international reallocation of resources do exert adjustment pressures on the factors of production involved. Put differently, it is exactly the propensity of mobile factors of production to follow new market signals, which enables enterprises to rearrange their activities efficiently on the international level. Out of a higher level of productivity, then, they are able to distribute higher incomes to shareholders and workers alike, that is, to promote economic growth.

What is also implicit in this model (and often overlooked by its critics) is that changes of economic structures are not at all confined to internationalization but are essential to any economic growth scenario, be it an open or closed economy. This fact is of course well known from the early work of Clark, Kuznets, Chenery and others who have developed and tested diverse models of sectoral change. These studies show that dramatic sector changes are taking place within any (developing) country as growth proceeds (Chenery/Robinson/Syrquin, 1986; Syrquin/Chenery, 1989). One important lesson from these studies is that the need for economic adjustment, which is often attributed to globalization, is in fact an essential attribute of any (developing) society.

What is indeed a distinct attribute of global growth and change is that there exists a multiple of chances and choices as compared to the closed economy, and these can be exploited to increase productivity more rapidly. Consequently, within the multilateral system of international trade and investment, economic growth is enhanced and at the same time structural change is speeding up. In this sense the global economy offers a higher rate of growth but also demands a higher rate of change from the actors involved.

In theory, all these changes are taking place within the prescribed scenario of higher economic growth. Consequently, any 'potential' loser could be compensated by the winners (which would still remain in a pareto-optimal position). Nevertheless, many concerns with globalization are caused by unresolved disputes over the distribution of the gains from trade within society and between particular groups of society. Some of these disputes are on purely economic issues, others reflect particularly sensitive social relationships.

One argument holds that a specific challenge of globalization arises when a greater speed of change causes higher distributional tensions within the society. Put differently, this hypothesis claims that the society's capacity to manage change is limited. Take, for example, the case of a slowly growing and relatively closed economy. Within this economy, adjustment pressures are supposed to be weak and those who manage to improve their relative position during the growth process are gaining relatively little. That is, the winners gain little and the losers don't lose very much. Further, suppose that there is a consensus within this relatively homogeneous society that losers are to be compensated (for example by a redistributing tax system). Now suggest that the economy becomes integrated into a dynamically growing world market, and its rate of growth rises. This is of course happening because the country's entrepreneurs are now able to take advantage of the opportunities provided by the global market and begin to specialize (reallocate) accordingly. That is, growth is speeding up for those who are (and get) employed in the expanding export industries while others get under pressure from foreign competition. Even they will probably gain from free trade in the long run (when all adjustments have taken place), but in the short run the balance between winners and losers may get lost. In order to establish social stability in this society, the balance between winners and losers would have to be readjusted. More precisely, the winners would have to agree on more redistribution in order to finance the increased demand of the losers for adjustment assistance. If this task does not find a political majority then the consensus about the 'fair' management of change may become doubtful and resistance to change may grow. This will also be the case if the losers' propensity to accept change diminishes because 'unfair' strangers are perceived to be the cause of their hardship rather than 'inevitable' national developments. Without elaborating on this point it is clear that the internal acceptance of change may become weaker with global integration, while the need to adjust increases. As a result the factor mobility that would be needed for the reallocation of production becomes hindered and (ceteris paribus) the rate of growth will drop.

The internal propensity to follow changing market signals may also be influenced by changing factor mobility over time. Following Hiscox (2002), the mobility of labor and capital between industries has in fact declined in the advanced Western economies since World War I.[20] The main causes of this development are technical and economic innovations, which have 'generated more specific forms of human and physical capital and ... greater complementarity between technology and labor skills' (Hiscox, 2002, 10). Inter-industry mobility became more costly as a result of these developments and new political coalitions based on industry groups (rather than class-based coalitions, such as landowners, capital and labor) gained importance. As a consequence of the new powerful coalitions between industry specific capital and labor, politicians saw themselves exposed to increasing protectionist pressure.

Another potentially disruptive factor for the acceptance of change is cultural distance. With an increasing participation of different types of economies (societies) in the international system, diverse political, cultural and economic concepts have to be reconciled to become compatible with the multilateral system. This sensitive aspect of globalization did not find much attention during the first decades after World War II. At that time, the relatively homogeneous Western industrialized societies were the dominant producers and traders of manufactures, while culturally more different countries were either fixed on primary exports or altogether absent on the international market. This relatively comfortable situation from the point of view of the Western industrializing economies became challenged seriously for the first time with Japan's rise to global exporter, and later on by a growing number of so-called newly industrializing countries (NICs) following up.

In recent years, the increasing interdependencies of the global markets began to embrace a growing number of culturally most diverse regions and economies, which are relying on distinct national policies. That is, at the time when national and international economic policies became more mutually dependent and common international rules were established that penetrate into the sphere of sovereign national politics, the diversity of national concepts of the management of political and economic issues itself has increased. Consequently, the definition of 'non-discrimination', the corner-stone of the multilateral system, has become subject to different interpretations and the scope for disputes is likely to increase. Under these conditions, structural change, too, may increasingly become subject to non-monetary costs of adjustment coming along in terms of pressure put on specific cultural norms.[21]

From the point of view of the advanced industrialized societies, one particularly important economic aspect of the internationalization process is that ever more LDCs are becoming part of the international division of labor. As a consequence of this development the reference price of unskilled labor has become quasi-fixed (or has even fallen) internationally, and this situation is unlikely to change even if growth is proceeding over years. While this is an especially desirable consequence of the international division of labor from the point of view of the world as a whole (maximizing employment generation in the poor countries) it poses a core problem for the low income (unskilled labor) sector of the advanced countries:[22] while national income rises constantly on average, the wage rate of unskilled labor is lagging behind – at least in relative terms. The adequate response to this 'globalization trap' would of course be the formation of a well performing educational system, which allows the transfer of unskilled into skilled labor, flanked by an adequate compensation mechanism for those left behind. If both strategies do not work sufficiently well, resistance against globalization is likely to grow.

In fact, rather than taking measures to increase the capacity to adjust to changing comparative advantages,[23] many Western societies (those of Europe in particular) have used the proceeds of the initially most successful internationalization period after World War II to expand the so-called 'welfare states'. These welfare states, though highly appreciated at the time of introduction because of their capacity to spread the fruits of economic growth more equally (thereby increasing the acceptance of the capitalist system), eventually became overloaded by mounting demands for redistribution, which undermined the economic pillars of growth.

Another important development that has to be considered in the context of adjustment flexibility is population growth. In almost all Western high income societies, declining fertility combined with increasing life expectancy has reshaped the traditional population pyramid dramatically. The new top down population structure, which developed over decades (though almost unnoticed by the public), is now threatening to disrupt all those social security systems that are based on an intergenerational and interpersonal re-distribution mechanism of income. More than often, the inevitable melting down of aspirations of redistribution in the face of a changing relation between contributors and recipients is attributed to the pressure of globalization.

Last but not least, the welfare states, by intervening heavily in individual risk insurance, have contributed to distinct changes in human behavior, which hinder crisis recovery and revival of the economies. In particular, by reducing the propensity to accept change, and by weakening the incentives for work and to bear risk, the welfare states have indeed undermined the conditions for their own survival. Nevertheless, recognition or even acceptance of this grave diagnosis appears to be difficult as long as lost competitive positions on the international market are easily attributed to 'unfair' international competitors rather than to economic 'sclerosis' at home (Lindbeck, 1982; Lübbe, 1986).

Altogether, these developments have weakened the capacity of many Western societies to adjust to globalization and change. Weak growth performance, increasing unemployment and rising opposition against the seemingly destructive effects of global international competition are the results.

While this scenario is frequently used to explain the timid reactions of many European countries to the challenges of globalization, things might be different in the USA (and possibly Latin America). In the USA, sluggish economic growth during the 1970s has brought about fundamental changes in economic policies since the 1980s. These economic reforms, including conservative public spending policies, have helped to revive the US economy during the 1990s and led to an extended period of rapid economic growth and full employment. Nevertheless, the resistance towards globalization appears to be particularly high and rising in the USA. Apparently, the challenge of globalization will be rated high even when the economic performance is extraordinarily good. The reasons for this apparently contradictory behavior of many Americans will be discussed in the chapter on NAFTA.

2.2.3 Globalization and the Environment

A second major concern with globalization is its potentially negative impact on the environment. Environmentalists believe that there are three fundamental effects of globalization that are working against their objectives. First, globalization, by fostering economic growth, may push the production of goods that are produced with environmentally damaging inputs or production technologies.[24] Second, globalizing trade and production intensifies the exchange of goods and people across borders and the use of scarce economic resources for transportation. Third, globalization is accused of initiating a 'race to the bottom' in terms of national and international environmental standards.

Based on these arguments, many environmentalists condemn globalization as detrimental to important objectives of environmental policy. They vehemently call for measures against liberal trade and investment policies and the spread of global economic activities. In principle, the claim is to minimize trade in order to minimize environmental destruction. To put it in the words of Esty, adherents to this extreme position would 'support trade only to the extent possible by bicycle' (Esty, 1994, 62).

However, a more thoughtful analysis of the environmental effects of globalization is essential in order to put environmental concerns into a broader perspective. Such an analysis will not only have to consider the perceived gains from trade relative to these costs, it would also have to investigate more accurately these three effects. Both aspects are highly interdependent!

As far as the balance between the benefits of globalization and the perceived costs to the environment is concerned, standard economic theory holds that any rational (economic) actor would expand globalization up to the point where the marginal benefits of globalization are equalized by the marginal environmental costs that arise out of it.[25] Based on this calculus the fundamentalist position (if rational at all) can be interpreted as one that does not recognize at all the benefits from free trade and globalization, but rates the (environmental) costs of economic growth and international transaction prohibitively high.[26]

What is obvious in any case from the previous discussion of the gains from trade is that ignorance concerning the positive effects of globalization is definitely not a well advised strategy and so are the unreflected critics on international trade. A more challenging question is whether globalization necessarily causes environmental degradation. At a first glance, this may appear to be a convincing thesis because additional economic growth and trade will most certainly cause an increase in activities that draw on scarce environmental resources. Nevertheless, the simple formula:

more production + more transportation = more pollution

is misleading because economic growth cannot be understood as a linear extension of existing trends. Rather, technological progress, one of the fundamental causes of intensive economic growth, increases productivity and income continuously. Both these developments, in turn, have an important impact on the structure of demand and supply. Thus, with increasing income per capita, the structure of demand, driven by different elasticities of income, changes from primary to manufactured products and from manufactures to services. More so, with the changing structure of demand the structure of supply also changes from resource intensive to knowledge intensive goods and services, which are produced at a continuously increasing level of technological sophistication including higher environmental standards. Put differently, the growing value-added of advanced high income countries is produced with a decreasing content of material resources and waste (environmental degradation).

Last but not least, when the level of economic welfare increases the propensity to spend parts of the additional income on environmental objectives is also likely to increase (the income elasticity of demand for a healthy environment is greater than one). By and large this means that in a growing economy the pollution content of total output decreases and it will do so the more rapidly the more dynamic is the economic growth process. If this perception of the growth process is correct, then globalization, by pushing economic growth, works in favor of environmental objectives.

There are two main criticisms of this positive view on globalization and the environment. The first one derives from the fact that the above analysis is limited to the discussion of the relative intensity of pollution in production. The second refers to the 'race to the bottom' issue. First consider the intensity of pollutionary production. A diminishing intensity of pollution means that (with growing income) every unit of GDP will be produced with a smaller amount of environmentally damaging inputs (pollutants, emissions etc.). But economic growth also means an increase of production, e.g., a rising quantity of GDP units. Therefore, the relative reduction of the utilization of environmental resources is not a sufficient condition for a positive environmental balance of globalization in absolute terms. Put differently, for globalization to have a positive impact on the environment, the absolute decline in environmental resource use due to increased environmental efficiency of production must be larger than the additional use of the environment brought about by increasing units of output (caused by economic growth). Whether this condition really holds in a concrete situation is an empirical matter.[27]

Evidence on this point is scarce and selective, but there are some indications from the advanced industrialized countries that the emissions of a number of important pollutants have been reduced in absolute terms during the last decades despite increasing production. Environmentalists never-theless claim that this positive balance does not hold, once LDCs are considered. They argue that most of them are just beginning to produce manufactures on a large scale so that their economic growth still relies heavily on the utilization of scarce environmental resources. As a consequence the balance between the output effect of growth and the effect of technical progress is believed to be strongly against the environmental objectives when the global dimension is considered. Taking also into consideration the fact that many LDCs still have a high rate of population growth the situation presents itself even more precarious. This is, of course, a correct and alarming statement. However, does it make a case against globalization? The answer is simply no:

1. If one agrees that LDCs are as much entitled to strive for economic welfare as the industrialized countries are (and have been in the past) and if they indeed insist on this option, the volume of industrial output that will have to be mastered environmentally in the future is quasi-fixed (predisposed) (except for the case that elementary human behavior will change quickly and radically and all people become dedicated environmentalists instantaneously).[28] Then, any given quantity of goods produced in the global economy will be produced at the minimum cost of environmental hazard if the international allocation of resources and trade are free.

2. Considering the problem of population growth does not change this result. Most of the population increase up to about 2100, when world population is expected to reach its peak at about 8 to 10 billion inhabitants, is fixed and these people must be fed. The best way to do this is to provide strong incentives for economic growth.[29] Given this provision, free international markets are again an important part of the solution of the problem and not a hindrance.

This conclusion leads back to the second critical point of the analysis: the 'race to the bottom' argument. Critics of the seemingly adverse impact of globalization on the environment claim that global competition enforces a decline of environmental standards. As a consequence, economic activities are becoming more instead of less polluting as economic growth proceeds on the global scale, even at a higher level of technological capabilities. In order to judge this argument more profoundly a rigorous discussion of the new developments of the theory of locational competition would be necessary. This is not possible in this context and I will limit my arguments to some basic notes.

The 'race to the bottom' argument starts from the simple textbook notion of traditional price competition. In that model, price is given for any competitor and cost efficiency becomes the principal means to gain and sustain competitiveness. Firms, therefore, have to go for efficient technologies and will soon find themselves producing at equal cost standards. Those who do not meet this standard will have to leave the market. Under these conditions any incremental cost reduction of an individual firm will provide this firm with a significant competitive advantage, and at the same time, destroy the competitive strength of its rivals. It is vital under these market conditions to use any chance for cost reduction. Now suppose that meeting environmental standards produces costs. Then, escaping these standards gains an important competitive edge for the forerunner. However, because every firm goes for the same strategy, they will also be heavily fighting for less costly environmental standards. Thereby, they force these standards down to the bottom and environmental policies become toothless.[30] In the global market this process is said to work in a particularly hazardous way because MNEs can economize on environmental costs by letting single countries compete against each other on environmental standards. In this competitive struggle of nations only the lowest environmental standard will survive.

However, in the environment of global innovational competition as outlined above, things are working differently. Heterogeneous rather than homogeneous markets are prevailing and firms are competing for innovational solutions to meet the continuously changing challenges that the markets provide. In the center of this competitive model is the notion that modern firms organize a team of skilled (specific) and non-specific factors in order to generate innovational rents. The competitive position of these firms derives from the efficient interplay of all these factors and the costs of environmental regulations are only one element within this complex set of factors that are determining competitive performance. It is not surprising, therefore, that the cost effect of environmental regulations – as a matter of rule – is not a dominant concern of firms operating on the global market. It might play a certain role at the margin and in distinct industries, but in many cases it is not decisive for an MNE's decision on the location of production. From this point of view the fears of a global 'race to the bottom' are clearly overrated because they are based on a misspecified concept of global competition.

Notwithstanding this conclusion, MNEs are indeed trying hard to lobby for their interests, which are more often than not incompatible with environmental objectives. Put differently, environmental (and other) regulations are most certainly subject to distinct lobbying activities, which will be employed in order to improve the relative position of a particular firm within its market. Pressure on environmental regulations that are believed to be too high (or discriminatory) can also be part of these lobbying activities. Depending on the specific position of an individual firm in its market and in the global economy these lobbying activities will meet quite different conditions for success, including an overthrow of particular environmental standards that democratically legitimized governments may have decided to implement. This kind of abuse of economic power is of course a very popular argument against MNEs and, because of their important role in the globalization process, against globalization. However, it must be emphasized that inferring from single cases of abuse of economic power to the overall competitive situation may be misleading. In fact, the conditions on the global market in general are more of the kind proposed by the transaction cost theory than of Hymer's power political views of the 1960s. And even if there should be concern about increasing abuse of oligopolistic or first mover positions on a worldwide scale, the adequate answer would be competition policy rather than protectionism.

Contrary to Hymer's perception, there are strong arguments in favor of the thesis that the limits of power of the MNEs in the field of environmental policies are not only determined by countervailing politics exercised by national governments and international institutions. Rather, they are developing ever more intensively out of a growing public concern for environmental problems. Put differently, lobbying of firms for their specific interests as producers is frequently faced by lobbying interests that are aimed at higher environmental standards. These lobbying activities can indeed count on the recognition of the most pressing problems of environmental degradation by growing parts of the population (at least in the advanced industrialized countries, but, increasingly, in third world countries, too). Driven by these changing perceptions of environmental problems, producers, and MNEs in particular, are forced by the markets to adhere to a more positive reflection on environmental objectives. These developments can clearly be recognized in the many (international) firms, which by themselves apply environmental standards that are higher than national legislation, which willingly avoid specific polluting inputs etc. (WTO, 1999).[31]

Furthermore, environmental technology has itself become a promising new market, which is expected to provide scope for the expansion of new high tech firms. These firms will most certainly share in and strengthen the lobby in favor of environmental policies. Rather than being in a 'globalization trap', environmental concerns will indeed become promoted more rigorously on the global level and under open market regimes, as these trends are gaining strength.

To sum up, the stereotype accusation of globalization as being a main promoter of environmental degradation does not find much support, once some important conceptual issues have been clarified. That is, theorizing on the nature of innovation competition and on the way in which MNEs are operating in open markets paints a more differentiated picture of the global market. In this picture, globalization is recognized as an indispensable mechanism to increase economic welfare and to deliver the technological and material foundations for the implementation of sound environmental policies. Growing public concern with environmental objectives has an important part to play in this scenario. It grants politics the mandate for sound environmental policies, and – if exercised skillfully and prudently – may become a useful lobbying power and an efficient control mechanism. However, this does not free politics from prudent decisions on economically sustainable (that is growth promoting) environmental policies.

Within this framework, global markets do not force environmental (and social) legislation of the nation state down to the bottom. Rather, they help to speed up technological development and economic growth, thereby providing the means to produce any given quantity of output at a higher level of 'environmental sustainability'.

2.2.4 International Migration

Migration was an important mechanism of wealth transfer during the first wave of globalization (1870–1914). At that time, about 120 million people (nearly 10 percent of world population) emigrated from densely populated Europe (60 million) and China. Europeans at that time predominantly went to North America, Australia and Latin America, while the Chinese preferred countries in East and South East Asia (World Bank, 2002a, 25).

While this early wave of migration had been highly welcomed by immigration and emigration countries alike (European emigrants in particular, took pressure off the European labor market and helped to colonize large parts of the New World), migration today is confronted with considerable dislike by the target countries. These countries have erected subtle systems of entry barriers, which are foremost meant to prevent unskilled workers from immigration, and to give incentives to attract high skilled workers. The reasons for these different policies today are manifold. For one thing 19th-century migrants went to so-called 'countries of recent settlement'. These countries were scarcely populated at that time (and are so even today compared with Europe and China). The newcomers easily found virgin soils and organized highly extensive growth and development processes, which eventually turned the North American region into the most prosperous one of the world (Rosenberg/Birdzell, 1986, 71 ff.).

Nevertheless, even under these conditions the dramatic relocation of labor had tremendous effects on wages. Lindert/Williamson (2001) have estimated that immigration into the so-called 'countries of recent settlement' has lowered wages between 8 percent in the USA, 16 percent in Canada and 22 percent in Argentina and at the same time raised it in Ireland, Italy and Norway by 32, 28 and 10 percent respectively. From a theoretical point of view this change in international wages reflects a mechanism that can easily be explained by the Rybczynski theorem. According to this theorem a country's relative wage rate will drop when the supply of labor increases more than that of capital, a typical situation of countries with a high rate of immigration. Likewise, when labor leaves the country, wages will tend to increase. In the US–European economic relationship still another production factor, land, played a crucial role. Land had been abundant in the USA (and Canada) during the 19th century and many immigrants used this land to expand agricultural production. US comparative advantage in agriculture was significant vis-à-vis Europe, but could not be exploited on overseas markets before transportation and storing facilities had been significantly improved. When this happened during the first wave of globalization European landlords came under severe competitive pressure from American (and Russian) farmers. Thus, in Europe, the position of landlords deteriorated significantly while wages increased, and the opposite took place in America.

This redistribution of income between the Old and the New World took place under particularly harsh conditions. In Europe, where job losses in agriculture exceeded new employment opportunities in industries, potential emigrants faced a bleak future at home, so that the mere hope for a better fortune elsewhere became a driving force of change. For them, low wages abroad coupled with a relatively high probability of social upgrading (compared with unemployment and hardship at home) formed a strong incentive for emigration.

Abroad, with any effective means of lobbying against the challenge of immigration being absent, those suffering from declining wages were forced to adjust in order to survive. Fortunately, the experience of rapid and sustained economic growth taught them most impressively how flexibility can be transformed into economic success. As a result, the vital linkages between growth and change could be sustained for years and helped to create a virtuous circle of economic development.

Migration today is still predominantly based on wage differentials. According to Stalker (2000), hourly labor costs in 1995 in Germany were 31.88 US$, in the USA 17.20 US$, and in China and India 0.25 US$. Even if one takes into account that these figures substantially overestimate the true difference in the average standards of living among nations, the fact remains that the remaining 'true' differences between rich and poor countries constitute a significant incentive to migrate. However, apart from wage differences migration today differs from the 19th-century experience in some important ways. First, emigration and immigration countries are different. Nowadays, emigrants use to come from LDCs, while Western Europe has been transformed into a principal recipient country (along with the USA, Canada and Australia). Second, the immigration countries are mature economies with only low average rates of economic growth, but effectively organized social groups, which strongly resist any negative change of their relative income position (Olson, 1982). Third, land has become a scarce factor in Europe and is hardly available for additional agricultural production in the USA. Under these conditions, many unskilled emigrants used to become employed in low wage jobs in agriculture (most often on a seasonal basis), services and industry, and directly put pressure on wages in these particularly sensitive segments of the local labor markets of the advanced economies. Last but not least, population growth and worldwide communication and transportation networks contribute to increasing pressure to migrate.

Altogether we find a scenario of increasing migration pressures provoked by high and rising wage pressures (non-globalizers falling behind!) and a decreasing propensity of potential recipient countries to accept immigrants. Compared with the 19th-century experience this mismatch between demand for and supply of new entrants into the Western industrialized countries signals that one important mechanism of (worldwide) wage equalization of the past does not function sufficiently well in the present period of globalization.

Reasons for the hesitant immigration policies of western industrialized countries are manifold, and they are not only economic by their nature. The basic economic barrier is the apparent fear of unskilled labor in developed countries to lose even more ground when more migrants are allowed to enter. Both theory (Rybczynski theorem) and experience with the 19th-century globalization process seem to make it clear that these fears are not unfounded as long as a short time horizon is taken and relative changes of the distribution of income become the ultimate target of wage policies. In the long run, however, the effects of migration are clearly different. Drawing on the same historical evidence underlines this statement. It is obvious from a longer-term perspective that both groups, emigration and immigration countries, have profited from migration. And contrary to many fears in Western industrialized countries at the beginning of the 21st century, migration, if it is analyzed with respect to declining population growth and over-aging, may even become more important than ever (not to say essential) in maintaining welfare.

Non-economic reasons hindering immigration are mainly based on cultural divergence. Apparently, the capacity of historically grown up societies to assimilate foreigners is limited. These limits may be open to change if prudent integration policies help to assimilate foreigners, but they appear to be present at any point of time.

Last but not least, the linkage between immigration and trade has to be emphasized. It has been shown theoretically that the pressure for poor people to emigrate, which has been built up by the tremendously growing differences in living standards, can either be calmed down by trade or migration or a combination of both (Mundell, 1957). This thesis must be qualified in the light of recent experience. Early theory based on the Mundell model saw trade and migration as close substitutes. Contrary to this we find evidence today that both may in fact be complementary: when trade and investment became liberalized and rose, so did immigration (Solimano, 2001, 15).

However, this apparent contradiction can easily be solved. Mundell discussed trade within a static framework, which was constructed to show the effects of trade and migration in isolation. Under these conditions the forces of substitution will work and operate in the same direction (that is, factor price equalization).

In a world of growth and change, this equilibrating mechanism will become superimposed by at least two additional effects. One is population growth, which takes place most of all in the emigration countries and refills the pool of potential emigrants. Second, opening up trade and investment will bring in information on life in other (rich) countries, and this will be the more so as global communication improves. Growing awareness of the tremendous international welfare differences, in turn, meets decreasing costs of transportation. Altogether this will help to increase the propensity to migrate. Under these conditions migration is likely to increase as long as real convergence does not take place internationally. Real international convergence, if sustained for a longer time period, is a key to drying up the pool of migrants, because high and sustained rates of growth increase job opportunities at home, feed expectations of a better future, and reduce population growth. But it is not able to generate any significant short-run effects. Consequently, the Mundell theory cannot be expected to materialize except for the long run.

There is still another reason why migration is most likely to increase initially as trade liberalization takes place. Consider the fact that trade liberalization initiates reallocation of capital and labor both internationally and nationally. As a matter of fact, these structural changes take time and are not without frictions. Thus, during the restructuring period, the economic situation may even become worse for quite a number of people. Consequently, migration is likely to increase until the positive effects of trade and international investment become felt more broadly.

Again, the real challenges of globalization are not how to keep migration from growing but how to secure open markets to enhance growth, and how to channel migration in a way that is economically advantageous to all participants, and also acceptable from a cultural (social) point of view. Here, the link to regionalism becomes evident.

2.3 SUMMARY

1. Global markets, by increasing economic welfare and growth, also speed up changes in the structures of production between national economies

(regions) and between and within sectors and industries, and these developments are taking place at a continuously increasing level of technological sophistication. Altogether, these changes put a premium on mobility but discriminate against immobility, thereby giving rise to distributional conflicts. One of the most important challenges that policy-makers are faced with in this situation is channeling the structural changes implicit in the dynamics of economic globalization in a way that is compatible with people's aspirations and capabilities. It is crucial in this context to understand the dual impact of globalization on both economic growth and structural change. In the recent critical discussion of globalization, the growth aspect of international trade appears to have been downgraded, if not neglected. It has been demonstrated in Chapter 1, that such a downgrading obscures the political–economic decision-making process and lends support to a biased outcome that might eventually lead to an inferior overall strategy.

2. Increasing international interdependencies do not only transfer new opportunities to increase welfare, but also a number of new challenges. One particular challenge is increasing factor mobility that allows for stiff international competition for mobile factors of production and renders national rents of immobile factors obsolete. Another one (not explicitly included here) is increasing volatility of the international financial markets. Both effects are consequences of globalization, which oblige national policy-makers to take international repercussions of their national decisions more seriously into consideration. That way, globalization imposes a disciplinary effect on both macroeconomic and redistribution policies, that might give rise to dispute.

3. Globalization, though posing a challenge for environmental policy, is also a phenomenon that may contribute to solving rather than stimulating environmental concerns.

All together the benefits and challenges of globalization shape the way in which people are thinking about regionalism. Some in fact argue that the New Regionalism is, to a significant proportion, a response to the challenges of globalization. Therefore, in the following chapter, regionalization will be discussed in the context of globalization.

NOTES

1. It remains unclear at this point why a multinational enterprise prefers to produce in a foreign market rather than export or sell a license. These questions are exactly the topic of Dunning's OLI-paradigma, discussed later in this chapter.

2. In terms of Vernon's product cycle theory this means that product cycles have shortened – a development that has been observed in most of the global markets.
3. Notwithstanding this conclusion, these (sometimes) very big companies are by no means powerless 'price takers' and occasional abuses of 'transitory' power positions are not definitely ruled out.
4. Firms that lose specific advantages during the product cycle may decide to organize production abroad (that is, in the country where the comparative advantage is located), rather than leaving the market to foreign competitors (Vernon, 1966).
5 See for example Casson and Associates (1986) for an extensive discussion of a number of these cases.
6. For a discussion in the context of intellectual property rights see Preusse (1996a).
7 These costs arise mainly from asymmetric information, discrimination etc. (see Caves, 1982).
8. Note, when markets are imperfect, comparative advantage is no longer the only factor that determines the quality of the country as a location of production. Rather, comparative advantage is now only one out of a whole bundle of factors, which altogether define the location quality of a particular economy for the production of a particular product. Others, for example, are tax regulations, market size, availability of skilled labor, political and economic stability, trade barriers, environmental laws etc. The optimal decision on the location of production then becomes a challenging task. I will come back to this point later.
9. Note that the following OLI framework is not confined to MNEs but includes purely national enterprises as a special case. National enterprises just exclude the FDI option and concentrate on trade. This implies that they will produce only in industries or market segments in which the home market offers a location advantage.
10. Note that market driven FDI are not limited to the case of a high sales potential. Rather, big markets may also be trendsetters and give an early indication of new technical developments (especially if it is a high income country).
11. Note that this is still an incomplete draft of the process of globalization. Simply taking into consideration the fact that licensing is a negotiable property right that can be extended to quite different versions, will complicate things tremendously. See for example Borner on the so-called 'New forms of internationalization' (Borner, 1986).
12. In terms of the endogenous growth theory, for example, learning and enhanced technical transfer on a global scale affect the rate of economic growth permanently. Among its most important transmission mechanisms are of course FDI and trade flows (trade in intermediate products in particular).
13. I use this term here in order to avoid the 'ideal typus' of multilateral free trade, which has never been realized despite its constant proclamation by political leaders and the support of more than 140 members of the WTO.
14. Despite the fact that it is extremely difficult to trace causation from trade to growth, the growing literature on the effects of 'open' markets supports the conclusion that 'neutral incentives systems' (Krueger, 1985) are superior to 'inward looking' strategies of development and growth. Critics of this claim argue that open trade regimes (along with sound macroeconomic policies based on the principles of the so-called 'Washington Consensus') may not be sufficient conditions for sustained economic growth (particularly so in LLDCs). Nevertheless, they are unable to challenge the basic notion that (multilateral) free trade along the GATT/WTO principles has been indispensable for economic development to flourish after World War II. For a presentation of this dispute see Mosely, 2000, Dollar/Kraay, 2002; and the debate on a World Bank publication on the 'East Asian Miracle' (The World Bank, 1993; Fishlow et al. eds, 1994).
15. Econometric work on this subject can be found in: Balassa (1977), Tuong/Yeats (1980), Michaely (1981), Mohs (1983) among others.
16. Factor endowments are typically changing from capital scarcity to capital abundance as economic development proceeds.
17. In the following, capital intensity will be defined in terms of the NFP theory, that is, including human capital.

18. Yeats has demonstrated that the relative intensity of capital between industries has been stable over the 1966–86 period (Yeats, 1989).
19. Heckscher–Ohlin trade structures are still prevalent in North–South trade. However, sometimes it is more difficult to detect them in the modern world economy, because firms (MNEs) split up the value-added chains and trade within the firm and within relatively homogeneous product groups. See the chapter on the Mexican Maquiladora industries (Section 4.2.3.2) on this point.
20. Hiscox (2002), for example, has investigated on the change of the mobility of capital and labor in six countries since the 19th century. He found increasing factor mobility over most of the 19th century. About 1920 this trend broke down, and, since the 1950s, a significant decline can be observed.
21. See, for example, World Bank, 2002a, 12 ff.
22. Meanwhile, many newly industrializing countries, too, are losing comparative advantage in low wage industries.
23. Also in most of these countries the wage structure has not been allowed to change in favor of skilled labor. As a consequence, unskilled labor became too expensive and employment dropped while the incentives to invest in high skilled professions became relatively unattractive.
24. Radical environmentalists would even argue that economic growth is bad for the environment per se because growing output always draws on scarce environmental and primary inputs.
25. A particularly serious evaluation problem arises from potential environmental damages, which are expected to fall on future generations. In this case, future costs and benefits will have to be discounted in order to provide policy-makers with an adequate decision-making tool. Bayer/Cansier have shown that well established discounting procedures in economics systematically underestimate the environment costs transferred to future generations (Bayer/Cansier, 1998).
26. In fact, one important point in this highly emotional debate derives from the fact that neither the economic gains nor the extent of environmental damage can be substantiated by more than crude approximations. This uncertainty about the true size of the problem may indeed call for a conservative (strong!) environmental policy in the case of a non-reversible future damage to be expected from a further abuse of global commons (e.g. global warning). Nevertheless, giving absolute priority to this environmental objective would still be an overreaction for reasons to be outlined later.
27. This situation has recently been discussed in terms of the so-called 'Environmental Kuznets Curve' (Grossman/Krueger, 1995, 353 ff.; WTO, 1999, 48; Esty, 2001, 115).
28. This is, of course, what environmentalists call for, despite the devastating experience with ideologies that focused on the creation of 'new' human beings.
29. Economic growth is also the most important factor promoting a slowdown of population growth. Therefore, it improves the environmental balance twice: first by raising technological capacities (knowledge), and, second, by its impact on population growth. In fact, Fritsch concludes that increasing knowledge and decreasing population growth are the key factors 'in achieving any kind of sustainability' (Fritsch, 1995, 361).
30. This process can be shown to function quite similarly if the static oligopolistic textbook approach is employed.
31. These arguments also apply to the question of labor standards. Brown/Deardorff/Stern (2003) have shown that there is a clear tendency for MNEs to pay higher wages and accept higher labor standards in LDCs than their local competitors.

3. The Economics of the New Regionalism

Chapter Two has discussed globalization as a result of multilateralism. Basically the benefits from globalization derive from static and dynamic gains from trade (enhanced by international capital flows) while most of the perceived challenges derive from the increasing pressures to adjust to changing market conditions.[1] These pressures become the more intensively felt the more tightly the national economies become interlinked (increasing interdependency). Growing concern about adverse environmental effects and increasing pressure of migration add to the list of global challenges even though they are not a direct consequence of (economic) globalization.

Economic regionalism may be interpreted as a different approach to the institutional organization and management of international issues, its main objective being to improve the balance between benefits and costs of international trade and investment. More precisely, the adherents of (economic) regionalism hold that a sound strategy of regional integration will help to enlarge the gains from (multilateral) free trade and capital flows and by the way calm down the challenges of globalization.

Regionalism may be coming along as an alternative to multilateralism or just as a complement. Most observers today reject the former version of regionalism because it would lead to the formation of highly protectionist regional blocs, which are unlikely to secure the level of efficiency of the multilateral system and might even contribute to a fragmentation of the international system (Bhagwati, 1999, 18).

Such a straightforward rejection of regionalism is not appropriate in the latter case. In fact, it is claimed that 'complementary' regionalism is compatible with multilateralism and may even help to enforce it more quickly and more comprehensively. This claim amounts to the thesis that regionalism under distinct conditions will be supportive to the management of globalization and its challenges.

In the following, the economic consequences of regionalism will be analyzed more profoundly. The lead question will be: does regionalism change the balance between benefits and costs of international specialization relative to multilateralism?[2] Based on the results of this investigation, the conditions will be formulated under which a regional integration agreement can be expected to succeed.

3.1 THE TRADITIONAL THEORIES OF ECONOMIC INTEGRATION

The birth of the traditional approach to regional economic integration dates back to 1950 when Jacob Viner's seminal work on 'The Customs Union Issue' was published.[3] Viner's main contribution to regional integration theory was to demonstrate the discriminatory character of the customs union (CU) (in fact, discrimination characterizes any preferential trade agreement), which produces both trade creation (among the members of the CU) and trade diversion (between members and the rest of the world). Meade (1955) extended Viner's model to include consumption effects. That is, whenever the price elasticity of demand is less than infinite, relative price changes do have an impact on demand that has to be considered too.

Considering both production and consumption effects makes it possible to analyze the effects of a CU from a welfare theoretical point of view (Grimwade, 1996, 241; Robson, 1998, 18). In this context a CU will be judged to be welfare increasing as a matter of rule, if trade creation exceeds trade diversion. This outcome is expected to be more likely:

* the larger the economic area of the CU is;
* the more states are participating;
* the lower the average external tariff level is;
* the more competitive the member states are.

Considering economies of scale (ECS) adds another welfare improving effect of a CU. Its relevance in open markets is not clear, however. For one thing, the CU broadens the local (regional) market and this will indeed be conducive to an extended realization of ECS. But the argument rests on the assumption that exports to non-members before the foundation of the CU are negligible because of high protectionist barriers. If this is not the case exports to the world market will guarantee sufficiently large production runs without regress to a CU. Thus, as long as the world market remains (relatively) open, the realization of ECS will not depend on the size of the local (regional) market.

Later, Cooper and Massell have shown that net trade creation is not a sufficient condition for a net welfare improving effect of the CU. They made the point that trade creation can always be achieved by a non-discriminatory tariff reduction that avoids the negative effects of trade diversion. The conclusion from this observation is that multilateral free trade is always superior to a CU (PTA) (Cooper/Massell, 1965).

The traditional analyses uncover the fundamental tension between multilateral free trade and preferential trade agreements. But they are not sufficiently sophisticated to capture even the most important parameters of deeper regional economic integration. Therefore, the traditional perspective 'is at best incomplete and at worst misleading' (Lawrence, 1996, 7). A more comprehensive analysis will have to recognize first that most regional integration agreements are more than just trade arrangements, and, second, it should include the expected effects of regionalism on economic growth. In order to include both these aspects the analysis of regional integration must be broadened.

3.2 DYNAMIC EFFECTS OF REGIONAL FREE TRADE AND DEEPER INTEGRATION

The dynamic effects of regional free trade are quite similar to the dynamic gains from multilateral free trade, which have been rediscovered from the work of the classical economists by Myint (1958). Applying these ideas to regional integration reveals, that, first, regional free trade allows firms to exploit regional comparative advantage more rigorously, and to realize a higher level of specialization as compared to the national economy. Both effects raise average productivity and income. Second, on the larger market, competition is expected to increase and to force firms to look more vigorously for new market opportunities and technological advances. Most often, the adjustment to the new market conditions goes hand in hand with rising average firm size, which, in turn, allows exploiting new technologies and gives rise to ECS. Innovating firms will find that under these conditions research and development (R&D) should be intensified in order to exploit the new opportunities or to challenge the innovators.

By and large, the higher intensity of competition combined with the effects of a bigger market and higher incomes drives both innovators and imitators to more activities: while innovators, by intensifying R&D, speed up the development of new products and productivity enhancing technologies, and expand production on the larger market, imitators are forced to react more quickly in order to keep pace.

This positive development trajectory will become even more pronounced if international capital flows are allowed for. Similarly to the welfare enhancing effect of trade, capital flows contribute to the efficient allocation of resources in the larger regional space and, through FDI, help to transfer technology (knowledge) both among industrialized countries and to the periphery. Between members of PTAs, which are differing by their level of development, this impact of FDI on growth is estimated to be particularly important (Mexico as a recipient of FDI from its NAFTA partners is a case in point).

Figure 3.1 sketches these dynamics of trade and factor mobility. Trade, by taking advantage of differences in factor endowments, larger markets and the availability of new technologies (mainly through intermediate inputs) generates gains from pure arbitrage, reallocation of resources, ECS and more sophisticated product differentiation, and extended innovations. The first two of these options lead to international exchange and specialization as explained by the traditional trade model. Taken alone they exhibit a positive (one time) effect on productivity and income. The latter contribute to the enlargement of the spectrum of potential specializations. But their specific importance derives from its dynamic impact on growth. The interplay of innovation (drawing on the higher international level of technology) and increasing product differentiation in the larger market is appropriate to create new markets and increases the intensity of competition. These developments, in turn, may help to initiate additional investment activities. If this sequence of changes comes to be realized, the one-time effect on income from exchange and specialization will be enhanced and eventually transformed into a permanent growth effect.

Factor mobility will intensify this growth effect in at least two ways. First, free capital flows are likely to improve the efficiency of international allocation of resources and diminish the scarcity of capital in LDCs. Thus, the increased demand of investment, which derives from the dynamic trade effect, meets additional supply of capital in the recipient countries. Second, FDI (capital) flows are not only providing physical capital but include a whole 'team' of intangible assets (Chapter Two), which directly enhances the availability of new technologies and skills abroad. As a result, a virtuous circle of growth is activated: new technologies initiate new innovation activities, which, in turn, are pushing product differentiation and so on. Last but not least, migration of labor may also contribute to this development.

In sum, the dynamic effects of trade, investment and migration do change the quality of their own determinants permanently: growing income and investment are continuously changing market size and relative factor endowments. Also, the ongoing innovations raise the level of technology. As a result, comparative advantages will change, allowing for a renewed reallocation of capital and labor and, starting from a higher level of technology, another round of innovation and product differentiation will be initiated.

All the determinants of growth discussed so far promise to provide economic advantages that derive from the use of the regional pool of

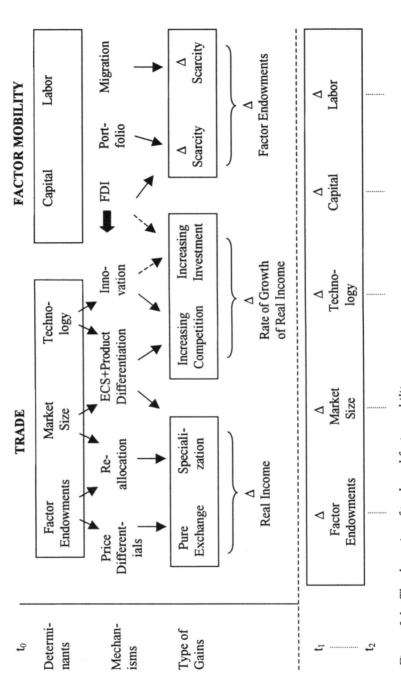

Figure 3.1 The dynamics of trade and factor mobility

knowledge and market opportunities. From this point of view it follows that
the economic gains from regional integration are virtually a mirror image of
the gains from multilateralism, but they will match the latter ones only if the
growth promoting factors within the region are as strong as on the global
level. It is obvious that in most cases this condition does not hold. Regional
integration, therefore, is not a promising strategy, if it comes at the expense
of multilateralism.

3.3   GAINS FROM DEEPER INTEGRATION

This preliminary result has to be reconsidered, if there are reasons to believe
that regional integration will (or can be made to) develop its own growth
dynamics. In fact, the new literature on deeper integration claims that these
particular growth dynamics would allow the transformation of regional
markets into 'pools of economic growth'.

Areas of 'deeper' integration are those that extend cooperation beyond the
FTA or CU. According to Lawrence, they include 'the elimination of
differences in national production and product standards ... credible and
stable government mechanisms and secure access to large foreign markets'
(Lawrence, 1996, 17). Leaving aside all problems of definition of the
intermediate stages of deeper integration,[4] the concept may help to clarify
some important aspects of regionalism.

Lawrence, for example, taking a functionalist perspective, argues that
globalization, by increasing international interdependencies, increases the
demand for 'common rules and institutions at supranational levels'
(Lawrence, 1996, 30). If these demands can be satisfied more easily at the
regional than at the multilateral level, there is scope for the implementation
of a well organized regional market. Regional integration, by that way,
lowers uncertainty and transaction costs and increases the credibility of economic policies among likeminded countries. Furthermore, member governments may agree to improve on existing national regulations and/or to
establish new growth oriented institutions that would not have found a
majority in the single nation states (Preusse, 1994).

Inter- and intra-regional capital flows and, in particular, FDI, play a central
role in any concept of deeper integration. Two impacts of regional integration
on these flows are crucial. First, the bigger common market changes the
conditions for the optimal allocation of resources – both spatial and between
sectors. As a consequence, firms are forced to reconsider their strategies and
to adjust. Second, the larger common market raises the attractiveness of the
location and induces FDI from the rest of the world.[5] Both effects lead to
increasing investment as firms respond to changes in relative competitiveness

(Bende-Nabende, 1999, 50), and they will be the more growth enhancing, the more integrated the common market becomes. If these policy effects materialize and are large enough to compensate for the limited scope of regional specialization, the regional grouping may indeed develop into a 'growth pool' whose performance exceeds that of the multilateral strategy.

More precisely, the theory of deeper integration states that economic integration beyond trade liberalization (FTA, CU) provides additional growth effects. These effects are positively related to the level of integration and – at a certain, not specified level of integration – outpace the negative effects of the smaller regional market. In this scenario, the balance of trade creation and trade diversion must also be reconsidered. When the region's growth performance improves and GDP rises (relative to non-members) so does the demand for imports. As a result, so-called 'external' trade creation will take place, and the adverse effects of trade diversion lose importance correspondingly.

Regional growth pools do have another important property: they are attractive for non-members, too, and thereby become a target for new applicants. If the region accepts new members, successive entry enlarges the integration area piece by piece (domino regionalism)[6] and will eventually include all countries. Multilateral free trade based on a highly integrated global market will be the final result. This 'nucleus theory' has originally been the spiritus rector of the GATT exemption of regional agreements from the principle of non-discrimination (Article 24). Adherents of the concept of deeper integration take one step further and claim that multilateral free trade may even be realized more easily and more rapidly when the 'indirect' path via regional integration is taken. For them, the increasing relative attractiveness of the region (growth effect) and the apparent political appeal of region building are generating a drive towards multilateral free trade that will eventually outpace the direct (multilateral) approach.

Ethier has emphasized another important systemic aspect of deeper integration. He argues that, from the point of view of an LDC, 'the ability to attract FDI is the key to a successful entry into the multilateral trading system' (Ethier, 1998, 1156). This ability might be positively influenced by regional integration both because of its effect on credibility and because of the improved conditions for market access within the region. However, as long as there are only one or a few regional areas, this effect will be FDI divergent, and this threatens to make reforms outside the region even more difficult. One regional agreement, therefore, 'produces reform destruction' (Ethier, 1998, 1158). This outcome changes for the better when regionalism becomes ubiquitous. In this case, reformers are free to enter into regional arrangements and the global externality of regionalism will be internalized.

As a result, the 'outcome [is] unambiguously superior to what can be achieved without regionalism' (Ethier, 1998, 1159).

3.4 CRITICS OF THE CONCEPT OF DEEPER INTEGRATION

The concept of deeper integration (DI) suggests that regional integration agreements that are going beyond discriminatory trade liberalization are serving both the need to manage growing interdependencies and to provide a better environment for economic growth. Based on these views trade diversion melts down to an almost insignificant phenomenon and the area of DI develops into an 'engine of growth', which complements and fosters multilateralism neatly. Also, in as much as regional integration strengthens the economic situation, it will contribute to an enhanced power political position. Thus security and growth will be fostered simultaneously and the positive balance of benefits and costs of regional integration improves even further.

Critics of the DI concept maintain that this positive outcome is doubtful, and in any case subject to the existence of some important preconditions. These preconditions are that the region really establishes market conditions that are conducive to economic growth so that the larger economic potential of the region can really be developed. More precisely, the growth effect from DI depends on the realization of the following integration program:

1. Internal market integration is fundamental for DI to function. Only if the DI area is capable of transforming the individual member markets into one single market, can the expected gains from the formation of a larger economic area be fully realized. This means, first, that liberalization of trade and investment (and a free movement of labor) must be implemented in the region without (major) exceptions. Second, part of any DI program is on the reforms of existing national institutions and regulations and the formation of entirely new (supranational) provisions. One fundamental target of these reforms is the adjustment of national rules to the new regional situation. Another one is the functional improvement of the institutions. In particular, traditional national regulations that might hinder the regional growth process have to be replaced by new growth enhancing (supranational) entities. Third, frequently the reforms under points one and two imply major institutional changes that apply to historically grown local markets. Thus, political resistance against these reforms will be most likely and may give reason to doubt the sustainability of the whole program. *Credibility* concerning

the seriousness of the project, therefore, becomes another important ingredient to successful regional integration.

2. Intensive relations to non-member countries are crucial in order to maintain the regional dynamics. Areas of DI face the problem that outside the boundaries of the region there are growth promoting forces at work that cannot be tapped on adequately from within the region (inputs, knowledge etc.). In order to keep this adverse impact on regional growth small and to improve the regional firms' ability to seize opportunities from outside the region, the DI area must make barriers to outsiders low. Furthermore, low barriers against non-members are an efficient means to keep competitive pressure high on the regional market. Last but not least, openness of the region may also mean that new applicants are welcomed (see above). Openness of this type is important because it avoids insiders establishing a 'closed' community over time. It is also indispensable if the transitory character of regionalism is to be secured. Because of the importance of these points *open* regionalism is claimed to be of utmost importance for the area of DI to function as a growth pool (Lawrence, 1996; Bergsten, 1997; Reynolds, 1997).

These fundamental elements of a successful DI concept are not in dispute. Proponents and critics alike do emphasize their importance as pillars of a growth promoting regional framework. Put differently, the economic success of the concept of DI intimately rests on 'openness' and 'good governance' in the sense that the growth promoting forces of regionalism must find an adequate institutional framework to flourish. Also, because of the complementarity of security and growth, the expected positive effect on foreign policy, too, rests on economic success.

In Chapter One, the New Regionalism had been defined as a concept embracing DI and openness. Good governance now arises as another important condition for the New Regionalism to succeed. Put differently, politicians must be ready and capable of taking advantage of the new opportunities by overthrowing outdated institutional arrangements and by finding and implementing a new policy framework that is appropriate to fully reap the benefits of the New Regionalism in the global world economy.

Adherents to the New Regionalism (implicitly) take it for granted that these reforms become realized and really improve on the status quo ante. They argue that resistance to change of national interest groups can be managed and melted down by common regional initiatives. Their claim is that strong national vested interests can be tamed by pressure exerted by the regional community.

Critics see the political willingness to establish such a framework more skeptically than its proponents (Berthold, 1996; Bhagwati/Panagariya, 1999).

It is important, therefore, to investigate more deeply into the nature of the management of regional reforms and the expected changes of the relative power of the parties involved. This will be done in the following section by referring to public choice theory, namely the interest group approach.

3.5 THE INTEREST GROUP APPROACH

The new political economy offers two opposing views of the impact of regionalism on the relative political position of protectionist and liberal forces within a given society:

1. The proponents of open (and deep) regionalism maintain that vested interests that hinder liberal trade and investment within the nation state will be weakened if they have to lobby for protection on the regional level. As a consequence, the described growth effect will most certainly materialize, new members will be attracted and the region eventually advances towards multilateralism (or, at least, it remains open and does not substitute for multilateralism).
2. In contrast, the critics would accept the thesis of weakened lobby groups only in the short (and medium) run – if at all. In the longer run they expect that protectionist interests will reorganize on the regional level and build even more powerful groups. These groups are expected to renegotiate the liberal policy stance of the formation period step by step and turn the 'open' into a 'closed' region. As a consequence, the growth performance will slow down in the longer run, the attractiveness of the region for outsiders will seize, and the expected drive towards multilateralism becomes illusionary.

Bhagwati and Panagariya (1999, 69ff.) have sketched these opposing positions in their 'time path' analysis (Figure 3.2). They discuss different trajectories of growth (world welfare) in t (time). The maximum level of welfare will be obtained if multilateral free trade is realized. This level will be approached via the WTO multilateral process according to curve (1). Now suppose a regime (2) of open (and deep) regionalism that exhibits a positive growth effect permanently. In trajectory (2a) it is supposed that trade creation (TC) exceeds trade diversion (TD), which results in an immediate positive welfare effect of regional integration. Thereafter, the growth effect of deeper integration and increasing membership initiate a relatively quick rapprochement of the multilateral maximum. (2b) assumes a less favorable starting point because TD exceeds TC (the welfare level drops instantaneously), but

World
Welfare

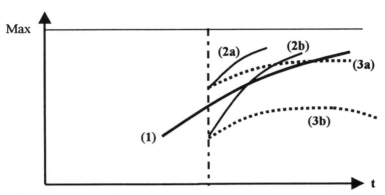

Max: Maximum welfare effect from WTO (multilateral) trade liberalization
      (independence of multilateral and PTA time paths)
(1) WTO (multilateral) trade liberalization process
(2) Open regionalism time path (permanent growth effect)
      (a) - TC > TD
           - positive growth effect from the start
           - increasing membership
      (b) - TD > TC
           - positive growth effect after initial decline
           - increasing membership
(3) Open regionalism (transitory growth effect)
      (a) - TC > TD
           - no permanent growth effect
           - stagnating membership
      (b) - TD > TC
           - no growth effect
           - stagnating membership

TC = Trade creation
TD = Trade diversion

Source: adapted from Bhagwati/Panagariya (1999,70)

Figure 3.2   Multilateralism and regional integration (time path analysis)

the still positive growth and membership effects are strong enough to approximate the maximum level quicker than in the multilateral case.

From the point of view of the critics of open regionalism the expected effects on growth are only transitory. Trajectories (3a + b) are sketching the long-term consequences of this thesis, starting from identical positions as in case 2. In the more favorable case of TC > TD regionalism performs better at the beginning. But, as the growth effect wanes and new membership becomes less attractive the drive towards the maximum contribution of international specialization slows down and eventually the performance of the region falls back and behind that of the multilateral trajectory. (3b) reflects the worst case scenario with TD > TC and a trajectory that lies always below the multilateral strategy and falls back ever more. Under this latter scenario a fragmentation of the global market would become a real threat.

Quite a number of arguments have been raised to justify the pessimistic views of open regionalism. Most of these arguments explain why the members of a regional agreement may lose interest in open markets against non-member countries:

1. Regional firms receive a privileged status relative to outsiders. Every new membership brings new sets of firms into the position of these established firms, so that the competitive pressure for insiders will increase. This will raise their interest in the maintenance of the status quo.
2. Large states or regions tend to regulate market accession selectively. This strategy aims at a discriminatory treatment of new members and increases transaction costs. Two particularly serious problems in this context are the 'hub-and-spokes' approach and the 'spaghetti bowl' phenomenon (see below). Thus, as these kinds of policies become more popular, the efficiency gains from the larger markets are getting lost and the attractiveness of the region will diminish.
3. The 'our market is large enough syndrome' (Bhagwati) states that in large regions people tend to underestimate the need to trade with the rest of the world. Pro-trade groups will become less insistent on openness and the relative power of protectionist lobbies will rise.
4. The spaghetti bowl problem. The theory of open regionalism usually analyses the situation of one (or a few) regions that exercise regional free trade within a WTO context of 'near to free trade'. If things run positively those few regions expand toward multilateralism.

This scenario does not reflect the present international economic situation sufficiently well. In particular, it underestimates the implicit dangers of an accumulation of regional agreements. The crucial point is that Free Trade Agreements are – contrary to what most theories build on – not perfect. That is, they are incomplete, and they are consciously designed to be so, because the regional option, as a matter of rule, implies a greater power political leverage for the larger participants. More precisely, governments use their increased scope for discretionary action to follow mercantilist strategies. That is, they execute economic and political power at the expense of weaker partners. Strategic trade policy[7] is one such approach, the 'hub-and-spokes' strategy is another. These (and further) deviations from the principle of regional free trade constitute a universe of 'free trade' and 'deeper integration' agreements, each of them departing in specific ways from the 'ideal' typus. One further aspect of this spaghetti bowl syndrome derives from the strategic use of rules of origin, which have originally been thought to define distinct properties of a product as qualification for the regional market. Rules of origin can easily be abused and transformed into significant non-tariff barriers (NTBs) (Estevadeordal/Goto/Saez, 2000).

As a consequence we find that, what appears to be a web of Free Trade Agreements at a first look, is in reality a complex system of selective regulations, which renders the term FTA (CM) virtually meaningless. Governments, instead of building DI areas along the principles of open regionalism, exploit mercantilist gains from bilateralism and selective sector treatment. This is equal to saying that governments in present day regionalism frequently overlook (or even consciously abuse) the welfare increasing effects that are proposed by the concept of the New Regionalism – not to speak of multilateral free trade.

Behind these basic objectives against the political-economic foundations of the New Regionalism lies the conjecture that regionalism – contrary to the convictions of its proponents – will change the balance between the defenders of free trade and the protectionists in favor of the latter.

Consider a simple interest group approach (political support function) in order to clarify this argument.[8] According to this approach individuals (consumers, labor), firms and politicians (and bureaucrats) try to maximize their individual welfare based on strictly self-interested behaviour. Politicians are organized in political parties. They maximize votes in order to gain political power. Voters have different interests according to their individual position within the society and/or ideological convictions. They vote for those parties that promise to best serve these interests.

In the context of trade (regional integration) the diversity of interests may be reduced to the two basic options, 'free trade' and 'protectionism'. In this scenario private individuals offer votes and demand free trade or pro-tectionism respectively. Politicians, in turn, offer free trade or protection and demand votes. Now suppose that politicians (governments) dispose of a spectrum of political options between the two poles 'pure free trade' and 'strongest protection'. This opens up the possibility for political parties to concede some more liberal (or more protectionist) policies according to the political situation (expected voting behavior). In this context, a rational politician (government) will decide to offer more protection (free trade) as long as this raises more votes from the protectionist clientele than are getting lost from the free traders and vice versa.

The exact outcome of this negotiating process between (organized) private interests and the political parties is due to a number of specific conditions. One is the parliamentary system itself, which may induce so-called log rolling phenomena (Frey, 1985). Another one is uncertainty about the true voter preferences (on part of the politicians) and/or the consequences of a distinct political program (on part of the voters). These kinds of uncertainties can be reduced by gathering new information. But gathering information is a costly process, which will lead many voters to rely on second-hand information. Second-hand information, however, may be biased to include specific information provided by lobby groups (rent seeking approach) to serve their particular interests. Under these conditions one would expect that the most serious efforts to gain information and to distribute it would be undertaken by those who are most seriously affected by a distinct political program. These groups, in turn, will also shape the outcome of the political bargaining process on the respective topic to their advantage.

Most important in the context of trade policy is the fact that the capability to organize varies among groups. Organization will be easier, if the groups' interests are homogeneous and if they are seriously affected from a given policy. In turn, organization will be difficult if many voters are affected to a small extent and uncertainty is high. Consider a typical situation in which firms and workers in exporting and import competing industries are voting in favor of more free trade and more protectionism respectively. Another group is consumers who are interested in low priced imports. Firms and workers in exporting industries and consumers should be expected to vote in favor of free trade. With equal organizational power and equal intensity of interests one would expect more free trade to be the outcome. In reality, however, a more protectionist policy will often triumph over the liberal strategy because consumers are virtually non-organized. Small interest groups from import competing industries in turn will vehemently oppose any policy that might be directed against their perceived interests. Furthermore, they also may enjoy the fact that they do not receive much attention from other groups because their overall impact is small. This free rider position can be exploited even more rigorously if specific interests are sold as being of a general interest (raising welfare of the society) or if they are presented in such a way that altruistic feelings in the society are addressed.

Without going into detail, the crucial point of these ideas is that interest groups actively (try to) influence politics and voters to opt in favor of their specific interests, and that strong vested interests defended by small but well organized groups may develop a disproportionately high impact on politics (Krueger, 1974; Hurrell/Fawcett, 1997, Ursprung, 2000). This will be the more so if opposing groups are weak (consumers) or can be convinced (persuaded) to accept rival claims because of altruistic considerations.

Applied to the regional integration issue the critics of the New Regionalism may gain support if regionalism can be shown to change the balance between the opposing interest groups in favor of protectionism. There are some reasons to believe that such an outcome is not unlikely. First, consumer interests on the regional market may be even less organized than on the national market. Second, the reallocation of resources under increased competitive pressures may lead to larger enterprises and growing concentration. Thus, lobbying for specific policies will become more effective. Third, these enterprises may feel less need to export beyond the boundaries of the region so that even traditional exporting industries may be tempted to slow down their activities in favor of open markets. Last but not least, in the longer run, supranational organizations (including labor unions) may evolve, which could become even more influential than they had been on their local markets (Berthold, 1996).

Not all of these arguments are entirely convincing a priori. Consumers for example will not suffer much from less ability to organize in a bigger market, if this ability had already been close to zero before the region was founded. High firm concentration, too, is not automatically linked to a higher propensity of protectionist lobbying. Under the conditions of globalization in particular, many of the bigger firms increasingly organize their diverse activities outside the region and the concentration effort on the regional market may in fact intensify this process. Because of this global involvement, MNEs are strongly in favor of low trade barriers that will enable them to optimize economic activities globally (global sourcing). The strong interest of globally operating firms in open national *and* regional markets turns out to be an important factor in defending the New Regionalism, because the liberalization of regional capital flows and the guarantee of non-discriminatory FDI, in particular, are important elements of this concept. Thus, the New Regionalism, by attracting FDI (both intra-regional and from non-members), strengthens the forces that are working in favor of multilateral openness.

However, what remains to be seen is whether the New Regionalism is generating institutions that eventually will shift the balance of interests in the direction of inward looking blocs.

3.6 THE NEW REGIONALISM AS A POLITICAL PHENOMENON

Up to this point we have discussed the arguments that have been raised in favor and against open (and deep) regionalism from the economic point of view. This discussion implicitly rests on the assumption that open regionalism eventually leads to either multilateralism or trading blocs. From a political perspective this question has been downsized in recent years. Many politicians and political scientists in fact argue that regionalism should better be understood as a phenomenon that is evolving out of the necessity to cope with some of the most urgent challenges of globalization. That is, the New Regionalism, rather than being a transitory phenomenon that leads to multilateralism, has emerged to become a permanent new option for the organization of world trade and investment. As far as this claim holds the basic objective of regionalism, which is ultimately the fostering of multilateral free trade, would indeed become a fiction. This would also mean that the new regionalism is going to challenge a cornerstone of the post World War II international economic order. It is worthwhile, therefore, to discuss this argument in some more detail.

Start by considering the fact that globalization raises international interdependencies. Strong international interdependencies put a limit on national governments' ability to carry out distinct economic and social policies at home. More precisely, national (economic) policies in the age of globalization have to be designed with due consideration of their impact on the countries' international competitive situation.[9] From a political point of view, this effect of globalization tends to erode national sovereignty. Regionalism could be an answer to this threat! It has been argued that the New Regionalism could become a defense strategy against this loss of sovereignty, if the region could be positioned as a powerful supranational organization that supports the weak individual nation state. Within the region sovereignty must, in fact, be shared among all participants. But this will be a minor sacrifice in view of the higher level of sovereignty that can be maintained vis-à-vis the global market (Schirm, 1999). Based on this calculus, regionalism cannot any more be interpreted as a transitory phenomenon but has indeed to be understood as a new permanent form of international (economic) organization.

If one looks at the concept of the New Regionalism from the point of view of sovereignty sharing, an important theoretical problem arises. Open regionalism has been defined as an approach that links the region closely to the world market. The idea was to take advantage of the global economy in order to maximize the region's welfare in a way that makes the region grow more dynamically than the global surrounding. Thinking about the close correlation between growth and structural change (in the long run) it is clear that successful open regionalism, by fostering growth, also fosters structural change.

Now consider sovereignty sharing. Sovereignty sharing intends to secure a higher level of sovereignty of the regional group, compared to the level that any single member country alone could have maintained. Thus, being part of a regional agreement that is capable of deploying a higher level of sovereignty, governments can improve upon their scope of discretionary policies vis-à-vis the global market. Suppose governments use this possibility to keep a higher level of inflexibility (substantiated for example by distinct forms of social and labor market policies) than would have been possible without the exploitation of the regional power political position, then the adjustment flexibility within the region will slow down. It goes without saying that this is exactly the opposite of an economic strategy to foster growth and development. As a result of this kind of open regionalism we would expect a growing mismatch between growth aspiration and adjustment capacity. In the long run, either economic growth will have to slow down in this 'sclerotic' scenario (the regional 'growth pool' cannot be sustained) or the adjustment flexibility must be improved in order to concede the structural changes enforced by economic growth. Then, however, sovereignty sharing as a means to defend outdated market structures becomes illusionary. This leads to the conclusion that 'permanent regionalism', understood as a means to maintain sovereignty in order to better resist global economic change, eventually will end up in a closed system. Thus, this kind of politically motivated regionalism is incompatible with the concept of the New Regionalism.[10]

Finally, the observation of constraints regarding the ability to adjust to economic change (especially in Western industrialized societies) gives credit to a quite different explanation of regionalism. In fact, many observers have stressed that a strong motivation of the New Regionalism of the 1990s has been (and is) to secure market access in the face of increasing global protectionist developments. From this perspective it is not so much the challenge of increasingly open global markets that brings about regionalism, but the fears that multilateral openness cannot be maintained. Under these conditions, tying one's fate to an important regional market may be an insurance against the breakdown of the international system (Perroni/Whalley, 2000). But a regionalism based on this objective can hardly be brought in line with the growth promoting concept of the New Regionalism.

To sum up, we find an array of arguments in favor and against the concept of open regionalism. Since many of the arguments ultimately rest on mere speculation about expected changes of human behavior under different integration schemes they cannot be definitely decided upon without profound empirical evidence. Thus, what is urgently needed is to improve knowledge on the dynamics of open regionalism, that is, to examine the experience of the existing agreements.

3.7 SUMMARY

Regionalism has grown to become an important element of the global division of labor, both as a political and an economic phenomenon. As such the distinct design of any regional agreement is the result of complex political decision-making procedures based on a large number of parameters. Drawing on conventional political models this complex set of parameters can be reduced to two fundamental objectives: security, an elementary political task, and welfare (economic growth), a specific economic objective.

In the long run, both objectives tend to be mutually reinforcing so that a political trade-off will not arise. In the short (and medium) run, however, power political intervention based on security considerations may be in conflict with the economic objective. A simple model of the interdependent decision-making procedure shows that the optimal degree of political intervention (that maximizes welfare defined broadly as the optimal combination of security and growth) depends on the relative importance that governments attribute to both objectives, and on the prevailing economic model of international trade. The political decision in favor of an inferior international economic strategy may have an adverse impact on the realization of both objectives in the long run. Thus, for a political regime to succeed it is essential to identify the optimal international economic order. This is the one that maximizes the contribution of international economic relations to national welfare (given a distinct level of security).

International economics, from a political perspective, is frequently reduced to power political (mercantilist) considerations based on a zero-sum philosophy.[11] This approach is quite different from the (liberal) economic perception of trade as a source of mutually reinforcing gains. Given these opposing views it is important to put the political vision on international economics in perspective. This has been done by discussing globalization in the preceding chapter.

Globalization is basically the result of the (non-discriminatory) multilateral GATT/WTO approach, which has been installed as the international economic order after World War II. It has been shown that the phenomenon of globalization can be broken down into a small number of long-standing trade (and international investment) theories including the theory of the international firm. This insight makes it clear that the static and dynamic gains from trade (and international capital flows), which have been extensively discussed in the economic literature directly apply to globalization. Overwhelming empirical evidence supports this statement.

The New Regionalism can be interpreted as a distinct version of the liberal trade and investment model that includes some particular power political elements. Proponents of this type of an international economic regime maintain that it might be even more growth enhancing than the multilateral model even though it is inherently discriminatory. Chapter 3 has traced these arguments in favor of the New Regionalism and examined them critically. Deeper integration is at the center of this discussion. It is aimed at the formation of regional integration agreements that go beyond the pure Free Trade Agreements. The success of deeper economic integration critically depends on the initiation of a dynamic growth process within the region. For this to happen, progressive institutional reforms and openness vis-à-vis non-members are critical preconditions. Adherents to this concept do see good chances for these pre-conditions to become realized.

The critics question exactly this belief. They claim that regional integration rather than freeing forces that are conducive to growth may indeed contribute to weaken them. This thesis has its theoretical under-pinnings in public choice theories and it warns against the danger that initially open regional agreements might, in the longer run, degenerate into inward oriented blocs. If these fears are real, the present state regionalism, rather than leading to multilateral free trade, will eventually threaten the whole international system.

Political theories tend to claim that regionalism in the context of globalization will be established as a non-transitory complement to free trade in order to facilitate sovereignty sharing between local governments; but they do not address the question of its potential welfare effect explicitly. It has been argued here, that the viability of this political approach to regional integration, too, rests on the sustainability of the conditions of an open regionalism. Given the fact that sovereignty sharing is often intending to build a fence against global competition it is doubtful whether this concept can guarantee openness in the long run. The question remains open, therefore, also from this political point of view, whether the New Regionalism will be as welfare enhancing as its proponents argue.

Empirical evidence on the economic virtues of the New Regionalism is scarce. The interwar period and Latin American regionalism during the 1960s have clearly been devastating experiences (Langhammer, 1992), but they were based on inward looking strategies. Open regionalism is clearly a different concept.

The European Community has often been cited as a proof of the viability of the concept of the New Regionalism. Indeed, it can be shown that the EC has brought about an ongoing movement towards deeper integration based on the formation of supranational institutions. Recently the implementation of a single European currency has added another spectacular supranational element. During this process the EC has repeatedly admitted new member countries. Starting from 6 members the EC now includes 15 members and is planning to add about another dozen within the next 10 to 15 years. It has also been demonstrated that trade among members has both increased economic growth and convergence (Ben-David/Nordström/Winters, 1999) while international relations with outsiders still grew rapidly (external trade creation). The European Community, because of this visible outcome, has found much attention worldwide, and it is quite often praised as a prototype of a successful project of deeper integration.

However, since the 1980s there has been growing concern that the EC might be unable to maintain a liberal trading system vis-à-vis outsiders. Most certainly, over time, the EC has already established a highly discriminatory trade policy regime (Preusse, 1994; Sapir, 1998) and increasingly adheres to administrative trade barriers (Messerlin, 2001). It is at least doubtful, therefore, whether the European experience will be able to belie the critics of the concept of the New Regionalism over a longer time period.

More evidence on regional integration projects is urgent under these conditions. The recent American Regionalism, though still in its early days, can serve as another laboratory for the disclosure of further insight into the functioning of the New Regionalism. This is the topic of Chapters Four, Five and Six of this study.

NOTES

1. In fact, it is only the differential effect of international activities on growth and change that is attributable to globalization.
2. Two other important questions that will not be addressed in this chapter are: 1. Does regionalism contribute to the solution of new cross-border problems that are emerging from growing interdependencies? 2. How does regionalism change the relative power political position of nation states? I will come back to these questions in the context of the Americas.
3. Robson remarks that there have been some important contributions to this topic before Viner (see Robson, 1998, 7 ff.).
4. If 'deeper' integration just means anything beyond shallow integration (FTA, CU) an almost infinite number of versions of 'deeper' integration arrangements may exist. A complete integration of national markets into one new regional market would be the final stage.
5. FDI may also be attracted because of higher import barriers. FDI that enters this way (tariff jumping) also increases capital inflows, however, it has quite different welfare implications as compared to the case discussed in this paragraph.
6. For a theoretical exposition see Baldwin (1995).
7. In an illuminating essay on 'Security and Trade' Nau (1995) interprets regionalism as part of the concept of strategic trade policy.

8. See Hillman (1982), Wellisz/Wilson (1986), and Grossman/Helpman (2002) for more profound theoretical presentations of this approach.
9. In order to avoid confusion concerning the concept of competitiveness (which sometimes is seen as strictly firm specific), here, a country's competitiveness means 'the quality of the environment for investment and for increasing productivity in a climate of macroeconomic stability and integration into the world economy' (IDB, 2001, 1).
10. Other political motivations, too, may of course be the driving forces of the 'power-sharing' decision. Nevertheless, the 'defense against globalization' argument ranks high.
11. This is most visible in international trade negotiations that are still based on the conviction that trade liberalization is an offer to the partner country rather than a measure in the country's own interest.

4. The North American Free Trade Agreement (NAFTA)

On 12 August 1982 the Mexican president Silva Herzog declared a debt moratorium against the USA. This declaration marked the beginning of a traumatic epoch for Mexico and Latin America. It is not without a symbolism, therefore, when exactly ten years later on 12 August 1992 the negotiations on the North American Free Trade Agreement (NAFTA) were brought to a successful end (notwithstanding the side agreements concerning labor and the environment which were added in 1993). The date emphasized the definite end of the 'lost decade', the credible devotion of Mexico to a new economic policy after decades of import substitution, and a radical change in the relations with its Anglo-American neighbors. After controversial political discussions in Canada, Mexico and the USA the treaty was ratified in 1993 and implemented on 1 January 1994.

Today, NAFTA is an established FTA with about 414 million people and a combined GDP of more than 11 trillion US$ (USTR, 2002d, 104). This makes it the biggest FTA in the world and the first one uniting two rich industrialized countries with an emerging economy (in 1994 the Mexican GDP p.c. was about one-tenth of that of the USA and Canada).

NAFTA did not only change the economic relations among and within its members but also the global international situation. A comprehensive evaluation of its economic impact, therefore, must at least consider three analytical levels: the national, the regional and the global level.

This chapter will be organized as follows: first a short characterization of NAFTA will be given. The idea is not to add another in-depth institutional analysis but to characterize the agreement with respect to the theoretical discussion in Chapter Three. Thereafter, the developments of trade and investment under the agreement will be analyzed. This will be followed by three sector studies, which identify distinct structural changes that have already taken place in response to the agreement. From these studies it will be possible to infer on some short- and medium-term effects of NAFTA. Next, some aspects of the longer-term consequences of NAFTA will be considered. This will be done by concentrating on some major trends in international (global) economic policies of the member states. The idea is to find out whether their global economic strategies under NAFTA are still compatible with multilateralism. The emphasis here will be on the US experience.

The findings of this chapter will be conducive to an answer to the question, whether the first (nearly) ten years of NAFTA experience do lend support to the thesis that the agreement follows the concept of the New Regionalism.

4.1   THE BASIC PROVISIONS OF NAFTA

Originally, the formation of NAFTA was a US–Mexican project. Starting in the second half of the 1980s the Mexican government under President Salinas had opened up the economy to the world market. This change of strategy from the import substitution regime of the post-war period was a major political and economic challenge for the country and it also made a reorganization of its international policies mandatory. Initially, Salinas had turned to the GATT to gain secure access to the global markets. But when the Uruguay Round talks on multilateral trade liberalization were about to fail in the early 1990s a more direct access to the US market became an important objective of the Mexican strategy. A trip to Europe in spring 1990 apparently convinced Salinas that the Old Continent was about to turn away from multilateralism and that a regional engagement in North America would be the only viable strategy to stabilize the new economic concept. In June 1990, he proposed an FTA with the USA. It is correct to state that an economic objective, the exploitation of the gains from liberal international (regional) trade relations, was central to Salinas' NAFTA strategy. However, turning to closer cooperation with the USA has also had an important political implication. That is, by stimulating growth and development at home, a closer relationship to its northern neighbors was thought to calm down the internal Mexican opposition against the reforms and help to strengthen the reform process.

For the USA, the economic effects of closer trade relations with Mexico, though much praised in the public discussions on NAFTA, are almost negligible in reality. In fact, for the USA, NAFTA at that time was basically a political instrument that was expected to serve different objectives. First, the Mexican political objective to stabilize the reform process at home neatly matched US security interests. Second, it has been claimed that a steadily growing Mexican economy under NAFTA would increasingly absorb the Mexican labor surplus and eventually slow down US immigration. Last but not least, many Americans hoped that an FTA with Mexico would also facilitate a more coordinated management of mutual border problems such as environmental degradation, drugs traffic etc.

On the global level it is apparent that the United States has played the regional card in order to put pressure on Europe and Japan in the Uruguay Round. It would be a superficial view, however, to reduce the United States' turn to the regional option to this single objective. In a broader context, the hegemonic power of the United States has been diminishing since the early 1970s. Regionalism in this context may be interpreted as an approach to secure relative political strength on the global market by the formation of firm alliances within the region (Mace, 1999). The turn of the USA to a multitrack approach as a strategy to defend its economic and political interests within the changed global environment dates in fact back to 1982, when the formation of 'GATT plus arrangements with like-minded countries' (Krueger, 1999, 108) had been proclaimed as a third pillar of the US international economic strategy.[1]

Canada initially opposed the US–Mexican project because it did not recognize any political advantage from such an FTA but feared considerable effects of trade divergence from increased US trade with Mexico. Though this argument rests only on a weak theoretical foundation (it takes for granted that Canadian and Mexican comparative advantages are highly overlapping, and it completely ignores intra-industry trade), the Canadian decision to participate in NAFTA was mainly born out of the belief that the damage to be expected for the Canadian economy from being shifted into a 'spokes' position within a North American 'hub-and-spokes' system would be even larger than being part of a trilateral FTA.

Taking into consideration the important political motives of all NAFTA protagonists, it is noteworthy that they nevertheless engaged in the formation of an FTA that is in large parts compatible with Article 24 of the GATT/WTO treaty. NAFTA includes all sectors of the economy and has initiated substantial tariff reductions, which will completely eliminate tariffs for almost all trade until 2004. Some remaining items (some agricultural products, glass and ceramics, footwear) are planned to be phased out until 2009. In the year 2000 this liberalization program had already reduced the average tariff level of US (Mexican) imports to 0.35 percent (1.27 percent), starting from 4 percent (10 percent) in 1994. Tariffs between Canada and Mexico performed quite similarly and US–Canadian tariffs had already been phased out by the end of 1998 under the bilateral FTA of 1988. This means, in fact, that currently tariffs on imports do not play any important role among the NAFTA members (external tariffs will be analyzed separately under section 4.5).

Another important element of the NAFTA is its treatment of capital flows. As has been argued before, a free flow of capital is an important characteristic of deeper integration agreements. Free capital flows, therefore, are a potentially large stimulus for the transformation of NAFTA into an area of deeper integration.[2] This aspect of deeper integration underlines the political claim to make NAFTA a 'catalyst of economic growth' (USTR, 2002d, 1).[3] It is worthwhile, therefore, to pay attention to these aspects of NAFTA.

One important part of international capital transactions is FDI. As argued in Chapter Three, FDI is not a simple transfer of capital but carries an entire team of specific assets. Consequently the transfer of embodied technical progress inherent in pure capital imports (and the corresponding capital goods imports, respectively) will be intensified through FDI. From this perspective, the provisions of NAFTA with respect to FDI are a decisive element of the project and crucial for the growth expectations to materialize. In fact, almost any Computational General Equilibrium (CGE) model on NAFTA has indicated that the growth effects from NAFTA for the Mexican economy strongly depend on FDI inflows (Brown/Deardorff/Stern, 1992).

The provisions of the NAFTA are indeed appropriate to enhance capital flows. They schedule equal treatment of investment, an unconditional transfer of remittances and the removal of export quotas.[4]

Based on these liberal provisions for FDI one should expect MNEs to reorganize production within the North American region, with Mexico becoming an attractive new location. Especially those enterprises that are looking for location advantages based on traditional factor endowments will be expected to invest in Mexico. However, a countereffect may also take place. MNEs that have been present in Mexico under the old protectionist regime because of the tariff hopping motive may now decide to relocate to the United States. In any case, this countereffect should only be of minor importance.

To sum up, from the discussion of trade and investment liberalization under NAFTA an increase of trade and investment flows has to be expected. Taking into consideration that trade flows between Canada and the United States are already intensive because of the much longer period of (relative) free trade under the automotive agreement and CUSTA (Canada–United States Free Trade Agreement), new trade and investment flows initiated by NAFTA should predominantly be taking place between the USA (and Canada) on one side and Mexico on the other.

Stepping down into the less transparent lowlands of non-tariff barriers (NTBs) and exceptions raises doubts concerning the characterization of NAFTA as a WTO conform agreement. One case in point is border road traffic. While US truckers are complaining of the discriminatory customs procedures in Mexico (Kornis, 2000, 5) the USA effectively blocked NAFTA provisions on the operation of Mexican trucks in the United States. In particular, the USA first delayed permission for Mexican trucks to operate in the US border states (1995) and later refused to concede access to the entire USA (2000). The rationale for these policies was said to be that neither Mexican trucks nor their drivers would meet US health and safety standards. There is no doubt, however, about the strong lobbying pressure that American trucker associations, the 'International Brotherhood of Teamsters' in particular, exerted on Congress (Kornis, 2002, 1) in order to prohibit the NAFTA obligations from being fulfilled. It needed a NAFTA arbitration panel to eventually force the United States to open its borders on 1 January 2002 for those Mexican trucks that meet US safety standards.

Another case is fruit and vegetables, which are not only liable to extremely long phasing-in procedures but are also operated by variable tariff rates. The official US rationale for this procedure is to smooth price changes between peak and slump seasons. The effect on (north) Mexican farmers, however, is that tariffs are high when they are ready to supply the US market and low when they cannot.

On the US side, in turn, producers of high tech products claim that international property rights (IPR) are not respected satisfactorily in Mexico. These problems are particularly worrisome in the case of copyrights because many violations in Mexico take place in informal markets that are not completely under official control. Still other cases of concern are regulations on rules of origin, which apparently serve protectionist objectives against non-member countries (Estevadeordal, 1999, 17) and the side agreements on labor and the environment. Though the latter are not part of the official NAFTA agreement, NAFTA would not have come to life without them. Most importantly for the future of the US trade policy is the fact that the side agreements, by making a package deal between trade and environmental policies (and labor standards respectively), have presumably altered a fundamental position of US international trade policy. These external aspects of NAFTA will be treated in more detail below.

At this point it is sufficient to note that there are a number of exceptions and discriminatory provisions of NAFTA that raise concern about the officially proclaimed degree of openness and WTO compatibility.[5] The point is that these kinds of hidden NTBs are invisible and do not influence much of the public debate, except for individual cases that only come to be known occasionally.[6] Put differently, they are not publicly discussed as political and economic obstacles to integration (or openness in general) but may nevertheless have an important impact on the regional economy.[7] Nevertheless, taking a realistic view of the present situation in international trade policies, one would have difficulties in qualifying NAFTA as an especially protectionist undertaking, just because of these exceptions.

4.2   IS NAFTA PROMOTING GROWTH?

In official statements on NAFTA one can find almost euphoric scenarios of growth, employment, trade, and investment effects of the agreement (USTR, 2002d). What is beyond dispute regarding these claims is the fact that all NAFTA countries underwent an exceptionally long growth period during the 1990s. Starting from a deep recession in the early 1990s the USA and Canada (lagging somewhat behind) showed an impressive growth performance throughout the 1990s, which came to an end in 2001. Mexico, which had a relatively good growth performance despite the US recession in the early 1990s (that is even before NAFTA) suffered a severe disruption of economic growth during the so-called Tequila crisis (1995) and recovered quickly thereafter to realize an average rate of GDP growth from 1996–2000 that exceeds its northern partners by far. In 2001, Mexico, too, was hit by the US recession and economic performance dropped to a zero rate of growth (Table 4.1).

Table 4.1   Real rates of growth of GDP, 1992–2001 (%)

	USA	Canada	Mexico
1992	2.3	0.8	3.7
1993	3.5	2.3	2.0
1994	2.3	4.1	4.5
1995	3.4	2.1	−6.2
1996	3.9	1.8	5.2
1997	3.9	3.7	7.0
1998	3.9	3.0	4.8
1999	4.1	3.7	3.5
2000	3.8	4.5	6.6
2001	0.3	1.5	−0.3
2002	2.3	3.3	1.5

Sources: US Department of Commerce; Banco de Mexico; Bank of Canada;
             OECD Economic Outlook No. 72, 2002

It is less clear, however, how much of this growth performance can be attributed to NAFTA. Trade and investment flows between the three countries can be measured relatively easily, but they are by no means entirely due to NAFTA. For one thing, driven by GDP growth, increasing openness and the specific opening-up policies in Mexico, trade has grown between the partner countries even before NAFTA came into being. Additionally, changes in real exchange rates, business cycles, relative changes in productivities, and national policies, which are not trade policies but may still have an impact on trade, would have to be netted out in order to come to a clear conclusion on the pure NAFTA effect on trade and investment.

Inferring from trade to growth is even more complicated. Again the impact of NAFTA on economic growth is only one out of a whole set of growth promoting factors and it may even be changing according to the distinct economic and political circumstances prevailing at a particular point in time. To say it in the words of Ferrantino, under these conditions it is 'extremely difficult to separate "the signal" of NAFTA effects from the "noise" of the other economic factors influencing ... the economies in the post NAFTA period' (Ferrantino, 2001, 2).

Notwithstanding the conceptual difficulties of identifying the effects of NAFTA seriously it is intuitively reasonable for simply quantitative reasons that the US growth performance of the 1990s cannot be attributed to any significant extent to increased trade relations with Mexico. The same reasoning suggests that trade and investment originating from the USA and Canada may have a potentially much more important effect on Mexico. Also the US role in stabilizing the Mexican economy during the Tequila crisis is worth mentioning in this context, because it highlights an important indirect effect of the NAFTA on Mexico, that is, the increased preoccupation on part of the USA with the economic fate of its neighbor.

Under these conditions the US–Mexican relations are critical for the performance of the whole project and Mexico appears to be the most important test case of NAFTA. Based on this insight, the following examination starts from the thesis that NAFTA has had a positive growth effect on the Mexican economy. In order to support this thesis it should be possible to identify two separate but mutually enforcing developments:

1. Trade and investment flows within NAFTA (and between the USA and Mexico in particular) should have grown at a higher rate than the respective external relations.
2. Trade and investment growth should have initiated structural changes in the region (and in Mexico in particular). That is, the Mexican (US) structure of production should have responded to the incentives provided by NAFTA.

In as much as support is found for both of these developments it may be inferred that, based on NAFTA, additional gains from exchange and specialization have been realized. These gains are likely to have been translated into higher real income and growth the more intensively and the more rigorously the structural adjustments have taken place, which the new regional economic conditions have provoked.

In order to analyze these hypotheses three questions will be raised:

- How did trade between the USA, Canada and Mexico under the NAFTA proceed?
- How did FDI flows between the USA and Mexico develop?
- Are there significant structural changes to be recorded on the sector level?

4.2.1 The Trade Effects

The thesis that NAFTA has had a positive effect on growth in its member countries would be supported if trade relations within the region had intensified relative to non-members during the first years of the agreement. Table 4.2 presents US exports and imports in nominal terms from 1993–2001. Reference is made to the development of trade relations with the 'rest of the world'. The 1993–2001 period can be regarded as a 'typical' period in so far as it starts at the beginning of the upswing of the 1990s and ends in the first year of recession, so that most exaggerations from the late boom years have probably been cancelled out.

Table 4.2   *US merchandise trade with NAFTA partners, 1993–2001 (billions of US$)*

	1993	1995	1997	1999	2000	2001[*]	% Change 1993–2001
Exports							
NAFTA	142.0	172.3	221.5	253.5	290.2	266.3	87.8
Canada	100.4	126.0	150.1	166.6	178.2	164.7	64.3
Mexico	41.6	46.3	71.4	86.9	111.3	101.6	144.2
Rest of the World	323.1	410.7	466.1	431.1	482.0	462.0	43.0
Imports							
NAFTA	151.1	206.8	253.9	308.7	366.7	351.8	133.1
Canada	111.2	145.1	168.0	199.0	230.8	219.9	98.2
Mexico	39.9	61.7	85.9	109.7	135.9	131.9	230.0
Rest of the World	429.6	536.7	616.3	721.3	857.7	808.8	88.1

Note: [*] annualized data based on January–December 2001

Sources: US Department of Commerce; own calculations

From these data it is clear that US trade with its NAFTA partners expanded much more rapidly (87.7 percent in exports and 133.1 percent in imports) than trade with non-member countries (43 percent in exports and 88.1 percent in imports). Within NAFTA, US trade with Mexico (144.2 percent in exports and 230 percent in imports) expanded far more rapidly than with Canada (64.3 percent in exports and 98.2 percent in imports). This amounts to rates of growth in real terms of 35, 93 and 20 percent for US exports to Canada, Mexico and the 'rest of the world' and 69, 190 and 59 percent for imports (Hillberry/McDaniel, 2002, 2). It is also remarkable that the overall trade deficit of the USA increased with all regions, but most rapidly in trade with the rest of the world and most slowly in trade with Canada (where two-way trade is dominant). By and large this means that, from the US perspective, there have been some remarkable trade creation effects of NAFTA, which are essentially pronounced in US–Mexican trade relations.

Mexican trade data (Table 4.3) covering the same period indicate that the Mexican penetration of the North American market amounts to an increase of exports of 223 percent which is much ahead of the 170 percent export increase to the rest of the world. Most of the NAFTA increase concerned the USA (227 percent), while Canada received 93.8 percent more Mexican exports. Mexican imports show a different performance. The expansion of NAFTA imports is only 153.8 percent as compared to 347 percent from the rest of the world. Within NAFTA a high increase of imports from Canada (250 percent) stands against an increase of 151.2 percent from the USA.[8] These figures are remarkable in so far as they suggest a more dynamic trade expansion with non-members and Canada as compared to the USA. A closer look at these figures reveals that the expansion of imports from Canada lagged behind the US performance until 1997, and outpaced US data only during the last years.

Leaving aside for the moment the performance of Mexican imports from the rest of the world, the NAFTA trade expansion gives a clear signal that trade liberalization under NAFTA has contributed to a rapid expansion of exports and imports within the region. Hillberry/McDaniel have shown that this trade expansion went hand in hand with an increasing variety of goods traded (Hillberry/McDaniel, 2002, 3). An increasing variety of traded goods, in turn, increases competition and improves consumer welfare.

Altogether the strong expansion of Mexican exports and (to a lesser extent) of Canadian exports to the USA suggests that NAFTA has enabled the US partner countries to participate more intensively in the exceptional US growth period of the 1990s than would have been possible without the agreement.

Table 4.3   Mexican merchandise trade with NAFTA partners, 1993–2001
            (billions of US$)

	1993	1995	1997	1999	2000	2001	Change 1993–2001
Exports							
NAFTA	44.4	68.3	96.3	122.8	151.0	143.4	223.0
Canada	1.6	2.0	2.2	2.4	3.4	3.1	93.8
USA	42.9	66.3	94.2	120.4	147.7	140.3	227.0
Rest of the World	1.0	1.3	2.0	2.1	2.7	2.7	170.0
Imports							
NAFTA	46.5	55.2	84.0	108.2	131.6	118.0	153.8
Canada	1.2	1.4	2.0	2.9	4.0	4.2	250.0
USA	45.3	53.8	82.0	105.3	127.6	113.8	151.2
Rest of the World	1.7	1.9	3.5	4.5	6.3	7.6	347.0

Sources: Banco de Mexico (2002); own calculations

4.2.2   Foreign Direct Investment

In a number of so-called Computable General Equilibrium (CGE) models, which calculated the potential effects of NAFTA, the (expected) expansion of activities of MNEs on the Mexican market has been identified as one of the crucial growth promoting effects of the agreement. Two important aspects of this development have to be considered. One is the FDI expansion within NAFTA (with a transfer of capital from the USA [and Canada] towards Mexico as the main focus). The second is the potential FDI inflow to Mexico (NAFTA) from outside the region. The latter effect may become important if MNEs from non-member countries are ready to trust the potential growth effects of NAFTA and decide to increase production on the regional (Mexican) market.[9]

First consider Table 4.4 which is derived from the UNCTAD database (UNCTAD, 2000, 2001). The figures show FDI inflows into NAFTA from 1988–2000. World FDI inflows are used as a point of reference. Comparing the values of the year 2000 with those of the 1988–93 period shows that during the 1990s a considerable expansion of FDI flows both within NAFTA and worldwide has taken place. It can also be observed that both series reveal an almost identical rate of expansion (an 8.5 times increase over the whole period), so that the average share of FDI inflows into NAFTA relative to global inflows remains almost constant (28.1 percent and 28.2 percent). From these data, NAFTA, despite the enormous absolute amount of capital inflows, still does not appear to have been an especially attractive area for international investment.

Table 4.4   FDI inflows into NAFTA, 1988–2000 (billions of US$), and shares of world total

	1988–93	1994	1995	1996	1997	1998	1999	2000
NAFTA	53.8	64.8	77.6	104.0	128.7	208.6	342.1	357.6
Canada	5.3	8.2	9.3	9.6	11.5	22.6	25.2	63.3
Mexico	3.7	11.0	9.5	9.9	13.8	11.6	11.9	13.2
USA	44.8	45.1	58.8	84.5	103.4	174.4	295.0	281,1
World	190.6	256.0	331.1	384.9	477.9	692.5	1,075.0	1,270.8
NAFTA World	28.2	25.3	23.4	27.0	26.9	30.1	31.8	28.1
Canada World	2.8	3.2	2.8	2.5	2.4	3.3	2.3	5.0
Mexico World	1.9	4.2	2.9	2.6	2.9	1.7	1.1	1.0
USA World	23.5	17.6	17.8	21.9	21.6	25.2	27.4	22.1

Sources: UNCTAD, World Investment Reports 2000 and 2001; own calculations

More detailed information on the relative attractiveness of the three member countries for FDI inflows derive from the single country figures. The USA is the most important single recipient country of FDI, but these capital imports did not keep pace with the global development (moving down slightly from an average of 23.5 percent of world FDI inflows between 1988–93 to 22.1 percent in 2000). Even more sobering is the frequently praised Mexican FDI performance once it is measured against the background of global development. On average, Mexico held a 1.9 percent share of world FDI flows during the 1988–93 period but, after an initial jump to 4.2 percent in 1994, this share dropped to 1.0 percent in 2000.[10] Canada is the only NAFTA member that managed to attract more FDI inflows during the last decade. Its share of total inflows jumped from 2.8 percent to 5 percent.[11]

Now turn to US FDI in Canada and Mexico from 1994–2000/01, that is, under the NAFTA (Table 4.5). According to the figures of the US Department of Commerce NAFTA has been slightly more attractive to US enterprises than the rest of the world (131 percent versus 126 percent increase). However, most of these additional FDI flows did not address Mexico but Canada (217 percent). Mexico's FDI inflows, though expanding on average from 1996–2000 (that is, after the Tequila crisis), continuously lost ground in relative terms. In the year 2000 the Mexican share in US FDI had dropped to 3.2 percent, down from 6.1 percent in 1994, while the Canadian share had increased from 8.2 percent in 1994 to 12.6 percent in 2001 (11.5 percent in 2000).

Table 4.5   US direct investment in Canada and Mexico, 1994–2001, and shares of world total

	1994	1995	1996	1997	1998	1999	2000	2001	% Change 1994– 2001
NAFTA	10.5	11.6	9.6	13.2	12.4	24.1	24.3		131.0
Canada	6.0	8.6	7.2	7.6	7.8	18.1	19.0	14.4	217.0
Mexico	4.5	3.0	2.4	5.6	4.6	6.0	5.3	D	18.0
World	73.3	92.1	84.4	95.8	131.0	174.6	165.0	114.0	126.0
NAFTA World	14.3	12.6	11.4	13.8	9.5	13.8	14.7		
Canada World	8.2	9.3	8.5	7.9	6.0	10.4	11.5	12.6	
Mexico World	6.1	3.3	2.8	5.8	3.5	3.4	3.2		

Note: D: suppressed to avoid disclosure of data of individual companies

Source: US Department of Commerce

Mexican data on FDI inflows from 1994–2001 are presented in Table 4.6. The 2001 figures are apparently biased by one-time effects (FDI in services increased by more than 9 billion in 2001 while FDI in manufactures dropped from 5.5 billion to 2.2 billion US$)[12] and will not be further examined. Drawing on the 1994–2000 data (which do not include the present recession) we detect a relatively small 38.3 percent increase of FDI inflows (new investments including Maquiladora industries) during the whole NAFTA period. Measured against the dynamic development of FDI worldwide during this period reveals that, in essence, the Mexican FDI position has stagnated in relative terms. And this stagnation appears to be basically due to the apparent non-attractiveness of the Mexican manufacturing sector for foreign enterprises (4.1 percent increase).

In contrast, the Maquiladora industries have developed into a particularly dynamic sector under the NAFTA.[13] Cautious signs of prosperity are also visible in the service sectors, which expanded rapidly during the last two years. However, taking in mind the general situation in Mexico, it would not be prudent to take these very recent developments as reliable grounds for a substantial future expansion of FDI in the Mexican services industries.

To sum up, contrary to some optimistic statements on the potential contribution of FDI to the formation of a NAFTA growth region (particularly with respect to Mexico), which have been made on the basis of CGE models, and which seemed to be confirmed by the observation of early FDI inflows, recent data suggest a different story. According to the UNCTAD data, during the 1990s, NAFTA as a region has been no more attractive to foreign enterprises than any other region worldwide. While the USA and Canada can keep pace with worldwide developments, Mexico clearly lags behind. Though it is true that Mexico has experienced a jump of FDI inflows from the pre-NAFTA (1988–93) to the NAFTA period (1994–2000) there is no sign of a stable increase since 1994 when worldwide FDI flows have increased dramatically.

This finding is supported by US and Mexican data on FDI flows within NAFTA. Data on US FDI outflows from 1994–2000 are indicating a 126 percent increase worldwide, but an increase of only 18 percent to Mexico. On average, the US FDI inflows into Mexico are stagnating over the entire NAFTA period and the Mexican share of US inflows dropped from 6.1 percent in 1994 to 3.2 percent in 2000. Canada presents itself as a most attractive location for FDI since 1999.

Mexican data show a 38.3 percent increase of new investments from all over the world (including the Maquiladora sector). Excluding the Maquiladoras makes this figure drop to 20.3 percent. This relative stagnation is due to the apparent non-attractiveness of the Mexican manufacturing sector for foreign capital, once the booming automotive sector and the Maquiladora industries are excluded. Due to the fact that the recently expanding services sectors may have been influenced by one-time events the situation appears to be even less promising than the data suggest.

It is illuminating to evaluate this state of affairs in the light of the worldwide expansion of US FDI during the 1990s. During this decade and contrary to the 1980s, new activities of US MNEs abroad were increasingly concentrated on non-OECD countries. Thus, between 1989–98 'US affiliates' experienced a rapid average annual employment growth in China (53.9 percent) and in Eastern and Central Europe (39.7 percent), but only 8.3 percent in Mexico (Hanson/Mataloni jr/Slaughter, 2001, 7). As most of these

Table 4.6 FDI in Mexico, 1994–2001 (millions of US$)

	1994	1995	1996	1997	1998	1999	2000	2001	% Change 1994–2001
New Investments (excl. Maquiladora)	9,741.0	6,864.0	6,282.0	10,330.0	5,780.0	9,756.0	11,723.0	21,729.0	20.3
Manufacturers	5,288.0	3,395.0	3,286.0	5,597.0	2,881.0	5,886.0	5,506.0	2,224.0	4.1
Services	2,100.0	1,468.0	1,700.0	1,926.0	1,464.0	2,128.0	6,198.0	15,336.0	195.1
Maquiladora	895.0	1,366.0	1,417.0	1,680.0	2,111.0	2,778.0	2,983.0	2,172.0	233.3
Reinvestments	2,367.0	1,572.0	2,590.0	2,150.0	2,864.0	2,303.0	3,704.0	3,588.0	66.1
New Investments	10,636.0						14,706.0		38.4

Note: based on accumulated figures 1994–2001

Source: Comisión Nacional de Inversiones Extranjeras, *Informe Estadístico sobre el Comportamiento de la Inversión Extranjera Directa en Méjico* (Enero–Marzo de 2002, Apendice estadístico)

activities were motivated by cost considerations it becomes clear that the Mexican competitive position vis-à-vis low cost competitors is still insufficient.

By and large, this state of affairs casts strong doubts on the validity of the thesis that NAFTA, by providing considerable amounts of additional FDI will promote growth in Mexico to any considerable extent. One notable exception is the Maquiladora sector, which has expanded rapidly. This raises the question whether either the supply conditions in Mexico outside the Maquiladora sector are still so much deficient that the growth impulses from NAFTA do not materialize at a sufficiently large scale or that the expected growth effects from NAFTA itself are overrated in theory.

It is beyond the scope of this book to go into a detailed analysis of the Mexican supply side bottlenecks. But a short examination of the literature on this topic reveals that the key weaknesses of the Mexican economy are well known:

1. The financial sector is still not brought in line with international standards, and Mexican institutes in particular still did not manage to recover fully from the Tequila crisis. Consequently, the enormous amount of investments needed for restructuring and growth does not find an adequate financial infrastructure (Krueger/Tornell 1999; De Luna-Martinez, 2000).

2. The educational system still has not been brought in line with the increasing demand for human capital and skills that arises in an emerging economy. As a consequence, the investments in advanced production facilities and technologies which are a key component of any successful upgrading strategy, may be limited by the scarcity of skills.[14]

3. Mexico still has to solve an endemic agricultural crisis that increases the burden of structural adjustment far beyond that of a simple industrial restructuring strategy (Barry, 1995; OECD, 1997) .

4. According to many observers the Mexican peso is grossly overvalued at the beginning of this decade. This hinders the development of a sound export sector (beyond the emergence of strong automotive trade relations among highly interconnected MNEs). In particular, it is not conducive to the development of competitive local export industries.

5. The slow progress of reforms under the new administration suggests that the transition from the one-party regime to a functioning democracy is costly and more time-consuming than some optimistic observers might have believed (Dussel Peters, 2000; Nunnenkamp, 2002).

Altogether these bottlenecks suggest that the future prospects of Mexico in the NAFTA strongly depend on the country's continued preoccupation with sound political and economic reforms.

4.2.3 Structural Developments

Modern international trade (integration) theory states that trade liberalization opens up new and enlarged opportunities for mutual exchange, specialization, the exploitation of economies of scale (ECS) and increased product differentiation, which can be turned into productivity growth and mutual welfare improvements. In discussions of the virtues of open markets it is often quietly assumed that the permanent structural adjustments, which are the basis for any gains from trade beyond pure arbitration take place quasi-automatically once the trade account has been opened up. However, experience based on many unsuccessful reforms in LDCs, and in Latin America in particular, suggests that political resistance to change may become an effective threat to economic reforms, even if they are believed to be welfare enhancing on the community level. Under these conditions and if structural adjustments are blocked, the desired positive impact of the reforms on the economic performance will remain small or even be totally absent, and the whole reform project may eventually be turned down.

The observation of distinct changes of the structure of production following regional integration under NAFTA could therefore serve as an indication of the seriousness of the transformation process and support the hypothesis that trade and investment have had a positive impact on economic performance.

Drawing on conventional trade theories one should expect two basic patterns of structural adjustment following the formation of NAFTA:

1. The USA and Canada are both highly developed industrialized economies. It is true that they differ in some respects (Canada is a particularly resource rich country while the USA disposes of a highly developed market for industrial products and modern services), but they are not much different in their relative endowment with capital and (skilled) labor. Consequently, the Canadian market is of interest to the USA mainly because it promises to provide free and secure access to natural resources, energy in particular, and new opportunities to expand (sophisticated) production and sales networks into Canada. The automobile sector, which has been integrated long before NAFTA, is one case in point. Under NAFTA (CUSTA) these kinds of trade and investment links are expected to extend to ever more industries.

For Canada, in turn, improved access to the large US market is important for the realization of ECS and for the advancement of tight links to the leading US centers of science and technology. Structural adjustment between Canada and the USA due to NAFTA should, therefore, be predominantly of the intra-industry type of specialization that is also prevalent in the European Union (Greenaway/Hine, 1991). The development of trade and investment structures between both countries during the 1990s supports this view.

2. The division of labor between Canada and the USA on one and Mexico on the other side will also contain some elements of intra-industry trade and investment and these elements will gain importance if Mexico manages to converge under the NAFTA regime.

Nevertheless, these emerging new structures will be dominated for many years to come by a structure of specialization that builds on Heckscher–Ohlin-type arguments (Chapter Two). In fact, when NAFTA was brought to life in 1994, the average income per capita in Mexico was about one-tenth of that of its rich northern partners. Income differentials in turn are indicative of corresponding wage differentials, which qualify Mexico as a relatively labor abundant economy. Accordingly, conventional trade theory predicts that Mexico under NAFTA will be predominantly engaged in exports with a relatively high content of unskilled labor and import capital and skill intensive goods.[15]

A superficial look at the Mexican trade performance under NAFTA seems to question this statement. The trade data reveal a higher share of trade in more sophisticated industries than the Heckscher–Ohlin theorem would predict. Put differently, the intra-industry component appears to be prevalent. However, these data are misleading in so far as they obscure the fact that much of the intra-industry trade between the USA (Canada) and Mexico is in fact 'false' intra-industry trade. The point is that much of the 'measured' intra-industry trade between these countries is in intermediate goods and results from the ongoing disentanglement of complex value-added chains. By this procedure, labor intensive subcategories of a multistage production process are becoming separated and dislocated according to comparative advantage. The trade figures do not uncover this fact in many cases because intermediate products are crossing the borders in both directions without a change of the official product category (e.g. within one single three-digit or four-digit SITC [Standard International Trade Classification] group). This behavior is most pronounced (and in fact politically enforced) in the Maquiladora industries, but it is not confined to this sector.[16]

In order to detect the true factor content of Mexican trade with Canada and the USA it is necessary to go into a more detailed investigation of each sector. Three sectors that are of particular importance for at least one of the NAFTA members are apparel, the Maquiladora industries and the automotive industry. These industries will be analyzed in the following sections.

4.2.3.1   The apparel sector

The apparel industry has been a classical labor intensive (and low skill) industry for decades (Yeats, 1989). As such it forms the basis of the early industrialization process in almost every successful industrial development strategy.[17] In the reverse case this implies that advanced high income countries like Canada and the United States have a clear comparative disadvantage in this industry and should allow these activities to shrink. In reality, the strong resistance to change in the apparel industry of the United States has led to the development of a highly restrictive worldwide quota system on textiles and apparel since the early 1960s. This so-called 'multi-fibre agreement', by claiming to provide 'fair trade' has increasingly separated this industry from the liberal GATT codex and forced international trade relations into a straightjacket of 'managed' trade (operating largely at the expense of producers in low income countries and American consumers).[18]

The Uruguay Round trade talks, followed by the foundation of the WTO and the NAFTA liberalization process (complemented by the US–Caribbean Basin initiative) have broken up the anti-trade coalition of the industrialized countries (at least partly) by reintegrating the textile and apparel industries into the multilateral GATT/WTO framework. All quota restrictions are to be suspended until 2005.[19] For the USA and Canada, like in any other high income country, this new institutional setting is likely to increase adjustment pressure in this sector.

Given this global context, NAFTA, in many popular statements, is supposed to be an additional challenge for the North American textile and apparel industries. In fact, because of (the more demanding) regional trade liberalization schedule under NAFTA a still more rapid and profound reallocation process is likely to be induced on the regional market.

Part of this restructuring process can be captured by the trade data. Table 4.7 shows the development of US apparel trade with Mexico and the Caribbean Basin Economic Recovery Act (CBERA) region. In this table, the trade performance of Asia is taken as a point of reference, because these countries have been the dominant competitors on the US market before the foundation of NAFTA. Starting with the trade balance the 'revealed' comparative disadvantage of the USA in apparel trade becomes visible. The USA exhibits high and widening trade deficits over the entire period and with each of the three regions. What is also remarkable from these data are the dynamics of trade expansion over time. Mexico has widened its apparel trade surplus more than tenfold from 566 to 6,691 million US$ from 1993–2001. The CBERA region follows second (189 percent). The US deficit against Asia, however, widened only slowly.[20] A look at the import data helps to explain this development. While US imports from Asia grew at approximately the same rate as the trade deficit, imports from Mexico grew more that fivefold and nearly match those from the CBERA region in 2000.[21] It is apparent from these data that NAFTA has had a significant effect on apparel trade flows and induced Mexican exports to grow at an exceptionally high rate.

Table 4.7 Apparel: US trade with Mexico, the Caribbean and Asia, 1993–2001[a] (millions of US$)

	1993	1995	1997	2000	2001	% Change 1993–2001
Exports						
Asia[b]	118	143	183	235	270	129
Mexico	849	1,159	2,205	2,763	2,288	169
CBERA	1,822	2,068	3,576	4,229	3,244	78
Imports						
Asia	20,006	20,075	21,827	27,214	27,100	35
Mexico	1,415	2,876	5,350	9,590	8,979	534
CBERA	4,015	5,487	7,664	9,729	9,576	139
Trade Balance						
Asia	−19,888	−19,906	−21,644	−26,979	−26,908	35
Mexico	−566	−1,506	−3,145	−6,827	−6,691	1,080
CBERA	−2,193	−2,967	−4,088	−5,501	−6,332	189

Notes: [a] data for 1993–97 are SIC 22, 23 classification, 2000–01 are based on SITC rev. 3 (made-up + apparel),
[b] P.R. China, South Korea, Hongkong, Taiwan, ASEAN.

Source: US Department of Commerce (2001)

It is less clear, however, if this Mexican apparel surge has really increased adjustment pressures in the USA. For one thing, the relatively slow growth of imports from Asia, from 1993–97 in particular, supports the thesis that NAFTA has caused trade diversion, with Mexican substituting for Asian exports.[22]

Another factor that might have brought alleviation to US producers can be derived from the US export data. US producers have hardly at all established new export relations with Asia during the NAFTA period, but exports to Mexico and the CBERA region have increased remarkably (169 percent and 78 percent). Apparently, some kind of two-way trade in apparel has developed between the USA and Mexico (CBERA region). Further investigation reveals that this two-way trade is mainly the result of production sharing activities by which US producers export intermediate inputs and reimport goods for final demand. These activities are politically promoted by the specific production sharing provisions of HTS (Harmonized Tariff Schedule) Chapter 98, but they are also the result of conscious market driven enterpreneurial strategies that are aimed at a more successful adjustment to import competition from Mexico.

According to a USITC study (1999), actors in the US apparel industries can typically be classified as manufacturers, jobbers (design and marketing) and contractors according to their position on the value-added chain. While in former times many firms had concentrated these activities in one location at home, the survival strategies under present day conditions aim at splitting up these processes and transfer low skill and wage intensive productions abroad. As a matter of rule this is the case with the contractors' activities. They are organized in low wage countries in Mexico and the CBERA region in particular. More skill intensive tasks are maintained within the US boundaries. In many cases these local activities include the production of intermediate inputs, which are exported and reimported when the operations of the contractors have been carried out.

In the sector trade balance these activities become visible from the rise of US exports despite the high and increasing comparative disadvantage in this field. They are also indicative of the thesis that the US apparel industry, though it will remain under severe adjustment pressure, must not fear to become entirely dysfunctional as long as multinational production sharing activities of the kind discussed above are tolerated. In fact, according to a study of the American Apparel Manufacturers Association (AAMA), it is exactly the possibility of responding to increased adjustment pressure by international outsourcing activities that gives national producers (and employees) an opportunity to stay in the market – and even to expand in it.[23]

Notwithstanding these observations, the challenge from NAFTA and the CBERA region for the US apparel sector remains high, indeed. First, the integration process within NAFTA will proceed as Mexicans learn to handle more sophisticated technologies and acquire jobber qualifications. Second, the implementation of the Caribbean Basin Trade Partnership Act, which concedes Caribbean and Central American countries a NAFTA equivalent access to the North American market, is likely to add to the adjustment pressure on the US market. Third, new technological developments may further change the relative competitive positions within NAFTA and towards outsiders. One important new development of this kind is the establishment of integrated textile mills in Mexico, which substitute for imports of fabrics. Last but not least, the global obligation to liberalize trade in textiles and apparel under the WTO regime remains on the agenda and with it the obligation to reduce trade diverting measures of protection. These obligations will most likely be extended if the new Doha Round of multilateral trade talks are brought to a successful end.

To sum up with respect to the case of a NAFTA induced reallocation of resources in the apparel sector it can be concluded that the North American liberalization process has indeed enforced structural change. In particular, it has enforced the specialization according to comparative advantage within NAFTA and, at the same time, provided relief from external competitors. That is, there have been trade creation and trade divergence effects that tend to produce countervailing effects on economic welfare. The net effect from these developments, therefore, is likely to be small even if trade creation prevails.

4.2.3.2 The Mexican Maquiladora industries

'La Industria Maquiladora de Exportación' came into being in the 1960s as a means to foster industrial development along the Mexican border region with the USA. The economic mechanism inherent in the Maquiladora system is the exploitation of comparative advantage in labor intensive production sectors by allowing inputs to be imported free of duties under the condition that the final product be re-exported. On the part of the USA the program was supported by allowing the Mexican re-exports to enter the USA without tariff duties, provided that distinct conditions were met. That way the Maquiladora industries developed as assembly industries that continuously attracted more US firms and provided a rapidly increasing number of jobs in Mexico.

NAFTA is expected to exert different effects on this sector. For one thing, a more intensive and stable relationship between Mexico and the USA and Canada should work as a further stimulation for the Maquiladora zone. Also, the fact that Mexico has accepted the phasing out of the Maquiladora program by allowing Maquiladora products to be sold on the Mexican market should increase the scope of investments in low skill and labour intensive activities. But there are also some important developments working against the future of the Maquiladoras. One factor is that decreasing protection in the NAFTA zone will erode the advantage from producing under this program. Another is that Article 303 of the NAFTA treaty has brought the duty drawbacks on Maquiladora imports from non-member countries to an end. This will force Maquiladora firms either to look for inputs and machinery on the North American market or pay tariffs. In both cases the relative competitive position of the Maquiladora industries is likely to erode. In order to slow down the effects of Article 303 on the Maquiladoras, some new preferential programs like PITEX (Programa de Importación Temporal de Productos Manufactureros para la Exportación) and PPS (Programa de Promoción Sectoral) have been installed. They are thought to counteract the adverse competitive effects of Article 303 on Mexican producers (Watkins, 2001, 20–21).

By and large, these new regulations of the Maquiladora system along with the overall liberalization effect of NAFTA are likely to make the sector disappear as a separate analytical unit in the long run. Presently, however, it is still of utmost importance.

These future perspectives of the Maquiladora industries motivate a splitting of this paragraph. In the first part, the recent effects of NAFTA on the Maquiladora industries will be analyzed under the conditions of the old regulatory framework. Data for this analysis are available up to 1998. In the second part the perspective will be changed and the Maquiladora industries will be analyzed along with other preferential programs under the new conditions. Data for this procedure are limited to the years 1997–2000.

NAFTA and the old Maquiladora system   Table 4.8 shows some indicators of the development of the Mexican Maquiladora industries since 1981. Since then, this sector has expanded rapidly. Between 1981 and 1993 the number of firms registered under the scheme increased from 605 to 2,114. Parallel to this rise in production facilities employment increased from 131,000 to 542,000. Under NAFTA the dynamics of the Maquiladoras even accelerated. In 1998 more than 1 million workers were engaged in 2,983 firms. During these years the average firm size has considerably increased and ever more firms decided to choose a location more distant from the US border. As a result, the concentration of the Maquiladoras in the four border states (Baja California, Chihuahua, Sonara and Tamaulipas), which was 83 percent in 1980, dropped to 75 percent in 1993 and 67 percent in 1998 (Table 4.9). Since 1990 about 485 Maquiladora firms have been founded in the inner parts of Mexico (Puebla, Estado de Mexico, Yucatán, Durango).

More important from the point of view of economic development is the fact that under NAFTA the diversity of industries has also increased. Measured by the distribution of sector employment (Table 4.10) there are no major changes between the established sectors (except for the rapid increase of employment in the apparel industries and the relative decline of the transport sector). But the strong increase of the share of 'other sectors' (from 4 percent to 14.2 percent from 1993–98) again points to the greater diversity of the new developments.

Table 4.8 Maquiladora industries in Mexico, 1981–98

	Number of Firms	Employees (in 1000s)	Value-Added (national in 1000 pesos)	Wages and Salaries (in 1000 pesos)	Imported Inputs (in 1000 pesos)	Local Inputs (in 1000 pesos)
1981	605	131	23,957	14,644	54.7	0.7
1985	760	212	325,250	167,665	980.5	8.9
1990	1,703	446	9,918,504	5,106,776	29,445.1	513.6
1993	2,114	542	17,264,031	9,598,665	55,028.8	971.2
1994	2,085	583	20,425,827	11,536,071	69,250.4	1,039.4
1995	2,130	648	33,182,509	16,231,279	140,055.4	2,381.8
1996	2,411	754	49,638,234	24,088,900	217,054.3	4,445.7
1997	2,717	899	70,086,751	34,883,936	278,143.3	6,514.4
1998	2,983	1,008	96,703,531	47,162,575	348,347.4	9,654.6

Source: Instituto Nacional de Estadistica Geografia e Informatica (INEGI) (1999): 'Industria Maquiladora de Exportación',
Estadisticas Económicas INEGI, S. 2, Julio

Table 4.9 Regional distribution of Maquiladora plants, 1980–98

	Total Amount	Baja California	Chihuahua	Sonora	Tamaulipas	*
1980	620	230	121	81	81	83
1989	1,655	686	252	95	204	75
1993	2,114	804	337	168	279	75
1998	2,983	1,018	383	245	342	67

Note * Percentage share of the four most important states

Source: Instituto Nacional de Estadistica Geografia e Informatica (INEGI) (1999)

Another small but important change concerns the use of local inputs. Traditionally, the Maquiladora industries had relied nearly exclusively on foreign inputs (98.2 percent in 1981). That is, the local value-added was about 1.8 percent. This share has not much increased until 1993, but rose to 2.8 percent in 1998.

Table 4.10   Employment in the Mexican Maquiladora industries, 1981–98

	1981	1993	1998
Food	1,572	11,436	11,470
Apparel	18,059	63,999	203,575
Shoes and Leather	1,821	7,268	9,096
Furniture	3,319	32,688	48,502
Chemicals	143	11,887	19,721
Transport	10,998	126,650	194,000
Tools	1,401	5,322	10,477
Electronic Assembly	76,185	189,142	344,180
Toys and Sports Goods	2,665	9,055	13,773
Miscellaneous	8,023	56,715	113,285

Source: Instituto Nacional de Estadística Geografía e Informatica (INEGI) (1999)

The small local content of the Maquiladoras has always produced criticism that the development in this sector is not very attractive for Mexico because most of the value-added is produced abroad and the linkages to Mexican producers are minimal. This view is correct in as much as the present situation is concerned. From the point of view of a longer-run industrial development perspective things may find a different interpretation, however. The Maquiladora industries are relying heavily on specialization and comparative advantage and exploit the opportunities rigorously, which are provided by differences in factor endowments. At the beginning of this process, such a strategy does indeed prohibit the use of high cost and low quality local inputs that would weaken or even destroy comparative advantage and make a rapid expansion on the world market illusionary. Instead, this strategy limits local content and, thereby, increases international competitiveness. As a result, high growth rates on the international market compensate for small local content. Furthermore, as the experience in international markets accumulates and upgrading takes place, diversification increases and more local content will be used. This pattern of development can clearly be

*Table 4.11 Mexican exports to the United States * under temporary import programs (Maquiladora and PITEX), by leading product sectors, 1997–2000*

Product Sectors (HS range)	Exports under Temporary Import Programs (TIP)				TIP Share of	
	US$ million				Total exports to the US in	Total exports to the US in
	1997	1998	1999	2000	2000	2000 %
Motor vehicles	12,064	13,607	15,798	19,344	19,366	100
Certain motor vehicle parts	7,305	7,729	9,085	10,006	10,184	98
Apparel and other textile articles (61–63,65)	5,539	6,605	7,843	8,648	8,933	97
Color television receivers and parts (8528.12, 8529.90, 8540.11, 8540.91)	5,259	6,316	6,892	7,859	8,434	93
Radio transmission and reception apparatus (8525, 8527 and 8529 [pt])	3,767	3,929	5,324	7,749	8,946	87
Computers and components (8471)	3,097	3,769	5,701	7,186	7,319	98
Electrical circuit apparatus (8534, 8535, 8536, 8537, 8538)	2,472	2,786	3,358	4,898	4,929	99
Measuring, testing and controlling instruments (9024, 9025, 9027, 9028, 9029, 9030, 9031, 9032, 9033 [pt])	799	1,080	1,314	1,588	1,623	98
Major household appliances (8418, 8422.11, 8422.19, 8450, 8451)	302	364	434	454	473	96
All other	35,784	42,766	49,275	59,061	77,432	76
Total	76,388	88,951	105,024	126,794	147,639	86

Note: * for details see original source

Source: USITC, *Industry Trade and Technology Review*, Production Sharing Tables (Mexican Data), July 2001

recognized in the Maquiladora industries in the 1990s, though this process proceeds stubbornly slowly in Mexico compared to other emerging markets.

The new Maquiladora regime According to Table 4.11, total Mexican exports to the USA increased from 76.4 billion US$ in 1997 to 147.6 billion US$ in 2000. From the latter amount, 86 percent have been exported under temporary import programs (TIPs). One of these programs is the Maquiladora program, the other one is the PITEX (see above). About 54 percent of all TIP exports are under the eight sub-headings ('motor vehicles' to 'major household appliances'). For these, the TIP coverage is between 96–100 percent. Table 4.12 allows discrimination between Maquiladora exports and PITEX exports for some of the more important subcategories (carrying more than 75 percent of total trade). HS positions 50–59 and 60–63 are textile and apparel exports respectively. About a quarter of these exports are traded under PITEX and about 40 percent of textiles and 70 percent of apparel are covered by the Maquiladora system. The HS positions 84–87 represent different categories of machinery exports, including electrical machinery (85) as the dominant category. It is worth noting that more than 90 percent of the exports in this category is still supported by the Maquiladora program. In the category HS 87 (other vehicles) it is only 16 percent. Apparently, the traditional Maquiladora industries like apparel, electronics, opticals and furniture are still holding a very high share of the Maquiladora operations. More advanced industries like machinery and automobile production (and even textiles) are advancing along the PITEX system. Comparing imports and exports supports the suggestion that these industries also produce a higher value-added in Mexico.

What is particularly surprising is the fact that within a Free Trade Agreement, which claims to have already brought down tariffs to negligible levels, most trade takes place under specific preferential regulations (85.9 percent in exports and 61.8 percent in imports). One explanation of this observation would be that NTBs are still prevalent so that it is attractive to use the special preferential agreements. Rules of origin (which will be discussed later) may be another reason.

If the first explanation holds it would be reasonable to expect that the impact of the special provisions will rapidly diminish as NAFTA becomes a mature FTA. Some indications of such a process can already be observed. Watkins, for example, claims that 'official US statistics ... are increasingly unable to quantify the magnitude and scope of production sharing activity ...' (Watkins, 2001, 11, footnote 2). The main reason is that 'a significant and growing proportion of production sharing operations does not enter under chapter 98 provisions because the goods are eligible for duty-free treatment under other agreements or tariff preference programs' (Watkins, 2001, 11).

Table 4.12   Mexican exports to the USA in 2000 (totals, Maquiladora and PITEX for selected HS groups) (in millions of US$)

Harmonized System	Maquiladora	PITEX	Other	Total	% Maquiladora	% PITEX	% Other
50–59 (Textiles)	541	337	412	1,290	39.8	26.1	34.1
60–63 (Apparel)	6,225	2,461	285	8,971	69.4	27.4	3.2
84 (Machinery)	10,656	7,926	684	19,226	55.3	41.1	3.6
85 (Electrical machinery)	41,767	4,119	345	46,231	90.3	8.9	0.8
87 (Other vehicles)	3,970	21,278	152	25,400	15.6	83.8	0.6
90 (Optical instruments)	3,012	1,152	78	4,242	71.0	27.2	1.8
94 (Furniture)	3,047	586	265	3,898	78.2	15.0	6.8
Total	78,248	48,546	20,845	147,639	53.0	32.9	14.1

Source: USITC, Industry Trade and Technology Review, Production Sharing Tables (Mexican Data), July 2001

Table 4.12 (continued)   *Mexican imports from the USA in 2000 (totals, Maquiladora and PITEX for selected HS groups) (in millions of US$)*

Harmonized System	Maquiladora	PITEX	Other	Total	% Maquiladora	% PITEX	% Other
50–59	2,649	833	1,114	4,596	57.6	18.1	24.3
60–63	2,637	608	336	3,581	73.6	17.0	9.4
84	3,623	3,828	9,430	16,881	21.5	22.7	55.8
85	26,833	2,953	5,558	35,344	75.9	8.4	15.7
87	817	5,806	5,783	12,406	6.6	46.8	46.6
90	996	702	1,595	3,293	30.2	21.3	48.5
94	214	439	422	1,075	19.9	40.8	39.3
Total	55,679	23,254	48,633	127,566	43.6	18.2	38.2

Source: USITC, *Industry Trade and Technology Review*, Production Sharing Tables (Mexican Data), July 2001

NAFTA is one such agreement, and it should become the dominant one as integration proceeds.

To sum up, the sector developments up to the end of the 1990s support the thesis that NAFTA has speeded up the exploitation of comparative advantage under the Maquiladora regime. The complementary rules for product sharing (PITEX), too, have contributed to a more rigorous intra-regional division of labor. Meanwhile, this division of labor takes continuously more hold in the more advanced industries (automobiles and components in particular). In these sectors, too, the outsourcing of labor intensive and low skill operations has played a certain role (though the regional reorganization of the automotive sector follows more complex strategies, which will be discussed in the next chapter), so that the initial period of the formation of NAFTA has indeed contributed to a more efficient and growth enhancing reallocation of resources.

Recent developments of the Maquiladora industries are far more difficult to analyze. Other than in the 1993–98 foundation period an ongoing success of regional integration under NAFTA would make the Maquiladora program and similar preferential agreements redundant. Thus, a decline of these activities during the following years, along with a rapid increase of 'normal' NAFTA trade, would be an indication of an ongoing positive integration process.[24] A further extension of these programs, in turn, would most likely be an indication of stagnation.

4.2.3.3   The automotive industries

In contrast to the apparel sector and the heterogeneous Maquiladora industries, which altogether exploit Mexican comparative advantage in labor intensive, low skill activities, the automotive industry is a medium to high tech industry with complex production and sourcing features. In the USA as in other industrialized countries it is also a mature industry in the sense that the market is almost saturated. In the USA, for example, about 90 percent of the demand for new vehicles concerns a replacement of the existing car park. Consequently, the net increase of demand for cars on the local market is close to zero. In fact, the 1998 sales of light vehicles of 15.5 million units (USITC, 1999) on the US market are estimated by many analysts to be close to the upper limit for the coming future.

Given these demand conditions and the fact that the global automotive industry is heavily engaged in rationalization strategies, the US automotive industry will only be able to grow on the local market in the future (and stabilize employment) if it succeeds in the realization of a more rapid productivity growth than their main international competitors and/or if local consumers switch to higher value-added vehicles. This situation is the more challenging as the international automotive industry is plagued with a considerable amount of over-capacity.[25] While consumers have switched to more expensive cars during the last decade,[26] the US rationalization strategies have not been matched by much success relative to its international competitors in recent years. On the contrary, since the Japanese car offensive of the 1970s the US automotive industry has been under severe pressure from foreign competitors both in the USA and on the global market. In the 1980s the USA responded to this pressure by a series of so-called 'voluntary export restraints' (1981, 1985), which turned out to be extremely expensive for US consumers but had little or no positive impact on the global competitive position of the American automotive industry (Dinopoulos/Kreinin, 1988; Feenstra, 1988). During the 1990s the highly protectionist automotive pact with Japan and the strong yen have hindered Japanese exports from growing, but the setback of Japan did not give relief to US producers, because European and other Asian competitors stepped right in to fill the gap. Also, growing FDI in the USA helped Japanese and European producers to circumvent entry barriers and to compete with the big three directly on the US market. By and large this situation indicates that the US automotive industry was fighting heavily to defend its relative position on the local market long before NAFTA was founded.

Against this background, the formation of NAFTA brought both an additional challenge for US producers (and employees on the US labor market in particular) and a chance to rationalize production more successfully and reap ECS on the larger North American market.

A similar situation had already been created vis-à-vis Canada under the automotive act of 1965. Free trade and investment under this agreement pushed the integration of the US and the Canadian automotive industries to form an ever more homogeneous market even before NAFTA came into being. Under NAFTA, the integration process proceeded further and in 1999 the US international trade commission was ready to state that 'the US–Canadian auto industry is fully integrated, and GM, Ford and DC consider the United States and Canada as a single unit for production planning purposes' (USITC, 1999, 12).

Table 4.13 shows US–Canada automotive trade from 1995–2001. During this period the bilateral US trade deficit with Canada has only slightly increased from 15.7 billion US$ in 1995 to 17.3 billion US$ in 2001.[27] This deficit is mainly the result of divergent developments in vehicles (rising deficit) and parts trade (rising surplus). While trade in all categories has been growing,[28] in parts it did so at a particularly high rate in both countries. This indicates that the mutual penetration of both markets is still proceeding.

The US–Mexico trade and investment relations in the automotive sector also have a pre-NAFTA history. US firms have maintained production facilities in Mexico for many years and production sharing activities were

Table 4.13 US–Canada trade in the automotive sector, 1995–2001

	1995	1997	1999	2001	% Change 1995–2001
Total Exports	23.9	28.4	30.6	40.6	70
Vehicles	11.3	14.2	14.4	13.9	23
Parts	12.6	14.2	16.2	26.7	112
Total Imports	39.6	43.3	55.7	57.9	41
Vehicles	33.2	35.9	46.6	41.3	34
Parts	6.4	7.3	9.1	16.6	159
Trade Balance	−15.7	−14.8	−24.9	−17.3	
Vehicles	−21.9	−21.7	−32.1	−27.4	
Parts	6.2	6.9	7.2	10.1	

Sources: McNay/Polly (2000) and USITC (2002)

enforced during the 1980s. However, there was a clear asymmetry in trade policies between the two nations before NAFTA. While the US market was relatively open for Mexican products,[29] the Mexican market was heavily protected. Import tariffs ranged from 10–20 percent and were complemented by a stiff quota system. Furthermore, trade balancing served as a popular and particularly anti-market oriented instrument of trade regulation. Under this system firms were obliged to export in a fixed relation to imports (which implied that the firms must produce in Mexico, obeying Mexican local content rules).

NAFTA is going to wipe out these regulations. Most of the fading-out procedures have taken place since 1998 and will fully incorporate the Mexican automotive market into the Canada–US production system until 2004. One should expect, therefore, that firms already respond to the changed conditions and rearrange their trade and production structures. Other than in the apparel industry, however, wage costs are less important in automotive production (less than 10 percent according to McNay/Polly, 2000, 23).[30] But they still play a prominent role in the production-sharing activities of the PITEX and Maquiladora programs and in the production of components. The latter is likely to be particularly important in the restructuring process, because components production is relatively labor intensive and wages are only about 50 percent of those in the construction plants.

Under these conditions, one would expect the large firms' decisions on production and trade to become a complex task by which proximity to the market, manufacturing competence (skilled labor) and the existence of adequate infrastructure facilities have to be considered. Wage costs will not have a major impact on this location decision, directly. Indirectly, however, they still have a significant impact because production sharing and components production are sensitive to wage costs and location decisions of auto firms and suppliers of components are interrelated. In fact, producers tend to gather major component producers at short distance from the plants so that the decision on the plant location has an important impact on the wage level of the components producer. Further, direct suppliers will tend to recruit their suppliers out of the region and these may produce with an even higher labor intensity.

Wage rates are also important from another point of view. They tend to influence the level of automation, which, in turn, is a determinant of adjustment flexibility (McNay/Polly, 2000, 23). Thus, Mexican plants will tend to be more flexible in their operations, capturing a competitive advantage in servicing distinct markets with a demand overhang (sports utility vehicles [SUV] and light trucks were such cases at the end of the 1990s).

Free trade and investment under NAFTA has already contributed to a significant restructuring of the North American automotive industries.

Though precise FDI data are still scarce[31] because of data security considerations, long lists of investment projects in Mexico and the USA show remarkable investment activities of North American, Asian and European firms in Mexico, but also in the USA (DC, BMW, Toyota). The automotive producers, in turn, have attracted component producers to join these firms abroad. Meanwhile, all major US component producers are present on the Mexican market along with an increasing number of European firms.

Producers are not just expanding their activities in Mexico but they are also restructuring their production profile. That is, they reduce production lines in Mexico that had to be expanded under the former regulatory system. As a result of NAFTA, small production lines will be cut, specialization will be increased, and the exploitation of ECS intensifies. As a result two-way trade will expand at a higher level of productivity. The same holds true for components that will contain a higher element of low wage trade, however.

Another important consequence of the restructuring procedures is an increased transfer of technology to Mexico, which has already contributed to 'significant improvements in labor productivity, product quality and competitiveness' (McNay/Polly, 2000, 23). This development increases the level of sophistication of production in Mexico and contributes to the convergence of Mexican producers towards North American (and world) standards.[32] Even today, Mexico appears to have upgraded towards the average quality level of US production facilities. Some new plants have even been ranked among the most competitive units in North America (Ford Hermosillo, DC Saltillo, and GM Silao) (Harbour and Associated Inc., Harbour Report 2000, cited in McNay/Polly, 2000, 23). The situation today is that most producers still prefer the USA (or Canada) for the production of the more sophisticated products. But in the longer run this situation may also change if the Mexican upgrading process proceeds.

It will be interesting to see how these developments have changed the structure of automotive trade between the two countries. I shall present two sets of data that are remarkable because they suggest quite different messages. The first message derives from recent data (1995–2001) compiled from official statistics from the US Department of Commerce, the second is from the fifth automotive report of 1999[33] and draws on data from the US Census Bureau.

Table 4.14 shows the development of US–Mexico automotive trade from 1995–2001. According to these figures a substantial intensification of the automotive trade relations has taken place since 1995. US exports have grown somewhat stronger than imports, but this has had little impact on the growing overall deficit. The export of vehicles has grown dramatically (900 percent), but the export of components, which is the single most important subcategory (3.8 billion US$ vs. 0.4 billion US$ for cars in 1995) grew only

Table 4.14 US–Mexico trade in the automotive sector, 1995–2001

	1995	1996	1997	1998	1999	2000	2001	% Change 1995–2001
Total Exports	4.2	4.9	7.0	7.1	7.4	8.9	10.7	155
Vehicles	0.4	1.2	1.9	2.2	2.3	3.2	4.0	900
Parts	3.8	3.7	5.1	4.9	5.1	5.7	6.7	76
Imports	10.6	14.2	15.3	16.4	19.5	24.7	26.1	146
Vehicles	8.4	11.7	12.3	13.2	15.8	21.0	21.5	156
Parts	2.2	2.5	3.0	3.2	3.7	3.7	4.6	109
Trade Balance	−6.4	−9.3	−8.3	−9.3	−12.1	−16.4	−15.4	141
Vehicles	−8.0	−10.5	10.3	−11.0	−13.5	−17.8	−17.5	118
Parts	1.6	1.2	2.0	1.7	1.4	1.4	2.1	31

Sources: McNay/Polly (2000) and USITC (2002)

modestly (76 percent). In turn, the import of vehicles has grown much more slowly than the export, but it has started from a higher level (8.4 vs. 0.4 billion US$). Due to the different weights of vehicle exports and imports a significant increase of the trade deficit in vehicles of 17.5 billion US$ resulted, despite the high rate of growth of vehicle exports. This deficit has been partly compensated by the trade surplus in components trade of 2.1 billion US$.

By and large, these figures suggest that the USA still has a relatively strong position in components trade (despite the high rate of growth of vehicle exports) while the product rationalization strategy in Mexico and the turn to a more export oriented production has had a positive impact on the Mexican vehicle exports. On balance, these two opposing developments helped to keep the US trade balance in a relatively stable position as compared to the overall trade deficit. Taking into consideration the discussion of the sourcing strategies of the MNEs in this sector, one would probably not be wrong to predict a further improvement of the Mexican position in components trade.

Now turn to Table 4.15. Two blocks of data have to be considered. The first block accumulates the five-year period before NAFTA (1989–93), and the second one the five-year period after the implementation of the agreement (1994–98). The last years of each period are shown separately. Figures on exports are not qualitatively different from those of Table 4.14. Overall, there has been a smaller increase between 1989–93 and 1994–98 (71.6 percent) as compared to the 1995–2001 data, but this difference might be due to the Tequila crises.

Imports under the new classification, however, grew far more rapidly and they produced a much higher trade deficit. This can be seen more clearly from the single year figures of 1993 and 1998. The trade deficit between these two years grew from −3.6 billion US$ to −15.8 billion US$ (339 percent). That is, the trade deficit is about 70 percent higher according to these data as compared to the former.

The difference is almost completely due to a different classification of the components sector, which shows a trade deficit of 5 billion US$ in Table 4.15 as compared to a surplus of 1.7 billion US$ in Table 4.14. A simple extrapolation of the trade deficit of Table 4.15 with the rate of change of the deficit according to the figures in Table 4.14 (rate of growth between 1998–2001) indicates the large gap between the two data sets. Based on the classification of the automotive report the trade deficit reported in 2001 would have been about two-thirds larger (25.4 billion US$) than the new official data indicate. It is worth emphasizing that under the old classification procedure there is no positive development of components trade over the entire period and the growth of the deficit is most rapid in this subsection.[34]

Table 4.15 US–Mexico trade in the automotive industry, 1989–98 (millions of US$)

	1989–93	1994–98	% Change 1989–93 to 1994–98	1993	1998	% Change 1993–98
Total Exports	27.5	47.2	71.6	7.5	11.9	59
Vehicles	1.0	6.6	560.0	0.2	2.4	1,100
Parts	26.5	40.6	53.2	7.3	9.5	30
Total Imports	40.8	108.0	164.7	11.1	27.7	150
Vehicles	13.4	49.2	267.2	3.7	13.2	257
Parts	27.4	58.8	114.6	7.4	14.5	96
Trade Balance	–13.3	–60.8	–357.1	–3.6	–15.8	–339
Vehicles	–12.4	–42.6	–243.5	–3.5	–10.8	–208
Parts	–0.9	–18.2	–1,922.2	–0.1	–5.0	–2,040

Sources: Trade Administration (1999); US Department of Commerce, Office of Automotive Affairs International

Drawing on these latter data, the thesis finds support that trade in components may be more heavily determined by comparative advantage than previously believed. Also it might be concluded that the integration of Mexico into the slowly growing North American market will come more at the expense of the established producers (that is, at the expense of the US plants of these same producers) than commonly held.[35]

It should be noted that these conclusions cannot be interpreted as an indication of a negative overall (welfare) effect of NAFTA on the USA and/or Canada. First, it would be methodologically wrong to analyze overall welfare problems on a sector basis. Second, NAFTA may contribute to an improvement of the competitiveness of the North American producers on the NAFTA and the global market so that the relative change within NAFTA will be more than offset.

4.3   CONCLUSION – THE INTERNAL INTEGRATION PROCESS

The evidence on trade, investment and sector adjustments reveals that the North American markets, by responding to the changed structure of incentives, are reorganizing towards the enlarged NAFTA space. That way, new investments have been made and trade structures have changed. While the US–Canada markets had already been highly integrated before NAFTA came into being the major new developments are concentrated on changes of the structures of trade and production of these two countries with Mexico. As this process advances, Mexico probably becomes a more important location of industrial production within the NAFTA.

The apparel sector and the automotive industry are two areas that are proceeding most rapidly along this path. In the auto industries large international producers are seriously engaged in reorganizing the intraregional allocation of production thereby upgrading Mexican plants to meet international standards. In the apparel industries, in turn, producers are following Mexican comparative advantage in labor intensive manufactures. The success of the Maquiladora industries, which form a heterogeneous set of subindustry labor intensive activities, underlines this direction of change of the ongoing adjustment process. That is, it is not too risky to predict that more and more Mexican industries will intensify trade relations with the USA and Canada, thereby taking advantage of their comparative advantage and eventually entering intra-industry type structures of production and trade.

However, it has also been found that FDI in Mexico during the second half of the 1990s fell short of the optimistic expectations of many experts. This finding warns against exaggerated expectations regarding the dynamics of the ongoing integration process. Until recently, FDI flows into Mexico have been driven by a very limited number of industries, the most important of which is the already highly multinationalized automotive industry (including components). The overall growth potential of this industry on the North American market is limited, despite an apparent backlog demand in Mexico.

The concentration of regional integration on only a few sectors supports the view that under the present conditions the broad majority of Mexican industries is neither well prepared to take advantage of the new opportunities that NAFTA offers nor particularly attractive for large scale FDI from the USA and Canada. Both observations suggest that supply side bottlenecks are still a severe obstacle to rapid progress of industrial development in the half-industrialized Mexican economy. If this conclusion is correct the potential growth effects of NAFTA will also remain largely unexploited by Mexico as long as these deficiencies are not removed.

4.4 NAFTA AND ITS EXTERNAL RELATIONS

The NAFTA, building on the WTO principles of (open) regional integration (Article 24), explicitly endorses the concept of open regionalism. In principle, therefore, the question whether NAFTA is on due course externally can be approached by analyzing the degree of NAFTA compliance with the WTO rules of regional integration. A superficial investigation of this topic would simply analyze the level of tariff protection before and after the implementation of NAFTA. Most certainly, such an investigation would presently find that, in general, NAFTA is in accordance with the WTO and did not change the multilateral course of any of its member states significantly.

However, after decades of successful GATT/WTO trade talks, nominal tariffs are hardly a reliable indicator of protection in the modern world economy any more.[36] Rather, the 'big' items today are NTBs,[37] bilateralism, tariff escalation (effective tariffs), rules of origin, and distinct exceptions to the general rules. Still another concern arises from the potential long-run protectionist dynamics as argued by Bhagwati's 'time path analysis' (Chapter Three). Drawing on this concept, regional integration may well exhibit the expected positive attributes of 'open regionalism' in the short run but will mutate towards a more discriminatory regime over time.

Given this state of affairs, a thorough investigation of the external positioning of NAFTA after eight years faces three fundamental problems:

1. Political–economic considerations hypothesize that regionalism has a dual effect on openness. While influencing trade liberalization positively in the

short run, its long run impact (say 20–30 years) may work in the opposite direction.

2. Given the multitude of 'bindings' of tariffs and trade rules that have been established under the multilateral system after World War II, a system change is unlikely to show up within a short time period.
3. The most significant protectionist measures in the present global system tend to be hidden rather than overt, so that nominal tariff rates alone are not appropriate to indicate any change in the relevant policy parameters.

Thus, in order to detect the true protectionist content of NAFTA and its potential change over time, an in-depth investigation of the entire system of protection (including NTBs, effective rates of protection etc.) would have to be carried out. However, even such an investigation, though highly deman-ding, would still not provide a sufficiently reliable basis for judging on the longer-term effects of NAFTA.

In order to catch these longer-run effects early, another approach will be employed here. The idea is to find reliable lead indicators of change of the relevant trade policy parameters. One such indicator is the revealed trade policy preference of the respective government, which is usually available to the public long before the institutional system really changes. However, a weakness of this indicator is that the government's proclaimed will may not find enough political support so that the distinct policies that are actually becoming realized after having passed the democratic process may deviate substantially from the original proposal. Also governments may willingly disguise their real intentions (e.g. NTBs). In order to avoid these pitfalls it would be appropriate to evaluate not only the government's proclaimed will but also the political and societal environment that might shape this will. Drawing on the new political–economic literature this would make it necessary to study both the national institutional system and the relative impact of voters on the political process. Changes of these parameters, then, would give an early indication of the changing political forces that eventually might change the future course of official politics.

Fortunately, the US political system and its implications for trade policy have been investigated in some depth in recent years (Baldwin/Magee, 2000; Thorbecke, 2000; Hiscox, 2002). These kinds of studies are appropriate to indicate fundamental changes in voting behaviour and in institutional provisions, before they become visible in codified rules, not to speak of changing structures of trade. In this context, polls on relevant trade topics may contribute to underpin this information.

In the following, I shall elaborate on this approach in order to shed some light on two basic questions:

1. Are there changes to be recognized in US trade policies under NAFTA that point to a changed balance between protectionist and free trade interests?
2. If so, can a proper link be established between these changes and the foundation of NAFTA?

4.4.1 Are there Changes in US Trade Policies Under NAFTA?

4.4.1.1 The institutional foundations of US trade policies

The American constitution has vested both the president and congress responsibility in trade policy matters: Article I, section 8 states that 'Congress shall have power ... to regulate commerce with foreign nations ...', but Article II, section 2, certifies the president's competence in foreign economic policies. Since it is the Congress that is entitled to define the president's political scope under Article II, it is the highest authority and it determines how the power sharing between both institutions is eventually handled in reality. This vague constitutional construction of trade policy responsibilities is not only 'an invitation to struggle' (Crabb/Holt, 1992) between both institutions but has an important impact on US international economic policy. The point is that the president and Congress differ in their interpretations of the respective interests of the USA in international economic issues. The president, being directly involved in foreign (economic) policies, must carefully evaluate the potential impact of America's political and economic strategies on its international position.

Congress, in turn, forms a legislative body that is deeply rooted in the representatives' national (local) political stance. Potential international repercussions of the US internal politics are not an important concern of most congressmen and women and frequently they are simply neglected. As a consequence, the president usually pays much more attention to US multilateral obligations than Congress does. In the field of international economics, this means that free trade (implying non-discrimination of partner countries) is a special concern of the president. For the sake of simplicity one might conclude that under this constellation the president represents 'the free traders' while in Congress 'fair traders' are more influential. In fact, the historical evidence of most of the 20th century shows that the USA usually turned to a more protectionist position whenever Congress restricted the president's responsibilities in trade policy matters. In turn, the country used to execute a policy that was more seriously dedicated to free trade, whenever Congress widened the president's political mandate.

Another important aspect of the political foundation of US trade policy is the distribution of 'free traders' and 'fair traders' in Congress and in the Senate. After World War II, and in recent days in particular, the Republicans in Congress tend to be the 'free traders' while the majority of the Democrats is more closely related to the 'fair traders'. But this distribution of attitudes towards trade is anything but stable. Before World War II, for example, the distribution of political convictions on trade have been quite different,[38] and during the last decade the views on trade policy changed considerably within both parties. In any case, the representatives from both parties are exposed to pressure from vested interests and voters that is sufficiently strong to change the representatives' views on this important topic even within relatively short periods.

Based on these observations the following institutional structure of US international economic policy can be sketched:

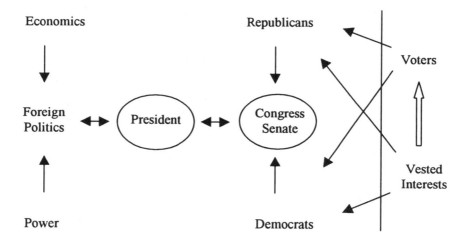

Figure 4.1   The institutional structure of US foreign policy

In this system, given ideological convictions of the political actors, the international political situation and the combined impact of voters and vested interests on the political decision-making bodies are driving the distinct international political strategies. Foreign politics, which might be split up into international economic policies (trade and investment) and power politics (Chapter One), will eventually be formulated as a reaction to this system of pressures.

Under the codex of the WTO the economic pressure on the president from abroad is clearly directed towards a free trade-oriented policy (subject to possible power political constraints). The possible direction of pressure on Congress concerning trade, in turn, is ambiguous. According to conventional trade theory, voters should constitute a powerful force in favor of free trade while vested interests, expressed by minority groups should not find much support. As a result, free trade should be the 'normal' outcome of this political bargaining process. However, interest group theory teaches another story that renders this simplistic view obsolete. Based on this approach it can be shown that special interest groups, because of their high propensity to organize and to fight for their privileges, are capable of deploying effective strategies to overcome the majority's interest in free trade (and increasing social welfare, in particular). They do this by influencing voters directly, by lobbying and by log rolling aimed at the formation of minority coalitions (Chapters Two and Three).

4.4.1.2 US trade policies before NAFTA

Congress, impressed by the disastrous consequences of the Smoot–Haley Act, had largely widened the president's trade authority after World War II (the turn of the tide being the Reciprocal Trade Agreements Act of 1934). During that time the USA led the revitalization of world trade and became the hegemon of the present international economic order. Since the early 1970s, however, the president's responsibility for international economic matters has been cut back by Congress step by step, giving way to an ever increasing impact of vested interests on US trade policies. The first step on this path towards a more restrictive foreign economic policy has been the implementation of the USTR[39] as a mediating institution between Congress and the president, and the removal of the responsibility for trade policy from the (relatively liberal) Foreign Office. Hand in hand with these institutional changes, several trade acts (1972, 1974, 1988) have paved the way for a trade policy concept that has become known as 'aggressive unilateralism' (Bayard/Elliot, 1992).

Aggressive unilateralism is a clear violation of the basic principles of the multilateral GATT/WTO system. The increasing efforts on the part of the USA to push the unilateral approach are, therefore, an indication that the USA itself slowly but steadily eroded the rules of the system that reflects its own vision of a sound international economic order. Based on the so-called 'dual track' approach (multilateralism being pursued along with a perceivably supporting unilateralism) the USA has repeatedly resorted to subtle NTBs (anti-dumping measures and voluntary export restraints in particular) in more and more industries (textiles and apparel, shoes, steel, passenger cars etc.). That way, it has contributed substantially to the world-wide spread of neoprotectionism while, at the same time, asking for a better compliance with multilateralism by its partner countries.[40]

Since the early 1980s the dual track approach has been complemented by distinct efforts to negotiate bilateral and regional agreements.[41] Since then, the regional option forms the third pillar of what is now called the 'multitrack approach'. Meanwhile, this new US trade option is reflected in a number of regional agreements of which NAFTA is the last and most important one. When the multitrack approach was initiated, the international economic system already suffered most heavily under the new protectionism so that it was not unreasonable at that time to interpret the regional option as a further extension of the anti-liberal stance of the dualtrack approach.

Leaving NAFTA aside for the moment and concentrating on the global level it is clear today that these fears have not been well founded. On the contrary, the foundation of the WTO in 1994 after the successful conclusion of the most ambitious Uruguay Round has given rise to new hopes concerning the future of an open international economic system based on the principles of multilateralism. In fact, the foundation of the WTO has not only strengthened the institutional underpinnings of international trade policy. It has also brought a clear commitment towards open markets. In particular, the reintegration of agriculture and textiles and clothing into the GATT regulatory system and the establishment of the single undertaking approach together have had a vigorous impact on the revitalization of the multilateral system. Case studies of the management of the US–WTO relations (dispute settlement, in particular) do indicate that the USA, in general, has been complying with the rules of the new multilateral system since its foundation.[42] Under these conditions, it is difficult to argue that the turn to the regional option during the 1980s has had any negative effect on the multilateral system until the mid-1990s. However, it is still open to dispute whether NAFTA might have changed the situation thereafter.

4.4.1.3   US trade policies and NAFTA

With the implementation of the WTO in 1994 early US objections against the functioning of the multilateral institutions (dispute settlement, in particular) have become largely obsolete. That is, when NAFTA came into being in 1994, it entered an international economic situation that promised a bright future for the multilateral approach. This situation also gave rise to the expectation that NAFTA, following the principles of the New Regionalism, would become a complement to rather than a substitute for the multilateral system.

Empirical evidence appears to be generally supportive to this thesis. According to conventional indicators (tariffs, NTBs), NAFTA presently sparkles brightly as a WTO conform Regional Integration Agreement (RIA), presuming to be a prototype of the New Regionalism – some incidents of trade diversion (Reuveny/Thompson, 2000; Romalis, 2002) and the apparent abuse of the rules of origin regime as a protectionist device (Estevadeordal, 1999), notwithstanding.

Under these conditions, a closer look at the trade policy mechanisms within the USA may help to generate some further insight into the present perceptions of multilateral and regional free trade in the country. Following a popular thesis, regional free trade, by providing a positive contribution to welfare and growth, should breed consent and ease further liberalization efforts (Krueger, 1999). That is, NAFTA after the successful start-up period should have built up political reputation and increased acceptance among people. Apparently, this has not been the case. Despite the fact that the USA has experienced a spectacular boom period during the second half of the 1990s (one result being a particularly small negative employment effect of NAFTA, even in sectors that are under severe adjustment pressure), NAFTA has raised much concern in public debates. In fact, NAFTA has contributed to an increasingly negative perception of free trade in the USA, and, as Weintraub has stated, has turned out to be 'a politically unpopular economic success'. Nowadays, the 'new' thinking on trade issues in the USA is so much influenced by protectionist sentiments that even 'free traders' feel obliged to regress to the politically correct term 'fair trade' (until then a mere synonym for protection) in order to find public recognition (Thorbecke, 2000, 90). Hufbauer (1999, 2) in a comment on the future of the Seattle conference has formulated the problem most clearly:

> Hard core backlashers ... want wide latitude to impose trade sanctions against offensive production processes. They want to extend textile and clothing quotas well beyond the 2005 phase-out period. They want tougher anti-dumping laws, and easier access to normal safeguards ... The 'new' backlashers want to put new trade agreements in peril until social issues are addressed. Both backlash camps [organised labour and environmentalists] would clearly love to rewrite or even dissolve NAFTA.

This 'change of the tide' of many Americans' perception of free trade after the foundation of the WTO and NAFTA has also changed the political climate regarding further trade liberalization initiatives in Congress. The blocking of Chile's application of admission to NAFTA and the repeated denial of a fast-track authority for President Clinton can be interpreted as the visible outcome of this change of attitudes.

In the centre of the present political disputes on international trade policy in the USA there are distinct demands for environmental and social standards. They are perceived as fundamental for the implementation of 'fairness' in international economic relations, and, in the case of environmental standards, they are also believed to be indispensable to secure vital ecological goals. Drawing on Chapter Two, the increasing acceptance of these objectives is not in dispute (at least in most high income countries), but their conjunction with trade issues is critical.

Apparently, the systematic objections against this conjunction from the trade political perspective have been downgraded in the USA during recent years and, in particular, under the NAFTA regime. NAFTA has heated up this discussion because of two basic reasons. First, for most of the post-war period, the two traditional lobby groups against free trade had worked independently and could not find much political support for their objectives. Environmental concerns, in particular, did not range high on the political agenda of the USA (and elsewhere) until recently.

This situation changed in the early 1990s. Non-governmental organizations (NGOs), gaining importance under the growing public sensitivity concerning environmental degradation unified with the trade unions to fight against freer trade. NAFTA became a focal point of this opposition: while NGOs managed to visualize apparent environmental problems in the US–Mexican border area, attributing them to NAFTA (free trade), the trade unions, led by agents of automobile and textile and clothing workers, vehemently complained of the tremendous job losses to be expected from free trade with Mexico. Together, environmentalists and unionists gained substantial political importance during the 1990s and began to influence the discussion on NAFTA effectively.

Second, right before the conclusion of the NAFTA a new president took office. President Clinton had fought against NAFTA during most of his election campaign and only changed his mind after the implementation of modifications of the original treaty under the so-called side agreements on environmental and labor standards. Though these side agreements are moderate in their substance (in particular, there is no link to trade sanctions), they broke a taboo of a long standing and successful American trade policy tradition. As Santos states, 'Clinton ... reversed 50 years of consistent efforts by Republican and Democratic administrations to separate trade from extraneous factors which might operate to diminish trade and the growth of the world economy' (Santos, 1995), and this was not without consequences.

While the side agreements may have facilitated the passing of NAFTA in the House of Representatives (the bill passed Congress by a small majority of 234 : 200 votes), they also divided Congress over the fundamental question whether non-trade issues should be linked to future trade negotiations or not. Republicans reject such a linkage following strong theoretical arguments. Democrats, in turn, tend to favor pragmatism. They argue that the inclusion of core environmental and labor standards in future trade negotiations is indispensable in order to gain acceptance for free trade (fair trade) in the American public.

The discussion of this topic has strongly influenced the US trade policy in the second half of the 1990s. Bill Archer, a former chairman of the US House Ways and Means Committee, has noted that 'the tone of protectionism (in congress) is harder than (he) had seen in twenty-seven years...' (quoted in Riley, 1999, 116). Given the fact that the president himself (who usually follows a more pronounced free trade policy according to his position within the institutional setting) had lined up with the fair traders in Congress, it is clear that under the Clinton administration the balance between free traders and fair traders has changed in favor of the latter.

It is also apparent that this change has been influenced by the changing public opinions on the subject. In particular, Congressmen and women can be shown to have voted the more in favor of 'fair trade' standards, the more pressure they feel from their voting district. Baldwin/Magee for example have shown that a high concentration of labor-intensive industries, a lower than average high school performance, and a high degree of import competition (each single parameter pointing to the prevalence of industries suffering from comparative disadvantage) are significantly influencing the voting behavior of Congressmen and women (Baldwin/Magee, 2000). Thus, whenever the perceived threat from international competition rises, the voting behavior will tend to react by putting more emphasis on market preserving measures. The voting behavior in Congress in the years after the foundation of NAFTA indeed underlines such a development. It can be shown that in important trade policy issues, such as the fast-track issue of 1998 (which has been rejected), Congressmen and women from both parties voted strongly against any renewal of the trade authority. Resistance was strongest from those who were relying on a voting population that felt threatened by NAFTA (and international trade in general) (Baldwin/Magee, 2000).

As a result, US trade policies during the last years of the Clinton administration became virtually paralyzed. One reason for this paradoxical behavior (given the strong economic position of the USA at the end of the century) is, of course, the political dispute on the link between trade and environmental and labor standards which led a number of free traders to vote against any new trade authority for the president in order to hinder the proliferation of non-trade issues in new trade agreements. However, even more important in the longer run may be the evolving sentiment against free trade in the American public that NAFTA has brought to light. In fact, at the end of the 1990s the polls confirmed that 'the most ominous aspect of NAFTA is the effect it had on public perceptions of international trade liberalisation' (Mena, 1999). One example is the Harrison poll of early 1999, which asked for the relative importance of job losses that Americans attach to the following four factors:

1. technological change;
2. over-regulation of the economy;
3. cheap foreign labor;
4. import competition.

Thirty-three percent of the respondents declared that import competition and cheap foreign labor are the most important factors challenging their jobs, and only 12 percent named technological change. From an economic point of view this result points to a pronounced ignorance concerning the impact of technological change on growth and structural change. Put differently, a majority of Americans are ignorant concerning the important impact of technological change on growth and employment, thereby overrating the negative impact of import competition. The fact that negative employment effects of NAFTA have been rare at that time and were limited to particularly small segments of the labor market reveals that partial views (steered by highly organized, efficient interest groups) dominate opinion-making on this topic.

By these groups NAFTA has been chosen as a symbol to demonstrate the negative employment (and environmental) effects of international trade. 'By creating an easily identifiable group of losers from trade, however small a proportion of the labor market it may be, NAFTA may have dealt a serious blow to the capacity of the US to lead global trade liberalization' (Mena, 1999). While these political–economic mechanisms have probably worked even before NAFTA came into being, an important new quality of the lobbying for protectionism in the USA has been developed by the coalition of (environmentally active) NGOs and labor unions from senescent industries (most often located in remote areas).

The new coalition apparently took the chance to visualize distinct border problems (environment) and adjustment burdens (labor) in order to make these issues a nation-wide public concern. That way, the political perception of free trade with Mexico in the public changed for the worse despite the clear economic success of the project.

What remains unclear is why and how a small number of opponents managed to introduce their specific views on NAFTA into large parts of the population. In order to answer this question, three propositions have to be considered:

1. A successful promotion of ill-advised theories by special interest groups has changed the views on international trade in the public.
2. Environmental and social standards are gaining importance in the American society, and this has helped these groups to engage successfully in logrolling activities.

3. Deficient systems of social security may contribute to making American citizens feel uneasy about their personal job situation even at full employment.

The third proposition opens up an array of questions concerning the organization of modern societies in general and of the US social system in particular, which are beyond the scope of this volume.

As far as the popularity of misguided economic explanations for the results of international competition is concerned it is obvious that two distinct labor unions have been front-running against liberal trade policies for decades. The first one is the textile and clothing workers union, which has been fighting for adjustment assistance since the 1950s when the USA has negotiated a first voluntary export restraint on cotton textiles with Japan. This early attempt to ease structural adjustment has been followed by a sequence of more and more restrictive follow-up treaties, which eventually ended up in the Multifiber Agreement (MFA). The second group is the automobile workers that managed to impose voluntary export restraints on Japan in 1981 and 1985.[43] It is worth emphasizing that both industries have been brought back to the GATT disciplines in the 1990s, the textile and clothing sector being a prominent success story of the Uruguay Round. At that time, by promoting the WTO, the USA apparently still endorsed the view that a permanent adjustment assistance for industries losing comparative advantage does hurt the international economic system (and, thereby, important US foreign interests) without being helpful for those being affected at home.

Measured against the background of multilateral standards, NAFTA, by establishing strict rules of origin, has in fact diminished the adjustment pressures for these industries. Nevertheless, the trade unions have proclaimed that NAFTA would introduce additional hardship for American workers. In order to underline this claim, the typical arguments are based on the study of trade balances:

> Plant closings and lay-offs attributable to increased US imports have been constant features of the past 20 years of massive US trade deficits. Studies have shown that a large share of the millions of displaced workers have been unable to find new jobs with compensation equal to the jobs that were lost ... their living standards decline and their communities suffer (Beckman, 1998).

That way, interest groups claim that the competitive problems that arise from declining comparative advantage in some industries today are the forerunners of economy-wide problems tomorrow. Looking for the perceived courses of this pessimistic scenario leads right back to the common reasoning of the American unilateralist approach. It is 'unfair' trade practice that is responsible for the difficulties of adjustment at home. While the 'old' aggressive unilateralism seemed to have been tamed by the US-shaped WTO (rendering the former claims of unfair pricing procedures and restrictions of market access largely obsolete), it quickly rose again under the new NAFTA label.

In this new scenario, ecological and social dumping are becoming the popular new challenge of international relations in general and NAFTA in particular. Drawing on Chapter Two, it is clear that a main point of dispute on international trade between economists and ecologists is on the link between environmental regulations and economic sanctions (in the form of trade restrictions). In particular, from the economic point of view, trade sanctions, which are becoming instrumental to securing ecological compliance, are prone to protectionist abuse and threaten to counteract the efficiency gains from free international exchange. This danger is openly visible in the case of NAFTA. Careful studying of official NGO documents reveals that, as a matter of rule, these groupings are not willing to differentiate clearly between well founded concerns regarding the negative inter-(bi-)national externalities in the US–Mexican border region (which are often resulting from insufficient standards of regulation under the Mexican Maquiladora program) and individual cases of ecological failure which are largely independent from NAFTA (and international trade respectively). By denying any success of environmental programs and claiming almost every ecological, social and economic hardship to be a direct consequence of NAFTA, environmentalists and trade unions have been consciously working together to change public opinions to make them their own.

The history of voting on international economic issues during the 1990s in Congress underlines that this strategy has been quite successful. Following Baldwin/Magee it would have been impossible to approve NAFTA in Congress at the end of the 1990s, even though the house majority had changed in favour of the more free trade-oriented Republican Party.

Due to these developments, the US commitment to a liberal international trade strategy was almost non-existent when George W. Bush took office in January 2001. Clinton, by insisting on social and environmental standards as part of any future trade agenda did neither succeed with the fast-track authority nor with the launching of a new round of multilateral trade liberalization in Seattle. New American regional options, too, could not be advanced under these conditions. It is not clear today whether Bush will deploy more than free trade rhetoric and bring the country back on course. For sure, the Doha Round of multilateral trade liberalization has been opened up, meanwhile, and new regional initiatives concerning the FTAA and Chile are underway.[44] But, at the same time, the USA has launched a new agricultural law (2002) offering generous subsidies for US farmers, and once again imposed emergency measures on steel imports. Optimists hold that the new temporary steel quotas and the agricultural reform act are part of a tricky political game that should eventually end up with more free trade in the end (Bergsten, 2002). But there is no clear sign today that the USA is really inclined to move in those areas of trade policy where its partners claim particularly stiff American protectionism (anti-dumping, agriculture, senescent industries). Such a move will probably become politically possible only if the fundamental views on international trade will reverse, which have gained ground in the public discourse during the second half of the 1990s.

From the present point of view, therefore, it has to be concluded that NAFTA has contributed to a less open-minded attitude on international trade by many Americans, while Congress is seriously disrupted over the dispute on the adequate treatment of non-trade issues. That way, protectionist forces have gained importance. This finding is in line with the claim of many political–economic theorists who fear a proliferation of protectionist forces in the long run rather than increased support for open markets under the New Regionalism.

4.4.2 External Economic Policies in Canada and Mexico

NAFTA started in a period of low tensions of the multilateral system. In fact, the foundation of the WTO and the commitments of all major world trading nations to further multilateral reductions of trade barriers in the Uruguay Round, fed the expectation in the early 1990s that the neo-protectionism could be turned into a new period of increasingly open international trade relations. Within this context, NAFTA, in order to qualify as a project of the open regionalism, should at least be expected to have kept external protection low (more precisely, it should have diminished its external level of protection along with the multilaterally agreed tariff reductions).

It has been shown that for the USA, in general, this task has been fulfilled. The average effective US tariff rate in 2001, for example, is at a historic low of 1.6 percent. Nevertheless, it is also clear that this average masks a number of important exceptions that put an especially heavy burden on less developed countries (Gresser, 2002, 10). In a more comprehensive evaluation of US protectionist behavior, it has also to be considered that this low average tariff rate does not include NTBs and the frequently deployed emergency measures. NTBs, as a matter of rule, are much more protectionist than tariffs, and a recurrent use of emergency measures breeds intransparency and questions the reliability of the international rules. Therefore, the recent temporary raise on tariffs and quotas on steel, the new agricultural act, and the incessant regress on anti-dumping measures in the USA are warning against a revival of neo-protectionism at the beginning of the new century. The change of US public opinions on international trade in general, and

NAFTA in particular, underlines the proposition that these fears are not unfounded. If this analysis of the present situation of US trade politics is correct, this also suggests that one basic condition of the New Regionalism, external openness, is at risk.

The situation in Canada does not appear to be much different from the USA. Canada entered NAFTA from a higher (though still GATT conform) level of external tariff protection but, due to its relatively weak power political position, with less emphasis on unilateral action. During the NAFTA (and CUSTA) years it diminished external tariff protection step by step both vis-à-vis the USA and Mexico, and multilaterally. But in Canada, too, the virtues of NAFTA do not seem to find general acceptance.

Mexico is a different case. It ventured into NAFTA by departing from its longstanding history of import substitution. That is, Mexico had started a fundamental reorganization of its economic model in 1985, thereby reintegrating the country into the multilateral system. In the field of trade policy this approach has led to progressive trade liberalization in both tariffs and NTBs between 1985–91. Entering NAFTA introduced an even more rigorous liberalization program vis-à-vis the USA and Canada that brought the import weighted tariff rate down to 5.7 percent in 1994 and 2.8 percent in 1999 (Table 4.16).[45] Under these conditions it is not surprising that external (multilateral) trade liberalization came to a standstill during the first NAFTA years. However, what is worrying is the fact that there are even some indications of a reversal. A look at the rates of tariff protection reveals that Mexico, under the NAFTA regime, has raised its tariffs towards non-members twice (1995 and 1999). In order to recognize the effect of these activities more clearly, the unweighted tariff rate is an appropriate indicator.[46] Table 4.16 reveals that the average unweighted MFN (most-favored nation) tariff rose from 12.4 percent in 1994 to 16.1 percent in 1999. The highest increase took place in consumer goods, where a 70 percent increase from 17.2 percent to 29.3 percent took place. Two points have to be remembered in order to put these figures in perspective. First, both these tariff adjustments took place during periods of severe internal and external economic pressure. The 1995 tariff rise, for example, was a defensive response to the so-called Tequila crisis, while the 1999 case can be attributed to a series of international currency crises (East Asia, Russia, Brazil), that threatened to spill over to Mexico. Thus, both developments may still turn out to be just temporary and should not be taken as a definite indication of rising external protection.

Second, Mexico currently trades predominantly with Canada and the USA. Thus, the (temporary) rise of the level of external protection only touches upon a small fraction of Mexican trade, and does not alter the challenge significantly that is imposed on the Mexican economy from opening up to the

Table 4.16 Tariff protection in Mexico, 1994–99 (%)

	1994	1995	1996	1997	1998	1999
Average Rate of Nominal Tariffs (import weighted)	5.7	3.4	2.9	2.6	2.6	2.8
Average Rate of Nominal Tariffs (unweighted)	12.4	13.7	13.3	13.3	13.2	16.1
Capital Goods	11.7	11.7	11.5	11.4	11.4	14.5
Intermediate Goods	11.4	11.8	11.3	11.2	11.2	13.9
Consumer Goods	17.2	24.8	25.0	24.9	24.5	29.3

Source: Presidencia de la República (1999)

world market, and NAFTA respectively. That is, the structural changes that Mexico will have to undergo during the ongoing North American integration process have not become much less demanding because of the higher external tariffs. Nevertheless, these arguments are not sufficient to calm down the fears completely that Mexico might already be preoccupied with raising its external protective position permanently, and concentrating on the NAFTA market at the expense of its multilateral engagement. This is exactly the claim that critics of the New Regionalism are making.

In order to get a more comprehensive understanding of the Mexican external trade policy under NAFTA, a closer look at some other fields of international economic policy-making is appropriate. One particular aspect of these activities is the Mexican policy concerning separate RIAs with non-NAFTA countries. In fact, while the agony of the US policy regarding new trade initiatives has prohibited any significant advancement of NAFTA, Mexico (and, as will be shown later, Canada) took the opportunity to develop a net of pluri- and bilateral RIAs. As can be seen from Figure 4.2, Mexico, apart from still being a member of LAIA,[47] is participating in 'el Grupo Norte' (together with El Salvador, Guatemala and Honduras) and 'el Grupo de los Tres' (together with Colombia and Venezuela). Furthermore, it has negotiated separate bilateral FTAs with Chile (1991, 1998), Costa Rica and Bolivia (1995), Nicaragua (1998), and the European Union (2001). Quite a number of additional agreements are in progress (Panama, Peru, Ecuador, Trinidad and Tobago, and Japan). Thus, it is not unfair to state that Mexico has developed into a 'hub' within an American hub-and-spokes pattern.[48] It is also clear that the Mexican approach is frankly mercantilist, aiming to exploit its favorable position within NAFTA (relative to non-NAFTA Latin American countries) and, at the same time, reap the benefits of preferential trade relations with Latin America.[49]

Canada, too has advanced a number of bilateral RIAs aside from NAFTA. A most interesting approach is the FTA with Chile (1996) that has been negotiated as a solid copy of the NAFTA. Thus, Chile now trades freely with Canada and Mexico. Nevertheless, it has been denied access to NAFTA because the USA rejected Chile's request until recently (the USA signed another separate FTA with Chile in December 2002).

Canada has also been most creative in negotiating new forms of regional integration and cooperation projects. One such venture is the Trade and Investment Cooperation Agreement. Such an agreement has been signed with both MERCOSUR and the Andean Community (1998). Another approach is the Memorandum of Understanding. This type of cooperation agreement has been negotiated with Costa Rica, El Salvador, Guatemala, Honduras and Nicaragua. A final type of trade (investment) agreement is the Reciprocal Foreign Investment Protection Agreement (FIPA) that is active with eight

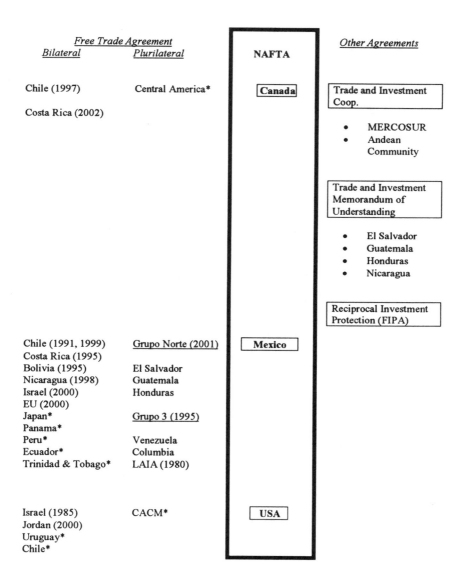

Note: * in progress

Figure 4.2   NAFTA's external regional cooperation network

countries while 13 projects are in progress. The different agreements, and the FIPAs in particular, emphasize the importance of both trade and investment, and are spreading the NAFTA provisions on FDI into the region.

Altogether these developments show that, while NAFTA did not evolve externally because of the US inability to overcome national resistance against further free trade initiatives, Canada and Mexico took the opportunity to establish closer trade and investment relations within the region and (in the case of Mexico) even to different continents. At a first glance, these developments seem to lend support to the domino theory of regionalism (Baldwin, 1997), and they may also be interpreted as a visible outcome of the dynamics of open regionalism.

A main concern regarding these views derives from the fact that 'regionalism in theory' differs from 'regionalism in practice' in some important points. Generally speaking, practiced FTAs and the like are only imperfect approximations of the 'ideal typus' that is usually discussed in the literature (Chapter Three). This is obvious from a comparison of the compliance of the existing agreements with GATT Article 24 (which itself by no means follows a purist philosophy). Most RIAs are a long way from the 'substantially all trade' rule of Article 24, and they are so in quite different ways. As a consequence, we find widely divergent free trade regimes among the existing agreements. These regimes are in fact consisting of quite different sets of 'areas of free trade and exceptions'.

These departures from the 'ideal typus' would still not be a cause of concern, if two conditions were met:

1. Only a limited number of imperfect RIAs do exist.
2. The existing imperfect RIAs are seriously driven by the commonly shared conviction of national governments that open markets are an indispensable precondition for the New Regionalism to succeed. That is, given the regional obligations, free trade is understood and accepted as an ongoing process that has to be pushed forward politically (just as it has been done on the multilateral level), in order to attain higher and higher levels of market integration.

Both conditions are vital for the success of the New Regionalism, and both are in doubt concerning the present external NAFTA experience:

1. The proliferation of imperfect pluri- and bilateral RIAs, which have been initiated by Canada and Mexico under the NAFTA regime, has led to an increasingly opaque structure of incentives between North and South American participants and non-participants. It is obvious that this development also has repercussions on NAFTA itself. The US automobile

industry, for example, feels increasingly discriminated by the Mexican hub-and-spokes strategy. Under the chaotic structure of incentives that has been created by means of increasingly overlapping regional jurisdictions and rules, transaction costs are rising and investment in export activities becomes riskier, so that the net gains from regionalism are likely to decline. As the rules of origin issue makes clear, this development has already become a distinct matter of concern for NAFTA. Firms that are willing to operate under the NAFTA regime do have to document the provenance of their inputs. Though the empirical evidence of the impact of ROOs (rules of origin) on welfare is scarce, there is no doubt that it causes costly administrative procedures, which are all dead weight costs. Krueger (1997, 15) for example, reports that EFTA (European Free Trade Association) producers had to calculate a 3–5 percent margin on their supply prices on the EU market in order to cover the costs of documenting the origin of their products. Appiah (1999) even came to the conclusion that the costs of the NAFTA ROO system are in the order of 2–3 percent of NAFTA GDP (quoted in Harris, 2001, 11). If this latter result is correct and can be compared to the welfare effects of trade liberalization, a sobering conclusion arises: the total (static) welfare effects of NAFTA plus the Uruguay Round as typically measured by CGE models[50] would hardly match the loss caused by the ROO regime.

As Krueger (1997) has noted, the costs of ROOs are rising progressively when firms have to comply with the rules of origin in a growing number of overlapping ROO regimes with different structural characteristics. This is exactly the situation that characterizes the North American Regionalism that has evolved as the result of the bilateral strategies of the two smaller NAFTA countries. Consequently, there is a growing number of firms that are renouncing NAFTA privileges in order to economize on the administrative costs of the ROO documentation systems.

2. The political will to seriously proceed towards open regional markets may itself be in doubt. The evolving bilateralisms of Canada and Mexico are not free from this claim. Given the fact that the individual FTAs and cooperation agreements are streamlined to fit the perceived bilateral interests of the partner countries it is obvious that the individual agreements differ in their structural characteristics, reflecting the distinct political and vested interests between and within the countries and regions. These interests are likely to strongly resist any broadly based liberalization initiative that is not led by the USA.[51]

Last but not least, integration theory teaches that bilateral treaties are likely to be biased in favor of the larger partners. Taking aside the special cases 'Mexico–EU' and 'Mexico–Japan' (still pending), these larger partners (in the Latin American context) are the NAFTA empowered Mexican and Canadian communities.

4.5 CONCLUSION – THE EXTERNAL RELATIONS

To sum up, as far as the New Regionalism is concerned, the impact of Canada and Mexico on their regional trade policy environment is not encouraging. Even if the Mexican tariff policy of the second half of the 1990s is not seen as an alarming sign of new protectionist sentiments, there are strong reservations regarding the compatibility of the flourishing bilateralism exhibited by Canada and Mexico. Both countries, but more so Mexico, have been sailing in the lee winds of NAFTA and the US inactivity in international and regional trade policies under the Clinton administration, to unfold a complex system of pluri- and bilateral RIAs. These RIAs widely ignore the GATT Article 24 provision of 'substantially all trade'. That way they have actively contributed to the formation of a 'spaghetti bowl' that currently characterizes the American Regionalism. These developments are in contradiction to fundamental principles of the New Regionalism.

Until recently, the agony of US international economic policies during the NAFTA period has been one important factor promoting these developments. Thus, it will be crucial for the future of the American Regionalism whether and how the USA will be able to overcome this period of reluctance. This problem is beyond the scope of any serious analyses currently. Nevertheless, there are some new regional developments beyond NAFTA that have opened up a range of new options for the further direction of the American Regionalism. These developments are in close context to the formation of the FTAA, which in turn will not evolve independently from the multilateral trade talks under the so-called Doha Round. Before discussing some of these new developments, MERCOSUR, the most important South American RIA, will be analyzed in Chapter Five.

NOTES

1. This interpretation has been challenged by Baldwin's domino theory. He explicitly rejects the mainstream explanation of the New Regionalism being the result of the turn to the regional track by the USA. In fact, the USA has had regional intentions long before the foundations of CUSTA (Canada-United States Free Trade Agreement), NAFTA etc. (Baldwin, 1997; Fawcett, 1997). Nevertheless he fails to explain why the new regional areas became so attractive recently.
2. The side agreements on labor and the environment are two other elements of this kind.

3. The acceptance of foreign capital, particularly FDI, also demonstrates impressively the dramatic change of the Mexican development strategy.
4 One major exception from this regime (which is not unimportant from the US point of view) is the Mexican petroleum sector, which is still constitutionally protected against foreign participation.
5. A comprehensive study on NAFTA's 'Outlier Sectors' has been presented by Miller (2002).
6. An indirect evaluation of this problem of hidden barriers to trade derives from the report of the president for the year 1998: 'The NAFTA investment and service group maintains an active agenda ... parties exchanged lists ... for transparency purposes ...' (USTR, 1999a, 161).
7. See also section 4.2.3.1 on the US apparel industry.
8. Note that these figures are heavily influenced by the fact that the USA is (and has been before NAFTA) by far the most important trade partner of Mexico. More than 90 percent of Mexican trade in both directions is with the USA.
9. Both effects are growth promoting for Mexico. However, if the latter effect is based on tariff hopping provoked by high NAFTA entry barriers, growth diverting effects for non-member economies also apply.
10. Dussel Peters (2000, 118) and Nunnenkamp (2002, 34) derive similar conclusions from a comparison of the Mexican experience with that of other emerging markets.
11. Note, however, that figures of one single year may be misleading because of large single projects. In the case of Canada, the 2001 figure does not appear to be reliable. Drawing on the average shares before 2000 indicates that the Canadian position has remained constant at best.
12. According to Emmot, the service figure (15,336) is heavily influenced by one single acquisition in the financial sector, that is, the acquisition of Banamex by Citygroup (approx. 12.5 billion US$) (Emmot, 2001, 70, cited in Nunnenkamp, 2002, 34).
13. The Maquiladora industries will be analyzed more deeply later.
14. This scarcity may be enlarged by an increasing brain-drain towards the USA.
15. In a broadened framework human capital would have to be considered separately. However, this more realistic approach would not change the overall structure of trade under NAFTA because the distribution of the human capital between these countries is such that the results of the conventional Heckscher–Ohlin approach would become even more pronounced.
16. Product sharing as a means of fostering the use of US components in foreign (labor intensive) assembly operations underlies special customs treatment (positions 9802.00.60–9802.00.90, Chapter 98 of the Harmonized Tariff Schedule).
17. That is, in those strategies that rely on world markets and concentrate on the exploitation of their abundant production factor.
18. The static welfare effect alone of import protection on textile and apparel has been estimated at about 13 billion US$ annually (USITC, 2002, 21).
19. In 1991, the quota regulations on US apparel imports amounted to an average tariff equivalent of 21.4 percent. Together with the average tariff rate on apparel imports of 11.4 percent this adds to a 32 percent duty equivalent (USITC, 2002, 21).
20. Note, however, that in Asia some new competitors have emerged (namely Pakistan and Indonesia) that are not included in these data (USITC, 2002, Publication 3510, 5–38).
21. Trade in 2001 dropped absolutely because of the US recession. That is, Mexico and the CBERA region have been affected by the US downswing much more intensively than Asia.
22. For a more detailed discussion see Romalis (2002).
23. The study concludes that for every 100 jobs that can be generated in Mexico and the CBERA region 15 new jobs will be created on the US market (AAMA, cited in USITC, 1999).
24. This would in fact mean that Heckscher–Ohlin-type trade, which currently has a special regulatory status, would be transformed into 'normal' trade under the official NAFTA provisions.
25. In 1998, according to an EIZ study, the world production potential was 71 million units as compared to 49 million sales (cited in Nunnenkamp, 2000, 5).

26. This change manifests itself in the growing demand for sports utility vehicles and light pickups. In 1997 the production of light trucks of 6.1 million units exceeded that of cars (5.4 million units) for the first time (USTR, 1999b, 6).
27. While the relative size of this deficit is in line with the general US trade deficit and may be interpreted as a reflex of an exchange rate misalignment, it is remarkable that the increase of the deficit with Canada was significantly lower than the overall deficit.
28. Canada is the largest US trading partner in the automotive sector, accounting for about 60 percent of US imports and 40 percent of exports in 1999 (McNay/Polly, 2000, Tables 4 and 5)
29. Except for the 25 percent tariff (duties) on pickups Mexican exports faced no serious constraints on the US market. Duties were zero on most components, 2.5 percent on cars and 4 percent on cab-chassis trucks (USTR, 1999b, 13)
30. And must be weighted against higher transportation costs in many cases.
31. One estimate is that automotive firms have invested more than 50 billion US$ in Mexico since 1994 (McNay/Polly, 2000, 26).
32. Still another important feature of the Mexican trade policy is the extension of bilateral FTAs with quite a number of European and Latin American countries. This development, which may have important consequences for the NAFTA market, will be discussed under section 4.5.
33. Fifth Annual Report to Congress regarding the impact of the North American Free Trade Agreement upon US Automotive Trade with Mexico (USITC, 1999b).
34. It is not entirely transparent from the literature which kinds of reclassifications of the components sector have been made. Table 5 in McNay/Polly is entitled 'Certain Motor-Vehicle Parts' as compared to 'Automotive Parts' in the Automotive reports. In any case, both tables are based on official data.
35. This leads to a more general insight concerning the restructuring procedures of MNEs on the global markets. In highly integrated global production networks, opening up or expanding one production facility very often comes at the expense of another facilty that is owned by the same company. Thus, within these markets, the reallocation of resources will take place relatively quickly, following new incentives, but breaking into established markets rigorously by a newly developing country is unlikely to be successful, because it comes at the expense of virtually the same producers. This situation appears to apply directly to the NAFTA automotive market.
36. Average nominal tariffs in the industrial sector of high income countries are estimated to be below 4 percent.
37. In many industries, the tariff equivalent of NTBs exceeds tariff protection by 300 to 500 percent (Messerlin, 2001).
38. The Smoot–Haley Act (1930), which had opened up the protectionist race that was one of the main driving forces of the 'Great Depression', was basically the result of a Republican initiative (Thorbecke, 2000, 87; Hiscox, 2002).
39. Attached to the USTR is an influential advisory board that offers private (entrepreneurial) interests a useful platform for the articulation of specific interests.
40. To be sure, these partner countries gave enough reason for concern, too. The point here is that the USA, the (former) hegemon of the GATT system, itself has hurt the rules that it had pushed forward and agreed upon multilaterally. It is a constituting property of multilateralism, that international economic rules will be negotiated and agreed upon by all participating nations. Disputes in this system have to be settled according to the commonly agreed set of rules and not unilaterally. For further discussions of this topic see Krueger (1995); Arndt (2000).
41. It will not be discussed here whether the initiative for regional integration came from the USA or from its partners (Baldwin, 1997). In this context, the crucial point is that the USA, if not the initiator, has been responsive to such proposals, and this has changed its international strategy.
42. This is not to say that the unilateral option has been dropped altogether. Rather, the point is that it has been used relatively cautiously since the conclusion of the Uruguay Round. A

clear departure from this general line has been the automotive deal with Japan in 1995, when the US administration was about to act unilaterally in an important trade dispute case. The fact that Japan complied at the last moment does not wipe out the recognition that the US is still prepared to disregard the multilateral rules if it is deemed to be necessary.

43. There are other industries which have repeatedly and successfully claimed adjustment assistance. Most prominent cases are the steel and the shoe industries.

44. The FTAA will be treated separately in Chapter Six.

45. In 1982 the average tariff rate had been about 100 percent and, additionally, almost all products had been subject to quotas and licensing. Official import prices (based on national prices) were applied to many products and added to these measures. See Ten Kate (1992, 659).

46. The weighted tariff rate is dominated by intra-NAFTA trade (90 percent) which has been liberalized according to the NAFTA provisions.

47. The Latin American Integration Agreement (LAIA) is one of the old-fashioned and relatively inefficient approaches to Latin American economic integration. It was established in 1980 as a predecessor of the Latin American Free Trade Association (LAFTA).

48. This hub position is not stable, of course, but reflects a typical free rider position that depends on the willingness of the USA to tolerate Mexican regional initiatives.

49. Official statements on the success of the Mexican regional policies emphasize the fact that Mexico has positive trade balances with all its (Latin American) partners.

50. It is, of course, highly problematic to compare these calculations directly. It may, nevertheless, be illuminating to have a crude idea of the dimension of the problem.

51. The FTAA, from this point of view, may become an approach that is capable of solving this Gordian knot. See Chapter Six.

5. MERCOSUR

El Mercado Común del Sur (do Sul) is part of the new wave of American Regionalism of the 1990s. This is not only so because it was founded in 1991 but also because it follows a concept that is close to the New Regionalism. In fact, the founders of MERCOSUR have repeatedly insisted on the interpretation of the agreement as a venture in open and deeper regional integration. Accordingly, MERCOSUR has been sharply demarcated from the former Latin American integration schemes of the 1960s and 1970s that heavily relied on the import substitution strategy (Langhammer, 1992). This change of regional integration policies did not take place in isolation, of course, but is part of the overall transformation strategy that has redirected most Latin American countries towards open development strategies since the second half of the 1980s (Edwards, 1995). It is also worth mentioning that the initial steps towards regional integration in the Southern Cone were focused on the de-escalation of the longstanding hostilities between Argentina and Brazil. Economic objectives gained importance only later.

MERCOSUR is different from NAFTA in quite a number of respects:

1. MERCOSUR is a regional integration agreement (RIA) between LDCs (less developed countries).
2. MERCOSUR is smaller geographically and economically than NAFTA and, though still the largest RIA among LDCs, it is politically less powerful.
3. The level of aspiration of the MERCOSUR policy-makers regarding the 'deepness' of integration of the Southern Cone exceeds that of NAFTA. While the latter basically retains the characteristics of a Free Trade Agreement (FTA) (despite the provisions for foreign direct investment [FDI], the amendments etc.), MERCOSUR has been founded with the clear intention of becoming a common market (CM).
4. MERCOSUR follows a kind of stages approach to regional integration. Though proclaiming the formation of a CM right from the beginning, today there is still no definite plan on how to advance the project beyond the customs union torso that it has remained since its implementation in 1995. Put differently, MERCOSUR, after 12 years, is still 'work in progress' without a reliable integration program.

Under these conditions, MERCOSUR has to be analyzed following a rather different concept than the one used in the chapter on NAFTA. Hence, this chapter will first concentrate on a short description of the history of MERCOSUR before and after 1995. The aim is to show that the successful first years were followed by increasing economic and political turbulences after 1995 that eventually brought the agreement to the brink of disaster. Then, the major causes of this failure will be analyzed in some depth.

5.1 THE EVOLUTION OF REGIONAL INTEGRATION IN THE SOUTHERN CONE

Since the mid-1980s, Argentina and Brazil began to advance bilateral talks on political security issues aimed at ending the long history of hostilities and distrust between the two nations (Smith, 1993; Peña, 1995).[1] During these talks it soon became clear that economic issues could not simply be separated from the political objectives, and the agenda was broadened accordingly. Thus, talks about closer economic cooperation began soon after the new political contacts had been established.

The early drafts of bilateral cooperation still drew heavily on the traditional integration model. That is, the 'economic complementary agreements' followed the ALADI (Latin American Integration Association) philosophy of limited and selective market access (Devlin/Estevadeordal, 2001a, 5). From this perspective regional free trade was not a serious concern, but rather a new label for the old results oriented model of managed trade. Only towards the end of the decade did the idea of an FTA based on open markets and limited selectivity gain support, and eventually succeeded in the MERCOSUR treaty.[2] The literature on the MERCOSUR treaty supports this claim. It reveals that the founders of MERCOSUR had hoped that regional integration would help to serve two major and interlinked objectives. The first was to establish MERCOSUR as a complement to global integration. That is, after the extended period of import substitution, it should help to foster the process of reintegration of the Southern Cone into the world markets. The second expectation was that regional integration would contribute to a more rapid upgrading process within the region and strengthen competitiveness abroad. The development of intra-industry trade and rising attractiveness of the larger markets for FDI played a prominent role in this concept. Altogether these ideas support the thesis that the founders of MERCOSUR argued along the lines of the New Regionalism as outlined in Chapter Three.

Argentina and Brazil have been the motors of regional integration in the Southern Cone, and they are also the major economic protagonists in the region. Over 90 percent of the region's GDP is produced in these two countries, and the industrial heartlands of Sao Paulo, Rio de Janeiro and Porto Alegre in Brazil, and the greater Buenos Aires area in Argentina are building a strong and relatively developed economic region. Paraguay and Uruguay, which joined Argentina and Brazil in 1990, did not have any major impact on shaping the integration process under these conditions. Nevertheless, not being left outside and not being cut off from the most important markets of the region appeared to be particularly beneficial for these relatively small partner countries.[3]

There are some important political considerations that have helped to push regional economic integration in the Southern Cone. Internally, under the pressure of the debt crisis, the longstanding rivalries between Argentina and Brazil became increasingly felt as a severe economic burden. At the same time, the (probably) inflated perceptions of the risk of war between both countries were downgraded when the new democratic governments took over. Thus, the balance between benefits and costs of political relaxation changed in favor of the former, offering new options for the management of peaceful ways of coexistence.

Within this new environment (personal) political contacts built up quickly and helped to initiate a virtuous circle of credibility formation that eventually led to new bilateral cooperation ventures. It is only later that, under the economic reform strategies, these political approximations gave rise to the consideration of common economic projects. The New Regionalism, by promising to strengthen the competitive position of the economies, became a symbol of both an open economic model and a political model of peaceful coexistence.

Presumably, some external power political aspects have also provided incentives for regional economic integration in the Southern Cone. At the end of the Cold War the political and economic situation of LDCs had changed dramatically. Those in particular that had bargained between the blocs during the Cold War, suddenly had to manage on their own and were eager to find new partners. Regional integration was felt to be an adequate answer to this problem, because it was believed to enhance market power and raise the attractiveness of the region as a trading partner and as a promising location for investment. The uncertain global situation under the impact of the neo-protectionism may also have contributed to the turn to regionalism (that is, to secure market access on the neighboring markets).

5.2 FROM THE FREE TRADE AGREEMENT TO THE CUSTOMS UNION

The official document of the MERCOSUR is the Treaty of Asunción (1991), which built on the Integration, Cooperation and Development Treaty that had been negotiated between Argentina and Brazil in 1988. Basically, the Treaty of Asunción enlarged the bilateral treaty in three different ways. First, it incorporated Paraguay and Uruguay as new members. Second, it explicitly formulated the goal to develop a common market. Third, it established a definite schedule to bring down tariff and non-tariff barriers until the end of 1994, following a linear and progressive liberalization sequence. To keep things manageable, sensitive sectors were exempted from the general trade liberalization schedule and were supposed to be negotiated separately in the following years. The founders of MERCOSUR also recognized the importance of macroeconomic coordination. In view of the severe macroeconomic disturbances of the preceding decades, this topic appears to be particularly critical. During the 1980s, highly volatile rates of inflation had led to unpredictable changes of the real exchange rates in the Southern Cone. As a consequence, the risk involved in investing in the tradable sector in particular increased and this hindered the evolution of trade and growth. Obviously, in an increasingly interdependent regional market, high volatilities of the real exchange rates would be an even larger obstacle for growth and development.

A common declaration striving for macroeconomic policy coordination addressed this problem. However, the presidents could not agree on a concrete policy framework for a coordinated management of the macroeconomic aggregates. The divergent macroeconomic concepts of Argentina and Brazil, in particular, should become a major burden for MERCOSUR in the longer run. I shall come back to this point later.

Another important aspect of the New Regionalism is capital movements. MERCOSUR does not provide for common rules of FDI in the region. But, after decades of ideological reservations, the potentially beneficial effects of MNEs for economic development in LDCs became widely recognized. Individually, each member country began to facilitate international capital movements. As a result, the conditions of FDI on the national markets improved substantially.

Altogether, the commitment to liberalized trade and capital flows within and outside the region, and to macroeconomic coordination reveal that MERCOSUR has incorporated some fundamental aspects of the New Regionalism right from its beginning. It is also apparent, however, that the treaty does not have an equally binding character in all of these elements. Macroeconomic coordination, for example, though having been recognized as critically important for integration, did not go beyond a mere declaration of good intentions without any proposal for implementation. Capital flows were deregulated on a national basis, but without any further obligation to proceed on a common scale. Put differently, even in 1991 the only area of a definite agreement on regional action was trade, while any commitment to common political strategies that would have demanded more serious regress to sovereignty sharing was carefully avoided.

This observation fits neatly into the overall institutional provisions of MERCOSUR, which are particularly weak. Aside from the tiny MERCO-SUR secretariat that operates from Montevideo, there are only two inter-governmental bodies, the Common Market Council (CMC) and the Common Market Group (CMG). The former is an institution that operates on the level of the ministers of foreign affairs, while the latter consists of high ranked officials. However, major decisions have usually been undertaken in occasional presidential meetings – often restricted to Menem (Argentina) and Collor and Cardoso (Brazil). The same type of institutional management prevails in the treatment of internal disputes and emergency issues.

During the first years of MERCOSUR this institutional construction of a highly personalized decision-making process seems to have worked fairly well. Apparently, the direct involvement of the leading presidents, who both felt a distinct personal responsibility for the project, helped to build up credibility and to overcome the frequently arising ad hoc problems of the implementation period.

Almost every analyst of MERCOSUR concedes that the first years have been particularly successful. This observation applies to the liberalization of tariff and non-tariff barriers (NTBs) as well as to the impact of regional integration on trade and capital flows. As Table 5.1 indicates, the average nominal MERCOSUR tariff rate dropped from 37.2 percent in 1985 to 11.5 percent in 1994. Brazil, starting from the highest level (55.1 percent), and Paraguay even managed to bring down their tariff rates to one-digit levels.

Preferential tariffs dropped even more on average. Again, Brazil has been the most dynamic tariff-cutter, bringing down the high 1985 rates to 3.2 percent (Argentina), 4.4 percent (Paraguay), and 4.9 percent (Uruguay). Argentina lagged behind Brazil in relation to Paraguay and Uruguay, but was most successful in cutting tariffs on Brazilian products. Thus, the important bilateral trade flows between the two leading countries have benefited most strongly from this process. This effect can also be recognized from the MERCOSUR preference margins that rose considerably in all countries except Paraguay. Again, the strongest effects apply to the Argentine–Brazil bilateral trade relations.

Another important observation is that most of the liberalization efforts took place during the pre-MERCOSUR period (1985–91). In some cases we even find a slight reversal thereafter: the average tariff rates of Argentina and

Table 5.1 Nominal tariff rates in MERCOSUR, 1985–94 (%)

		1985	1988	1991	1994
Average Tariffs					
MERCOSUR		37.2	29.5	17.4	11.5
Argentina		39.2	30.8	14.2	15.4
Brazil		55.1	41.5	20.4	9.7
Paraguay		18.7	18.6	13.6	7.3
Uruguay		35.9	26.9	21.4	13.6
Preferential Tariffs					
Argentina	–Brazil	36.6	24.4	7.2	5.1
	–Paraguay	35.2	22.2	7.8	7.6
	–Uruguay	36.0	20.8	8.1	10.7
Brazil	–Argentina	51.9	30.9	10.0	3.2
	–Paraguay	49.9	28.3	10.8	4.4
	–Uruguay	51.1	25.1	10.7	4.9
Paraguay	–Argentina	19.9	19.2	13.3	7.0
	–Brazil	19.9	19.2	13.8	7.0
	–Uruguay	19.7	19.0	13.4	6.9
Uruguay	–Argentina	34.6	21.1	15.5	12.0
	–Brazil	34.6	22.0	15.8	10.0
	–Paraguay	33.3	22.5	14.8	9.1
Preference Margins					
Argentina	–Brazil	1.5	4.6	6.0	9.5
	–Paraguay	2.6	6.4	5.4	7.0
	–Uruguay	1.9	7.9	5.2	3.9
Brazil	–Argentina	1.9	7.4	9.6	6.2
	–Paraguay	3.2	9.2	8.8	5.1
	–Uruguay	2.5	12.1	8.9	4.5
Paraguay	–Argentina	0.2	0.7	1.2	0.7
	–Brazil	0.2	0.7	0.8	0.6
	–Uruguay	0.3	0.9	1.1	0.7
Uruguay	–Argentina	0.7	4.9	5.1	1.5
	–Brazil	0.7	4.1	4.9	3.4
	–Paraguay	1.6	3.5	5.6	4.1

Source: Estevadeordal/Goto/Saez (2000)

its preferential rate vis-à-vis Uruguay rose again from 14.2 to 15.4 percent and from 8.1 to 10.7 percent respectively. Most of the preferential margins, too, were cut back between 1991–94.

Tariff protection is only part of the story, however. In many cases, NTBs formed the most efficient entry barriers of the old regimes. In 1989, for example, Argentina had still put quantitative restrictions on about two-thirds of its tariff lines. Since 1990 these barriers were substantially reduced, except for the automobile sector. Brazil, too, dismantled NTBs drastically since 1990 by abolishing the list of forbidden imports and turning to automatic licensing procedures for most products. The nearly complete abolition of NTBs has undoubtedly enforced the effects of tariff reductions considerably and brought the MERCOSUR countries closer to international standards.

Outside Latin America, this keen swing towards open markets has been registered with great sympathy. However, many observers seem to have been ignorant about the severe political–economic problems that such a change of paradigm involves. A closer look at the transformation process of the member countries reveals that these problems have always been prevalent (and, along with it, a permanent threat of a setback). The hectic experimentation in Argentina with different tariff regimes, for example, is a good example of the uneasiness of the political decision-making procedures. Between 1990–93 the country underwent several changes of the level and structure of tariff rates and also imposed a quasi-tariff in the form of the statistical tax that nearly doubled the tariff level at times (Estevadeordal/Goto/Saez, 2000).

A more general indicator of the potential conflicts concerning future trade liberalization is the list of excepted products. Each member was allowed to define such a list on its own. According to the concept these lists should be reduced step by step during the coming years. Phasing out proved to be difficult, however, and in some cases the lists were in fact extended. Still another most sensitive area of concern is the exclusion of entire production sectors such as automobiles and sugar from the general process of convergence.

Many early analysts of MERCOSUR did not pay adequate attention to the fact that these sectors form the backbone of the Brazilian and Argentine economies, and, therefore, their exemption put a high burden on the ongoing integration process.

These reservations concerning the reliability of the phasing out process notwithstanding, trade and investment in MERCOSUR expanded rapidly during the first half of the 1990s. Table 5.2 indicates that MERCOSUR exports expanded at 8.4 percent on average from 1986–88 and 11.3 percent from 1992–95. Imports even increased from 6.2 to 23.6 percent during this period. Intra-regional trade expansion is the most dynamic aspect of this

Table 5.2   *MERCOSUR average annual increase of exports and imports,*
           1986–95 (%)

	1986–88	1989–91	1992–95
Exports			
MERCOSUR			
Total	8.4	0.8	11.3
Extra-regional	8.0	−0.9	8.3
Intra-regional	14.5	20.3	29.6
Argentina			
Total	2.9	9.5	15.0
Extra-regional	2.2	6.6	9.1
Intra-regional	9.5	31.2	36.1
Of which Brazil	7.0	34.8	38.5
Brazil			
Total	9.6	−2.2	10.1
Extra-regional	9.3	−3.1	8.3
Intra-regional	16.4	13.9	27.8
Of which Argentina	11.2	25.0	28.6
Imports			
MERCOSUR			
total	6.2	14.1	23.6
extra-regional	4.7	13.1	22.6
intra-regional	18.5	20.0	28.4
Argentina			
total	11.7	15.9	24.9
extra-regional	10.0	15.9	24.4
intra-regional	18.8	15.5	26.4
of which Brazil	16.7	16.3	28.6
Brazil			
total	3.9	12.7	23.7
extra-regional	3.0	11.4	22.6
intra-regional	18.1	27.3	31.8
of which Argentina	14.4	33.2	34.7

Source: Estevadeordal/Goto/Saez (2000)

process. Both exports and imports grew at an average rate of nearly 30 percent per year from 1992–95. Extra-regional exports, in turn, did not expand at a higher rate in 1992–95 than in 1986–88. This is in sharp contrast to the extra-regional imports, which rose sharply.[4] Overall, Argentina has been the most dynamic trader of MERCOSUR during 1989–95. Brazil shows a strong import schedule but its exports only picked up towards the end of the period. This pattern is apparently due to the fact that the Brazilian economy still lacked a coherent reform concept until 1994 while Argentina enjoyed the 'high times' of its Currency Board system.

Altogether, MERCOSUR appeared to be on due course at that time. Internal trade relations increased at extraordinarily high rates and pushed intra-regional exchange. That way, the share of intra-regional to total exports increased substantially from 8.9 percent in 1990 to 20.3 percent in 1995 (Preusse, 2001, Table 1).

FDI, too, contributed to the economic integration of MERCOSUR. On average, compared to the 1980s FDI inflows almost tripled,[5] thereby changing their structure significantly. Most additional inflows at that time went to Argentina because a growing number of foreign investors began to perceive MERCOSUR as one single market, permitting the location of production freely within the region. In the automobile industry, in particular, the prospects of a common market gave rise to new investments, which promised to become a starting point of the development of a more deeply integrated MERCOSUR automobile industry.[6]

In the early 1990s the development of MERCOSUR was based on the growth dynamics in Argentina while Brazil was still fighting against inflation and a disappointing growth performance. However, soon after the implementation of the economic plan (Plano Real) by Fernando Enrique Cardoso in 1993/94, the Brazilian situation improved sharply, giving a further push to MERCOSUR. At that time the Southern Cone seemed to have successfully crossed the deep waters between inward and outward looking development; and the implementation of the CU in 1995 was commonly believed to be another proof for the thesis that the further advancement towards a common market was just a matter of time. Surely, the final adjustments of the external and internal trade measures still had to be implemented, the special sectors had to be negotiated and integrated into the common market system, and the harmonization of the still differing macroeconomic concepts had to be realized. Yet, after the experience of the smooth and successful management of convergence up to that point, no principal obstacle was believed to exist any more on the final way towards the common market.

5.3   FROM INTEGRATION TO DISINTEGRATION?

Under the CU regime MERCOSUR kept on developing sufficiently well until 1997. From that year on the rates of growth of GDP dropped significantly in every single member state (Table 5.3). After a short period of (relative) recovery in 2000 (due to a strong Brazilian performance) the depression in Argentina eliminated every sign of hope for a sustained revival of MERCO-SUR in the foreseeable future.

Looking at the data from a longer-term perspective reveals that MERCOSUR experienced its 'miracle' years from 1990–97, when Argentina led the group with an average growth rate of GDP of 6.9 percent. This country, starting from a shrinking GDP over the 1985–90 period (–1.1 percent on average), also managed the most impressive turnaround. The growth performance of Brazil and Uruguay improved modestly during the early 1990s (2.4 to 3.9 percent and 3.7 to 4.4 percent respectively) while Paraguay, in terms of GDP growth, could not take advantage of MERCOSUR at all. 1998 was another turning point. Subsequent performance up to 2002 was disastrous. Only Brazil managed to keep on growing, though at a relatively low rate, while Argentina and Uruguay suffered under sharply contracting economies. Paraguay, too, ended up with a negative average rate of growth.

Trade flows mirror the GDP data. From a five-year perspective (Table 5.4), exports in Argentina and Brazil picked up in the early 1990s but then, on average, dropped significantly during the 1995–2000 period. For Paraguay and Uruguay, MERCOSUR has never been a stimulus of trade. Both countries rapidly increased their trade flows before MERCOSUR was inaugurated, but suffered a continued decline of export and import growth rates since 1990. Table 5.5 gives some more details on the development of MERCOSUR exports since 1995. These data indicate that the Argentine and Brazilian exports have been growing ever more slowly since 1996 (except for Brazil in 1997). In 1998 and 1999 the whole region was severely hit by recession without being able to recover from this setback until early 2003 (notwithstanding the short period of relief in 2000). Similarly to the GDP data, only Brazil could prevent a negative rate of growth of exports between 2000 and 2002.

For the evaluation of MERCOSUR market integration, intra-MERCOSUR trade flows are an important indicator. Table 5.6 shows that the share of intra-MERCOSUR trade rose significantly from 1990 (8.8 percent) to 1998 (25 percent), but dropped to below 20 percent in 1999 and to 11.4 percent in 2002. Even taking into consideration that 2002, because of the exceptional developments that took place in that year, is not appropriate to give any

Table 5.3 MERCOSUR rates of growth of GDP, 1985–2002 (%)

	1985–90	1990–97	1998–02	1997	1998	1999	2000	2001	2002[*]
Argentina	–1.1	6.9	–3.3	8.0	3.8	–3.4	–0.8	–4.4	–11.0
Brazil	2.4	3.9	2.2	3.1	0.1	1.0	4.0	1.5	1.5
Paraguay	4.4	3.2	–0.4	2.4	–0.6	–0.1	–0.6	2.4	–3.0
Uruguay	3.7	4.4	–3.0	5.4	4.4	–3.4	–1.9	–3.4	–10.5

Notes: [*] preliminary

Sources: CEPAL (2002a); UNCTAD (2002b); own calculations

144

Table 5.4 MERCOSUR exports and imports, 1985–2000 (% change)

	1985–90	1990–95	1995–2000
Exports			
Argentina	9.9	10.6	5.2
Brazil	7.6	8.9	3.7
Paraguay	35.0	0.6	−3.0
Uruguay	13.5	4.6	2.8
South America	8.7	8.0	3.1
Imports			
Argentina	−0.3	36.8	4.0
Brazil	8.8	18.3	0.2
Paraguay	17.8	15.1	−8.9
Uruguay	12.7	17.1	2.9
South America	7.3	18.5	0.6

Source: UNCTAD (2002b)

serious indication of the future, the tremendous setback of intra-regional trade since 1999 is an alarming indication that MERCOSUR is really in trouble.

Drawing on the concept of the New Regionalism, expectations concerning the stimulating effects of capital inflows, FDI in particular, have been ranked high in MERCOSUR. Table 5.7 presents data on FDI inflows between 1985–2002. At a first glance, the FDI performance has been impressive until 1999. Average inflows doubled between 1985–90 and 1990–95, and they increased even further at an extraordinarily high rate thereafter. In 1999, the year with the highest FDI inflows, 49.8 billion US$ entered the region. FDI into Argentina expanded rapidly after the early 1990s but then dropped in 2000. Brazilian FDI only began to boom in 1996 and did not drop until 2001. Taking into consideration that the 1999 data for Argentina and the Brazilian data for 1999 and 2000 might be biased by some extraordinary transactions,[7] a more gradual longer-run expansion path of FDI inflows emerges. Undoubtedly, this trend has its origins in the opening-up policies and the foundation of MERCOSUR in the early 1990s. However, it is too early to

Table 5.5 MERCOSUR exports, 1995–2002, (% change)

	1995	1996	1997	1998	1999	2000	2001	2002
Argentina	33.9	13.6	10.7	0.3	–11.8	13.3	0.9	–5.0
Brazil	6.8	2.7	11.0	–3.5	–6.1	14.7	5.7	3.6
Paraguay	12.5	13.5	4.3	–6.9	–26.9	1.0	0.7	–3.0
Uruguay	13.8	13.8	13.7	1.7	–19.3	4.1	–10.1	–10.0

Sources: UNCTAD (2002b); CEPAL (2003a)

146

Table 5.6 The share of intra-MERCOSUR trade in total trade, 1990–2002 (%)

	1990	1995	1996	1997	1998	1999	2000	2001	2002[*]
Argentina	14.8	32.1				30.3	31.8	28.4	22.4
Brazil	4.2	13.2				14.1	14.0	10.9	5.4
Paraguay	27.4	12.5				13.3	23.7	22.0	22.1
Uruguay	35.1	46.2				44.2	42.9	39.1	33.3
MERCOSUR	8.8	20.6	23.0	24.8	25.0	19.9	21.1	17.2	11.4

Notes: [*]Jan.–Sept., preliminary

Source: IDB (2002)

Table 5.7 MERCOSUR FDI inflows, 1985–2002 (billion US$)

	1985–90	1990–95	1996	1997	1998	1999	2000	2001	2002[1]
Argentina	0.9	3.5	5.3	5.5	5.0	22.6	10.7	3.3	1.5
Brazil	1.3	2.0	11.7	17.9	26.0	26.9	30.5	24.9	13.4
Paraguay	–[2]	0.1	0.1	0.2	0.3	0.1	0.1	0.2	0.1
Uruguay	–[2]	0.1	0.1	0.1	0.2	0.2	0.3	0.3	0.2
MERCOSUR	2.3	5.7	17.2	23.7	31.5	49.8	41.6	28.7	15.2
Latin American Caribbean			40.0	55.9	60.9	79.7	67.7	68.1	39.0

Notes: [1] preliminary
[2] below 0.1 billion US$

Sources: CEPAL (2002a); UNCTAD (2002a)

decide whether this trend has ended or has just been temporarily interrupted by the present depression.[8]

In any case, comparing the changes of FDI inflows, GDP and trade leads to an important observation. While FDI still increased rapidly in the late 1990s when economic growth and trade were already declining, FDI was only cut back when the Argentine crisis broke out and threatened to spill over to Brazil. This behavior of FDI might be taken as a first indication of the quite different causations of the economic turbulences that hit MERCOSUR in the late 1990s and from 2001 onwards. While the 1999 crisis had a strongly exogenous causation (which was enlarged by insufficient national responses) but did not challenge the positive views of foreign investors on the new Latin American economies seriously, the 2001 crisis seems to have altered this situation significantly, because it was basically home-made.

5.4 THE CAUSES OF THE WEAK MERCOSUR PERFORMANCE

There is not one single cause that would be appropriate to explain the misery of MERCOSUR at the beginning of the new century. Rather, MERCOSUR had to operate within a highly complicated global environment during the second half of the 1990s, and it is beyond doubt that exogenous events had a significant impact on the region. It will be argued here that the pressure from the exogenous shocks on MERCOSUR did not find an adequate response in the region in some important cases, because both MERCOSUR and the individual countries still had to cope with an unfinished reform agenda. Consequently, the national economies did not manage to recover quickly enough from these global challenges and got caught by home-made economic and political deficiencies. Eventually, the region itself tumbled into a severe depression.

What are these home-made deficiencies and how are they linked to MERCOSUR? In order to analyze these questions it is important to recognize that the New Regionalism draws on the growth promoting effects of institutional up-grading. More precisely, it is claimed that the removal of national institutional deficiencies and the implementation of a superior regional framework are working jointly together to improve the region's competitive position. One important effect of these reforms should be an enhanced capacity to respond efficiently to exogenous shocks.

In order to elaborate a little bit on this point suppose that an economy's capacity to respond to exogenous shocks is crucial for a successful management of the integration into the global markets. In the case of regionalism this capacity is determined by two interlinked institutional systems. One is the national framework of action, the other one is the (emerging) regional framework. One of the compelling ideas of the New Regionalism is the claim that modern regional institution building helps to improve the existing national institutions by enforcing superior regional conditions for economic action (Chapter Three). Hence, an improved overall framework evolves that is appropriate to enhance the growth potential and makes the region more resistant against adverse external effects. Put differently, the new regionalism derives its economic power from a positive interaction of national and regional institutions that are conducive to growth and development. The crucial aspect of regional institution building is that it should become a driving force of institutional upgrading for the whole region.

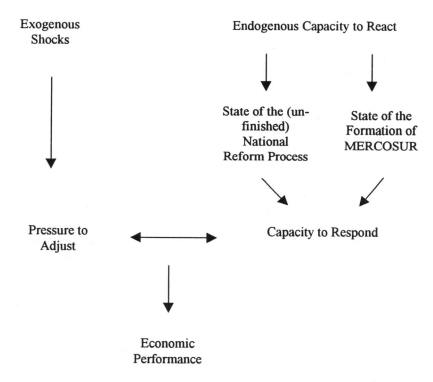

Figure 5.1   MERCOSUR and the challenge of the global system

For MERCOSUR, after the long period of import substitution and a period of almost dysfunctional institutional systems in the1980s, both aspects are crucial. In fact, MERCOSUR will only be viable in the longer run, if new sound institutions will be implemented on the regional *and* on the national level. Thus, it is not only the state of affairs of MERCOSUR that will determine its future. Rather it is the state of affairs of the whole reform project that matters. The endogenous capacity to react, therefore, will be determined by the success of the general reform process *and* the advancement of the regional agenda. Figure 5.1 summarizes the structure of the problem.

In the following, a short summary of the global situation and its impact on MERCOSUR will be given. Thereafter, the state of the national reforms will be briefly discussed and finally I will return to the specific problems of MERCOSUR.

5.4.1 MERCOSUR and the Global Economy in the Second Half of the 1990s

During the first five years of MERCOSUR the international economic situation was quite stable, but it was also the time of extended recessions in the major economic powers, the USA and Japan in particular. It is worth noting that this constellation did not hinder MERCOSUR from prospering. Since the end of 1994, things changed dramatically in the international markets. While the US economy recovered, the Mexican currency crisis (Tequila crisis) erupted. In the wake of this crisis international investors began to review their strategies in the emerging markets, and, in some cases, capital inflows were cut. Argentina, too, with its new currency board, became a prominent test candidate of international investors, and as a result of the speculative attacks against the peso, its rate of GDP growth dropped sharply in 1995. However, the Tequila crisis was soon overcome in Argentina and the economy recovered quickly in the following year. The prudent management of the crisis by the Argentine central bank on that occasion contributed very much to the credibility of the new Argentine economic policy in general and the Currency Board in particular.

The next major exogenous shock was the Asian currency crisis, which started with the crash in Thailand and quickly spread over the East Asian region and into Russia. Latin America was hit by this crisis in several ways. First, the substantial decline of economic activities in East Asia had an immediate impact on Latin American trade with this region. Second, international capital markets again turned their backs against the emerging markets and forced the Southern Cone countries to severely raise interest rates in order to prevent capital outflows. The situation threatened to escalate when Russia, too, had to float its currency and the rouble depreciated substantially in 1998. This new trouble-shooter threatened to turn the Asia crisis into a global crisis and hindered the global system to recover quickly enough to avoid an economic downturn in Latin America. While the high interest rates had to be maintained in order to defend the national currencies, they cut into production and consumption at home. The trade effects added to these negative impulses and forced the regional economies into a recession. The emerging boom in the USA could have countered this development, but the US performance became a two-faced creature. On one side, rising demand for imports tended to support Latin American exports, but, at the same time, the strong appreciation of the US$ hindered the expansion in other parts of the world. Argentina, in particular, had to follow this appreciation in order to defend its Currency Board, and lost competitiveness in Europe and much of Asia.

Nevertheless, foreign investors paid much more attention to Brazil in 1998. The Brazilian economy did not only suffer from the strong real at that time,[9] but had lost almost all the reform dynamics of the early days of the Cardoso government. It was clear that the future of the real plan was intimately linked to the solution of these problems. For one thing the fiscal balance could not be financed in the long run by ever increasing public debt, so that a restructuring of government expenditure was inevitable. Second, the low level of inflation and fiscal stability had partly been borrowed from the overvalued real and the maintenance of high interest rates. The strong real and high real interest rates, in turn, put pressure on economic growth and development. Still another part of the deficit was financed out of the receipts from privatization.

In the tense international environment of 1998, foreign investors realized these weaknesses of the Brazilian economy much more clearly than before and, given a generally increasing international risk awareness, became suspicious concerning the future of the Brazilian creditworthiness. In 1998 Brazil became a target of international speculation twice that way, but each time managed to calm the international queries down successfully. Towards the end of the year, when Cardoso was re-elected, the situation seemed to be under control. It was commonly believed that after the elections he would use the renewed public mandate to push for the missing reforms more rigorously. In fact, this was exactly what he tried to do. Right after the election, and still in the old election period, he brought in the new pension plan that was widely viewed as a symbol of the reform capability of the government.[10]

Unfortunately, the bill was rejected and the credits given to the new government were lost instantaneously. Some weeks later, in December, the governor of Minas Gerais (and ex-president) Itamar Franco again scared the international community, declaring that his state could not serve its debts against the federal government anymore. In January 1999 Brazil had to free the quotation of the real and the next currency crisis was underway.[11]

However, due to prudent macroeconomic management[12] Brazil surprised its critics and recovered extraordinarily quickly from the crash. Most important in this context is the fact that Congress, under the impact of the crisis, gave up its resistance against a number of important structural reform programs. Even the so much contested pension system passed the Houses in spring 1999, and eventually the country emerged from the crisis stronger than ever.

Nevertheless, the fact that Brazil needed this crisis to push forward its own reform agenda may finally turn out to have been the beginning of the end of MERCOSUR. The point is, that the severe depreciation of the real in 1999 has changed the relative competitive positions within MERCOSUR dramatically. Figure 5.2 shows the performance of the real effective exchange rates of Argentina and Brazil from 1993–2002. Starting in 1994 the Brazilian real appreciated about 20 percent until the end of 1998. The Argentine peso, too, did so between 1996–99, though at a much smaller rate. As a consequence, the relative competitive position of Argentina with respect to Brazil did slightly improve. For Argentina, being already in trouble internationally because of the strong US$, this situation at least helped to save the Brazilian market. But this constellation changed dramatically with the sharp Brazilian devaluation of 1999, which made the Brazilian market almost inaccessible for Argentine producers.

The effect of the movements of the nominal exchange rates on the relative competitive position of both countries can be seen from the bold line, which is defined as the real exchange rate index of Argentina relative to that of Brazil. According to this indicator, the Argentine price competitiveness increased from an index value of 130 (1994) to about 160 (1998) and then slumped to 90 in 1999 and 85 in 2001. In 2002 the crash in Argentina put an end to this constellation, raising again the relative real exchange rate of Argentina to about 180.

One interesting observation from this graph is the fact that the Argentine peso did not appreciate dramatically in real terms from 1996–2000. Thus, the Currency Board alone can hardly be blamed for the downturn of the economy. Rather, a more convincing interpretation is that from the very beginning of the Currency Board era the peso/US$ relation was fixed at a rate that was too much overvalued for the Argentine economy (and its tradables sector, in particular) to prosper. When the US$ appreciated, the peso had to follow in line. This had no major impact on the real exchange rate of Argentina but made it even more difficult to sell profitably in overseas markets. As long as the relative competitive position vis-à-vis Brazil remained unchanged, Argentina could keep the situation under control. But

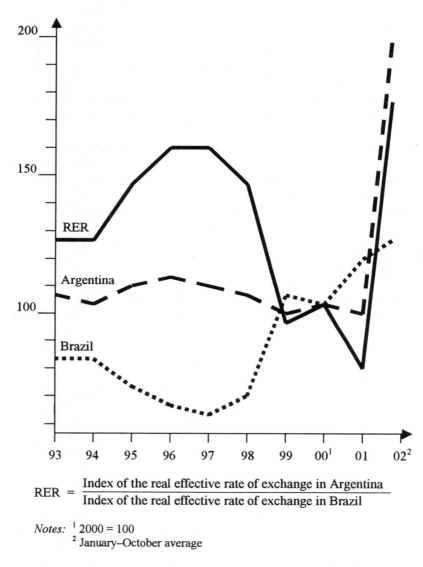

$$\text{RER} = \frac{\text{Index of the real effective rate of exchange in Argentina}}{\text{Index of the real effective rate of exchange in Brazil}}$$

Notes: [1] 2000 = 100
          [2] January–October average

Source: CEPAL (2002a)

Figure 5.2   The relative (real) exchange rate (RER) of Argentina/Brazil

when Brazil depreciated in 1999, Argentina found it impossible to adjust to this additional burden without running into a deflationary spiral. Brazil, too, did not remain untouched by the Argentine crisis, and for some time was seriously threatened to become another victim of this policy.

In 2001 still another exogenous development, the recession in the USA, worsened the situation for all MERCOSUR countries. Moreover, the 2002 presidential elections in Brazil threatened to build up another severe challenge, as the Partido Trabajador candidate Ignacio da Silva (Lula) scared national and international investors. As a result, the real slumped even further and made international debt obligations (mainly denominated in foreign currency) almost unbearable for Brazil. It is not surprising under these conditions that national policy-makers increasingly regressed to protectionism in order to get control of the escalating international imbalances. Due to the swing in the competitive positions between Argentina and Brazil, the situation became particularly critical between these two countries. That is, new protectionist measures boomed in and between exactly those countries that had once been the twin motors of economic integration of MERCOSUR (IDB-INTAL, 2001).

From this stylized presentation of some of the major economic events of the region from 1995–2002, some crucial aspects concerning the proper functioning of the new economic model in general and MERCOSUR in particular emerge. Some of these aspects derive from the fact that both reform projects are still incomplete, so that a satisfactory management of the open economies in the stiff global environment of the late 1990s proved to be almost impossible. In order to elaborate more deeply on these issues, two questions have to be analyzed. One is about the present state of the structural reforms of the member states. The other one is about the potential weaknesses of the MERCOSUR concept itself.

5.4.2 The Present State of the Economic Reforms in the Southern Cone

The transformation of Latin America from import substitution to open market economies and its success during the 1990s has been widely discussed. The first one who systematically gathered information on the reforms and related them to GDP growth was Edwards (1995). He estimated the reform efforts (macroeconomic stability, trade reforms, incentive systems) of each Latin American country and classified the economies as early, recent and late reformers. Edwards found that early reformers (Chile, Mexico, Bolivia) were those who had suffered most in terms of declining (and even negative) rates of growth of GDP during the 1980s. In turn, those doing relatively well during the debt crisis, like Brazil, for example, did not engage in successful reform efforts early. Edwards also realized that the early reformers had a better growth performance from 1989–93 than the latecomers.

One step ahead is the investigation of the relation between the intensity of the reform process and economic success. Preusse (1996b) developed a combined reform indicator based on the Edwards data, which took into consideration:

- macroeconomic reforms (weighted 40 percent);
- trade policy reforms (weighted 30 percent);
- growth policy reforms (weighted 30 percent).

Applied to nine economies this indicator showed a positive correlation between reform efforts and growth performance between 1992–94. Later, Morley/Machado/Pettinato (1999) advanced the idea and constructed an indicator that combined five different reform areas (commercial, financial, capital account, privatization, taxes). They gathered data on 17 Latin American countries that reflected the reform situation of 1995. Paunovic (2000) reorganized the reform indicators to reflect only stabilization efforts and structural reforms and correlated this information with the GDP growth rates of the 1990s. He found 'that the reforms explain one third of the variation in growth' (Paunovic, 2000, 15). It is useful to apply this procedure to MERCOSUR. Based on the Paunovic system one can construct a scale of reforms according to Figure 5.3. In this matrix we observe reformers that

Macro-economic \ Micro-economic	Strong	Moderate	Weak
Strong	strong reformers	moderately strong reformers	
Moderate	moderately strong reformers	moderate reformers	moderately weak reformers
Weak		moderately weak reformers	weak reformers

Figure 5.3   Economic reforms and performance in Latin America

have a strong performance in both macroeconomic and structural adjustment. These will be called 'strong reformers'. A second category of countries exhibits a strong performance in one area but a moderate one in the other.

Countries belonging to this category will be called 'moderately strong reformers'. The third category is 'moderate reformers', exhibiting a moderate performance in both areas. Similarly, 'moderately weak reformers' underwent moderate reforms in one but weak reform efforts in the other area, and 'weak reformers' have a weak performance in both.

Table 5.8   Intensity of economic reforms in Latin America in the 1990s and rates of growth of GDP (%)

Intensity[a] of Reforms	Countries[b]	Average Growth Performance (1991–99)		Countries Covered by Questionnaire
Strong	Argentina Chile Peru Dominican Rep.	5.1	4.5	Argentina Chile Peru
Moderately Strong	Bolivia Uruguay El Salvador Costa Rica	3.9		Uruguay
Moderate	Guatemala Mexico Paraguay	3.2		Guatemala Mexico
Moderately Weak	Brazil Colombia Jamaica	1.7	2.1	Brazil Colombia
Weak	Ecuador Honduras Venezuela	2.4		Venezuela

Notes: [a] Classification following the Morley/Machado/Pettinato (1999) index, which combines two subindexes of macroeconomic and structural reforms (as of 1995) which indicate three degrees of reform intensity: strong, moderate, weak. Strong in the table means that both subindexes reveal strong reforms. Moderately strong means that one index reveals strong reform efforts, the other one moderate reform efforts etc.
[b] The classification and the rates of growth are according to Paunovic (2000).

Table 5.8 employs this classification (first column) in order to identify the countries' reform intensities (second column) in relation to their growth performances in the 1990s (third column). Again, we find a remarkable difference in the growth performance of the different reform categories, ranging from 5.1 percent for strong reformers to 2.4 percent for weak reformers.[13] To put it more clearly it is useful to compare the average of the growth rates of the reform categories (*one + two*) and (*four + five*). From this comparison one finds that, on average, the 'strong' and the 'moderately strong reformers' have realized an average rate of growth of GDP of 4.5 percent while the 'moderately weak' and 'weak' reformers only obtained 2.1 percent. The intermediate category of 'moderate' reformers obtains an average growth of 3.2 percent.

An important point to remember is that the GDP growth rates of the 1990s include the negative effects of the Asian crisis that drowned Latin America into recession between 1998–99. Nevertheless, the relative growth performance of strong and weak reformers remained unaffected. This means the reform countries did not suffer more in relative terms than the weak reformers. It is also worth noting that the new figures are quite similar to those presented in Preusse (1996b). One important exception is Colombia which fell back significantly in the second half of the decade, in both reform efforts and growth performance.

Table 5.9   Reform efforts and economic performance in the Southern Cone, 1990–2002 (%)

	Rates of growth of GDP	
	1990–2000	2001–2002
Strong Performers		
Argentina	4.6	−7.7
Uruguay	3.2	−7.0
Weak Performers		
Paraguay	2.0	−0.3
Brazil	2.6	1.5

Sources: CEPAL (2002a), UNCTAD (2002b), own calculations

Now return to MERCOSUR. Following Table 5.8, Argentina ranks as a strong and Uruguay as a moderately strong reformer. Paraguay is a moderate and Brazil a moderately weak reformer. In Table 5.9, only the stronger and the weaker reformers have been differentiated and confronted with their individual rates of growth. For the 1990s we find the typical result. The stronger reformers exhibit much higher rates of growth. But the 2001 to 2002 depression has reversed the scale. The seemingly weak reformers are the (relative) winners, while the former champions are suffering one of their worst declines in recent history.

Does this new situation render the economic reforms of the 1990s obsolete or is the indicator unsuitable? Without going into a new discussion of the merits of open versus inward looking development strategies the answer concerning the reform policies is straightforward. There are good reasons to stick to the reforms of the 1990s even though not all of them are unquestionable in detail.

A profound judgment on the efficiency of the reform indicator itself is much more difficult. Three critical points are worth mentioning:

1. It should be clear that the 'combined indicator' is a very rough approximation of reform efforts. It is true that its subcategories call attention to some important aspects of the reform agenda, but it is not clear whether the reforms have really been implemented correctly. Privatization, for example, is one important aspect of the economic reform process in Latin America because the interventionist regimes of the past used to rely on state enterprises, which were rarely managed efficiently. As a result they produced much of the public deficits that have to be handled today, without having been able to generate the economic development and growth performance that had been hoped for.

   The reasons for this failure are manifold. In principle, the state-owned enterprises had to serve divergent goals (as, for example, in many socialist countries) that are not compatible with the principles of a sound economic management. More precisely, they often had to take care of politically imposed social objectives (subsidized pricing; employment generation etc.) and they also had to follow political targets that hindered them from giving priority to efficiency considerations. Under these conditions, privatization was and is an important reform category.

   But a successful implementation of these reforms is anything but easy and may end up in just another undesired situation. Many privatization ventures in Argentina and other Latin American economies had to suffer under these kinds of implementation problems. The indicator cannot capture these deficiencies. Obviously, the same arguments apply to the diverse approaches for capital account liberalization. Consequently, high positive values of these indicators may be misleading because they do not mirror the success of the respective policies adequately.

2. Even if the individual subindicators would show the effectiveness of the reforms correctly, the combined indicator may still be unable to correctly reflect the relative importance of the individual reform measures and their interactions. In other words, the weighing procedure of the combined indicator (giving each reform category equal weight) follows an ad hoc

judgment that lacks any theoretical foundation. In particular, it is not clear which the key reform areas are and which factors are complementary. Drawing on the experience of the East Asian success stories, for example, a prudent macroeconomic management, including low target rates of inflation, fiscal discipline and the maintenance of relatively stable (that is, reliable) real exchange rates have been identified as important preconditions for low risk investment. Thus, growth and development of industrial capacities is intimately linked to macroeconomic stability. In turn, given macroeconomic stability, the creation of competitive production capacities depends on a relatively unbiased incentive system (including openness towards the world market), and the availability of skilled labor. Foreign capital is another potentially very important factor contributing to growth. Nevertheless, a higher volatility of capital flows due to the participation in the global markets may also become a major challenge for the growth strategy, if the rules of the game are not taken seriously enough or if well functioning financial markets are still not in place. The combined indicator cannot reflect all these aspects precisely.

3. The combined indicator is one that intends to capture long-run trends in policy changes and their results. However, it is not at all capable of handling cyclical swings. From this perspective, it appears to be particularly risky (not to say methodologically wrong) to include the two years of depression (2001, 2002) into the analysis of the reform agenda of the 1990s.

Nevertheless, the Latin American (MERCOSUR) situation cannot be analyzed correctly without regress to exactly these recent years. The crucial point is the Argentine crisis which poses a severe problem for the whole region; and this crisis may be due to a macroeconomic mismanagement of a very distinct variant.

In order to learn a bit more about the combined indicator and its capacity to predict the successful reform politics, the newest version of the indicator can be employed. These data have been published by CEPAL for the years 1999–2000 (CEPAL, September 2001b, 49). They show the values of the five subcategories of the Morley/Machado/Pettinato index. The year 2000 data suggest that fiscal reforms are still a major area of preoccupation in Argentina and (to a lesser extent) in Brazil. In Brazil, the capital account reforms, too, are still lagging behind. This observation fits neatly into the explanation of the Brazilian currency crisis of 1999 (see above), but the Argentine experience with its Currency Board is still opaque. For one thing, there is the massive swing of the real exchange rate that has put pressure on the Argentine tradables sector. But why has the government been unable to find external financing that could have prevented a depreciation?

An answer to this question must be based on a more detailed investigation of the Argentine reform model and its deficiencies. Though the whole Argentine disaster is not yet fully understood, it is beyond doubt that one of the roots of the 2002 depression is to be found in the crisis management of 1998. Another possible point of concern is the far too optimistic view on the merits of a strong currency as a (sufficient) means to secure both stability and economic development in the longer run.

In order to explain the mutually re-enforcing effects of both these points it is convenient to start from the real exchange rate appreciation. As has been shown before, this appreciation took place along with the US$ and was reinforced by the Brazilian currency crisis. Under a Currency Board there is but one reaction to such an exogenous event. That is, the rapid adjustment of local costs in order to meet the new situation. In Argentina this would have meant that wages would have had to react flexibly in order to give way to substantial price cuts. Also, the public households would have had to be consolidated in order to cut back on foreign credits. To be sure, these kinds of adjustment procedures put a heavy burden on the local community, but, given the fact that the nominal exchange rate was definitely fixed they were inevitable.

In Argentina, a sufficiently high adjustment flexibility did not exist. On the contrary, the scope for wage adjustment was quite low despite the reforms of the 1990s (Pastor/Wise, 2001). While the adjustments of the early 1990s heavily drew on the forced reduction of the labor force in public services and state-owned enterprises, wage flexibility and mobility remained low. A far reaching consequence of this inflexibility is that the restructuring procedures after the switch to the export oriented development strategy were also hindered. More precisely, the Argentine model apparently lived from the one-time effects of the rigorous market reform programs of the early 1990s, which were focused on the elimination of the most visible inefficiencies of the old system. But the crucial next step, that is, the development of modern industrial capacities, which would help to raise international competitiveness, penetrate foreign markets and increase employment again, was not very successful.[14] If this interpretation holds, then Argentina never had reached the stage of a sustained growth process. Rather, as the strong productivity efforts of the early 1990s faded out, economic growth, too, fell back again.

Also public households were unable to react adequately to the crisis. In this field, too, the strong consolidating effects of the past seem to have been overrated and in any case, they seduced the public sector (the provinces in particular) to less fiscal discipline. During the second half of the 1990s the government increasingly regressed to foreign credits in order to prevent a consolidation of the public expenditures. That way, public debt was raised considerably,[15] and could not be brought under control when the situation began to become critical after 1998. Even without going into a detailed discussion of the reasons for this public agony,[16] it is apparent in hindsight that the Argentine reform model appears to have been much less perfect than many observers have believed.

Taking the lack of adjustment capacity as given, the Currency Board itself has to be discussed. This monetary system is fixed on the unconditional acceptance of exogenous shocks as an advice to internal adjustment. Even if a Currency Board is fixed to a major trading partner the pressure to adjust to exogenous events can become relatively large. But a well functioning market oriented economy may well be able to master these challenges. In the case of Argentina, however, trade with the USA, which provides the anchor currency, is much less than with Europe and Brazil. Brazil in particular accounts for more than 20 percent of the Argentine exports (against 12 percent of the USA). Under these conditions, the country became virtually squeezed between these much bigger partners when the US$ appreciated and the real crashed. This claim leads back to the question of policy coordination in MERCOSUR and will be treated in the next section.

Summing up this section leads to the conclusion that after a decade of reform policies, Argentina, despite some euphoric evaluations of this model in the 1990s, has still a lot of important reforms left before it can really get rid of the growth absorbing structures of the past. Brazil is a latecomer as a reformer. The 1994 Plano Real has brought the economy back on a growth path, but until 1999 the country had many difficulties in implementing the more demanding structural reforms. Hopefully, it seems to have progressed after the currency crisis of 1999. In both Argentina and Brazil, the fiscal problem that has been inherited from the old structuralist approach of inflationary development finance still appears to be a main weakness of the reform concepts. Under these conditions, international capital flows, which are so important for the region both because of the low savings capacity and the need to enhance technology transfer, will remain volatile and pose another obstacle to growth.

Last but not least a low growth performance and frequent cyclical downturns are not a good precondition for maintaining open markets. The New Regionalism model, which counts on a sound national framework for economic growth as a basis for the enforcement of even better institutions, does not meet very good preconditions in MERCOSUR currently. Given the severe and unpredictable situation in Argentina and Uruguay, only Brazil might become an economic anchor for the region if it remains on due course under the new government.

5.4.3 Weak Points of the MERCOSUR Concept

In the preceding section it has been shown that exogenous shocks and, due to an incomplete reform status in Argentina and Brazil, insufficient reactions to these shocks had severely hurt the regime and eventually led Argentina to fall into depression. The New Regionalism should have been a shield against such events. By providing a bigger integrated market it was thought to enhance economic growth and strengthen the whole region against the risks of the global economy. Increasing economic power was supposed to translate into political power and enforce the region's voice in international institutions. Altogether, these virtues of the New Regionalism were also supposed to help to prevent (or at least to calm down) the traditionally high volatility of the national economies. In early 2003 it is obvious that these hopes have not been met by reality. Neither is the region prospering any more nor has it managed to sufficiently cut back its high degree of volatility. The question now is what part the MERCOSUR has played in this tragedy.

The theory of the New Regionalism claims that regionalism threatens to become part of the problem rather than being part of the solution, if it is implemented in a way that neglects the basic conditions for its smooth function. In the following, two fundamental aspects of the MERCOSUR regionalization process will be critically examined:

1. the management of the growing interdependencies that regionalization automatically produces;
2. the establishment of open markets.

5.4.3.1 The management of growing macroeconomic interdependencies
The founders of MERCOSUR were aware of the fact that regional integration would increase intra-regional interdependencies. High and growing inter-dependencies, in turn, are stimulating the mutual exchange of macro-economic fluctuations such as differing rates of inflation, capacity utilization and cyclical swings of aggregate demand. These effects have a special meaning in MERCOSUR because of the history of Latin American macro-economic instabilities. In fact, a common market could hardly be expected to prosper if macroeconomic stability and a minimum of congruence of macro-economic policies could not be realized. Under these conditions it was clear from the very start of MERCOSUR, that integration of trade and capital flows should soon be complemented by some kind of macroeconomic policy coordination or harmonization.

In order to elaborate a little on this topic[17] the concept of the real exchange rate (RER) is a good starting point. The RER is usually defined as

$$RER = e_n \cdot \frac{P_T}{P_{NT}}$$

where e_n is the nominal exchange rate, P_T is the price of tradables, and P_{NT} the price of non-tradables. An often used approximation of $dP_T/P_T : dP_{NT}/P_{NT}$ is the relation between the foreign rate of inflation (more precisely, the weighted average of the rates of inflation of the major trading partners) and the national rate of inflation.[18] In the following, the argument will be presented using the latter (less precise) version.

The formula states that, given a fixed nominal exchange rate, the RER varies directly in response to the differential rate of inflation at home and abroad. An increasing RER indicates that the home rate of inflation is lower than the weighted average rates of the trading partners. Such a situation implies a real depreciation of the local currency and signals an increasing price competitiveness of the local economy on the world market and vice versa. In view of this relationship, it becomes clear that macroeconomic policies at home (and abroad) are of critical importance for the development of the RER and price competitiveness respectively: in order to secure competitiveness under a fixed nominal exchange rate system. Macroeconomic policies must keep the national rate of inflation strictly in line with the world level. Given the rate of growth of factor productivity this goal also defines the scope of monetary policy.

In theory, the devastating effects of inflationary policies on international competitiveness may easily be neutralized by frequent depreciations of the nominal exchange rate. However, more than often this strategy suffers from serious implementation problems. These problems largely derive from the fact that the nominal exchange rate is a highly sensitive 'political price' in many countries. It is most difficult, therefore, to employ a nominal exchange rate policy that strictly and continuously stabilizes the RER. The problem is particularly delicate if the exchange rate is also applied as an instrument to fight inflation (exchange rate anchor). High inflation economies, due to these two limitations, usually depreciate much too late and often only under severe external pressure. Under these conditions, rather than stabilizing competitiveness and the price level, an erratically changing RER adds to volatility and increases the risk of investment in long-run activities. This, in turn, aggravates the economic situation and renders any reliable growth strategy obsolete.

The situation becomes much more complicated when capital flows are allowed for. Starting again from a fixed nominal exchange rate regime, net capital inflows raise the demand for local currency and force the central bank to respond by increasing money supply. The resulting inflationary effect causes the RER to appreciate and the trade balance to turn into negative. That

labor. After the import substitution era, a lot of skilled labor is still concentrated in inefficient industries that are bound to shrink under the new economic regime. To make things worse, many of these industries have paid premium wages under the old system (due to oligopolistic market structures and aggressive labor unions that in many cases could firmly count on political support).

Thus, it is the relatively well paid skilled labor force that will be hurt from trade liberalization and the subsequent change to more labor-intensive industries: these people might in fact be forced to leave the high wage sector and (if lucky) will have to pick up a lower wage job in the newly expanding export industries. In essence, this means that in MERCOSUR (and in Brazil and Argentina, in particular) the Stolper–Samuelson type adjustment mechanisms will breed similar results as in high income countries where labor is the scarce factor. Since the workers who are exposed to this challenge in MERCOSUR are both well organized and able to defend their special interests, while those who are expected to win (the unskilled poor and the unemployed) are hardly organized at all, the opposition against this type of structural adjustment must be expected to be strong.

Above, it has been argued that capital specificity may increase immobility and resistance to change. Brazil with its relatively diversified industrial sector (having been built up without much emphasis on efficiency considerations) and, to a lesser extent, Argentina, too, are prime candidates for such a sector specificity of capital. Consequently, not only labor is likely to resist the opening-up process in the more advanced economies of MERCOSUR, but capital as well. Both factors are suspicious of unifying and lobby vehemently for extended protection.[32]

Under these conditions the type of changes suggested by the conventional SS process may be effectively blocked in MERCOSUR, and the whole reform project faces serious implementation problems. Given this state of affairs and any effective mechanism of compensation being absent, it is also not surprising that politicians have tried to find out alternative strategies of adjustment to trade liberalization that promise to avoid the most serious challenges of the conventional approach.

In MERCOSUR, the IIT strategy was supposed to perfectly handle the adjustment problem. With capital and labor forming a strong coalition in the most advanced industrial areas, upgrading along the existing lines of production in the IIT setting was expected to minimize the costs of adjustment and to calm down resistance against the reform process.

In fact, most analysts claim that IIT has a more favorable balance of adjustment costs than North–South trade (INT) (Greenaway/Milner, 1986).

The basic argument is that under the IIT conditions structural change usually takes place within the same industry so that the most sensitive forms of adjustment are largely avoided (the need to acquire completely new skills and regional migration in particular). Also the export expansion within MERCOSUR would be less labor-intensive, if IIT within the region dominated the growth process. As a result, the functional distribution of income would not be affected as seriously as under the (inverted) SS process, and this might help to calm down the resistance against the reforms on part of the skilled labor force and capital alike.

But this is not the whole story regarding structural change under an IIT regime. In order to recognize more clearly the different wage and employment effects of the IIT or upgrading strategy relative to the SS process, both employed *and* unemployed labor must be taken into consideration.[33] Under the SS strategy adjustment would take place according to the *present* structure of comparative advantage. Thus, this strategy would create more labor-intensive industries. These industries, in turn, would generate a maximum of new jobs albeit at the cost of a non-increasing or even declining level of real wages as long as large scale unemployment exists. This strategy would have an ambiguous impact on the distribution of income. First, the functional distribution of income would change in favor of capital along the lines proposed by the famous Lewis model as long as unemployment prevails (Lewis, 1954). Second, among labor we would expect both winners and losers. The rapid job expansion would clearly be in favor of the formerly unemployed, which are usually located at the lower end of the income scale. Skilled labor in turn would remain under severe pressure (see above). Thus, this kind of job expansion would help to decrease wage inequality *within* the labor sector but it is against the interest of the (employed) skilled labor force (at least in the short run).

Under the upgrading (or IIT) strategy the economy would proceed differently. In order to upgrade and expand the more advanced (capital- and skill-intensive) industries with a potential to be successful rapidly enough in an innovative IIT environment (that is, to upgrade quickly enough to generate full employment within a reasonable time) the scarcity of skilled labor would have to be tackled forcefully. If this strategy works, new jobs in the well paid skilled labor segment would emerge and this would raise the demand for low skilled labor, too. Hence, the diversified structure of production of MERCO-SUR could be saved, its relative competitive position on the world market would improve, and sustained economic growth would eventually dry out unemployment.

However, this strategy draws heavily on *higher* skilled labor, which is still scarce in the region. Its success, therefore, depends critically on an increased availability of this type of labor. Taking into consideration the weak education systems in many Latin American countries and the long gestation period of investment in human capital, it appears to be unreasonable to assume that the required expansion of jobs in skill-intensive industries can be managed in due time. Thus, the scarcity of skilled labor would most likely rise. The effect on the distribution of income, then, would be quite different compared to a functioning IIT process or the SS approach. That is, the functional distribution of income would move in favor of capital (as would be the case under the SS strategy), because capital intensity would have to increase. At the same time, the increased scarcity of skilled labor would push the wage structure at the expense of low skilled labor. Unskilled labor would be negatively affected by these developments in two different ways: first, because the generation of new jobs would be generally less than in the SS scenario, more workers would remain unemployed over a longer time period; second, the pool of unskilled unemployed would remain larger and the pressure on real wages in this segment of the labor market would remain high and may even increase over time.

To put it differently, the development along the (IIT) upgrading path offers an immediate and more equal participation of skilled labor in the growing (relatively) capital- and technology-intensive industries, and minimizes resistance against the reform program. However, it also goes hand in hand with the stabilization of the prevailing dualistic structure of the labor market. Thus, unemployment will stay at a relatively high level and the wage rate of unskilled labor will remain under pressure for a longer period of time, because employment generation would only be moderate.

The fact that the upgrading strategy builds on scarce (higher) skilled labor points to another important problem that is frequently overlooked when the seemingly low adjustment costs of IIT are discussed. IIT in the high income countries usually takes place in a highly demanding competitive environment. The point is that IIT is most often the result of stiff innovational competition, and the winners are those who are able to use specific skills in order to create new products and production processes in advance of their rivals. That is, IIT successfully evolves out of skill-intensive activities. In LDCs, in turn, skilled labor is scarce and the abilities to directly compete with the industrialized countries in these markets are not well developed.

Drawing on the product cycle theory, it can be inferred that the upgrading strategy will make progress only slowly if the MERCOSUR firms try to compete directly in the innovative segments of the product cycle. They lack the R&D facilities, the capital needed to acquire specific knowledge, and the experience to efficiently develop marketable products. Consequently, some isolated dots of excellence may develop, but progress on a broader scale will remain slow.

Because of these circumstances, LDCs, in order to compete successfully in the product cycle, are well advised to concentrate on the lower end of the cycle where the skill profile is lower and factor endowments determine comparative advantage.

The fact that MERCOSUR subsidizes regional trade and discriminates against outsiders for infant industry reasons makes it clear that the mechanisms of innovational competition (and the weak position of the region in this field) have clearly been recognized by its founders. But, apparently, the consequences for economic growth of a distinct IIT strategy are less obvious: for an emerging market, competing in the high end of the product cycle makes catching up on a broad basis almost impossible and causes economic growth to be confined to small market segments. As a consequence, the overall development performance is likely to slow down. To say it differently, a successful upgrading strategy in the region will have to concentrate on gaining competence in the lower ends of the cycle first, and then proceed towards the high end, high value-added activities. Starting at the lower end also brings in comparative advantage again, and stimulates the demand for low skilled labor.

If this argument holds, it follows that there is virtually no way around concentrating on comparative advantage for MERCOSUR. The proposed lower costs of structural adjustment under the IIT strategy are the misleading result of a static calculus. Once the differential growth effects of both strategies (if employed in LDCs) are taken into consideration it becomes clear that a less demanding adjustment process under the IIT strategy can only be expected at the expense of economic growth. Thus, if economic growth remains the overriding goal of economic development in MERCO-SUR (as claimed by the proponents of the concept of New Regionalism) a specialization according to comparative advantage becomes inevitable. And comparative advantage can most effectively be exploited in the global market.

To put it differently, in as much as the precarious situation of low skilled labor in MERCOSUR is really the core problem of development policy, the SS approach is preferable to the IIT approach because it maximizes economic growth and generates employment for those who are most seriously affected by poverty. However, in the short and medium run this strategy puts a heavy burden on those who are well organized and dispose of a sizable political impact. It is unlikely from this point of view that the job maximizing strategy will succeed over the coalition of vested interests of organized labor and capital in the established industrial regions.

Taking these political aspects of the reform process into consideration, a mixed strategy might be most promising. In this scenario, some new labor-intensive industries that largely take the burden of job expansion in the low wage sectors may develop. At the same time the more sophisticated industries with a relatively low degree of international competitiveness will try to upgrade in order to survive in a more open market or simply fight for renewed protection.

In any case, the economic consequences for MERCOSUR are obvious. The IIT strategy of the 1990s is unlikely to become successful because it leaves much of the growth potential of the region untapped. Upgrading within the given set of industries faces a lot of serious obstacles and threatens to undermine growth and development if it comes at the expense of global trade relations. Consequently, this strategy should be reconsidered seriously. The more open the region becomes against the world market, the more likely MERCOSUR can be revitalized. It is open to speculation at present if such a strategy will really become politically feasible, given the strong vested interests that dominate large parts of the manufacturing sector in Argentina and Brazil.

5.5   SUMMARY

MERCOSUR is a step by step approach to create a common market among four (plus two) developing countries. The first step has been quite successful and brought MERCOSUR to the level of an (incomplete) CU. The following steps, however, were less successful or did not follow at all. In early 2003 MERCOSUR seems to be paralyzed and near to failure. This chapter has traced some major external and internal reasons for this lamentable performance. It has been argued that MERCOSUR, after its most promising start-up period, has run into turbulent international waters in the second half of the 1990s. This adverse external environment, to be sure, would have been a hard test for the region even if it could have counted on a firm and solid economic basis. However, such a basis did not exist due to the following reasons:

1. The region found itself in a most difficult period of structural transformation from the era of import substitution to export orientation. This uneasy situation has increased its vulnerability against external shocks.
2. Institutional reforms proved to be difficult to introduce in some sectors and remain incomplete in others. Macroeconomic policies, in particular, could not be modernized quickly enough in the leading economies of the region and, following different exchange rate concepts, tended to work against each other. An area of particular concern is the financial sector, which became a critical bottleneck both in terms of international

monetary policy and the financing of investment at home. There was also a lack of intense and conscious efforts to encourage the overdue structural adjustments in the industrial sectors and to improve the investment climate in the region.

3. The weakness of the institutional regimes on the national level produced spillover effects on the regional integration process:

   • In as much as national restructuring policies failed (or were absent altogether) the international (regional) integration process slowed down.
   • A binding regional institutional framework being absent, the management of the integration process was all too often left to ad hoc decisions on the presidential level. That way, accidental events rather than a conscious strategy began to rule the integration process. As a result, rather than pushing for deeper integration, the presidents, in order to keep the MERCOSUR alive, were restricted ever more frequently by the management of emergency actions.

Besides the institutional deficiencies and the absence of a sound concept of macroeconomic coordination, MERCOSUR suffers from another serious conceptual weakness. This is its *intra-industry strategy*. This strategy was thought to be a means of avoiding too much inter-industrial restructuring, which is commonly held to be particularly costly. But its inventors neglected the fact that intra-industry trade rests on the prevalence of sophisticated high income markets in order to flourish. In these markets, intra-industry trade comes along as a complement to inter-industry trade but not as a substitute. Pushing IIT in an emerging market at the expense of North–South trade instead is not a viable alternative. The basic reason is that this strategy cuts on the high yields of trading on factor endowment differentials but does not deliver a large potential for intra-industry trade in turn.

In fact, the MERCOSUR IIT strategy is the regional manifestation of the large countries' reluctance to tackle the outdated structures of production of the import substitution period seriously.

Under these conditions one would hesitate to treat MERCOSUR as a good example of the New Regionalism. In fact, in the case of MERCOSUR the New Regionalism largely remained a (vague) conceptual outline of the presidents' well meant intentions rather than a testable case study. It would, therefore, be a failed judgment to sell MERCOSUR as a proof of the functional disability of the concept of New Regionalism as such. Nevertheless, the experience of MERCOSUR points to the fact that building a regional 'growth pool' is not an easy task and failure could have quite a number of different origins.

NOTES

1. The political tensions between Argentina and Brazil can be traced to the early days of independence, when both nations tried to position themselves as regional powers (Child, 1985).
2. Note, however, that some of the key sectors of the former managed trade concept (capital goods, telecommunications, automobiles) were defined as sensitive and treated separately. Their inclusion into the general free trade concept was postponed to a later stage of the integration process. In hindsight, this strategy appears to be responsible for some of the difficulties that have accumulated in recent years.
3. Basically the same arguments induced Bolivia and Chile to join the MERCOSUR as associated members in 1996. Note, however, that Chile is in a relatively comfortable, that is, less dependent position. Put differently Chile's participation or non-participation in the ongoing integration process might be crucial for the future of the whole project. This is the case both because of its economic strength and its geographical situation (permitting direct access to the Pacific Ocean) and because of its global interests. Another important point in this context is the much stricter adherence to the open market economy model on the part of Chile.
4. This is an important observation that will be considered more seriously below, when the trade strategy of MERCOSUR is analyzed.
5. FDI inflows averaged 2.3 billion US$ during the 1980s and 6.3 billion US$ in 1991–95 (US$ in prices of 2000).
6. Note that these developments were to a large extent anticipatory and based on the belief that the future automotive regime would concede a free flow of resources within the region.
7. For an in-depth analysis of the FDI performance in MERCOSUR see Chudnovski/López (2002).
8. In fact, the question whether or not FDI will pick up again in the near future is crucial for the evaluation of the prospects of MERCOSUR. In order to get some more insight concerning this problem the causes of the present crisis must be analyzed in more detail. This will be done in the next section.
9. Brazil had a system of managed floating at that time, but did not depreciate strong enough to keep the real exchange rate of the real close to equilibrium. The basic reason was that the country needed to attract FDI and put pressure on the inflation rate.
10. The generous pension system for public employees was responsible for the overwhelming part of the deficit of the overall pension system. Its reformation, therefore, was seen to be a major step on the way to consolidate public expenditures. At the same time its elimination was a major political problem because those benefiting from the system were almost identical to those who had to agree on its elimination.
11. This is not the place to discuss the difficult internal political situation in Brazil that helps to explain these developments. For detailed analyses see Dillinger/Webb (1999), Selcher (1999), Ames (2001), Faust (2003).
12. For a discussion of recent central bank policies and the implementation of an inflation target see Averbug (2002).
13. The 1.7 percent average growth of the economies in the category of 'moderately weak' reformers is due to Jamaica, which has an average rate of growth of 0.0 percent for the whole decade.
14. One possible exception might be the rapid development of the automobile production within MERCOSUR. I shall treat this point separately, later.
15. The good reputation that Argentina had built up with the successful implantation of the Currency Board apparently helped to sustain this policy far too long.
16. There are two principal causes of resistance against expenditure cutting. One cause is public employees (wage inflexibility and resistance against adjustment is not less than in the private sector), the other is the tense relationship between the state provinces and the federal

government. For detailed discussions see Baer/Elosegui/Gallo (2002), Mussa (2002), Nicolini/Saiegh/Sanguinetti (2002).

17. The macroeconomic implications of regional integration cannot be presented here in detail. For some more comprehensive discussions see IDB (2002), Chapters 7 and 8.

18. The two terms differ, because P_{NT} does not include tradables but the national rate of inflation (the consumer price index for example) does.

19. There are, of course, many examples of public investment that are complementary to private investment. Nevertheless, foreign credits may still be problematic because of extremely long gestation periods (education) and substitution effects. Some analysts warn against foreign debt financing in general because of the difficulties that are involved in separating consumptive from investment uses of foreign capital inflows. However, this position abstracts from the fact that low national savings rates enforce capital imports in order to facilitate economic growth. For a critical position see Bresser-Pereira (2002, 15).

20. Uruguay, too, advanced much in line with the bigger nations, and became a renowned banking center. Only Paraguay was left behind but could at least be hindered from falling back into dictatorship. At that time the joint political efforts of the other MERCOSUR members were celebrated as a strong sign of political maturity and willingness to cooperate in the region.

21. In hindsight it is obvious that most analysts were too much focused on macroeconomic advancements, but did not really recognize the seriousness of structural adjustments that would have to follow the improvement of macroeconomic conditions (not to speak of the severe political constraints that the still existing traditional vested interests would impose).

22. In 2001/2002 the situation escalated further because of the speculations about the presidential elections in Brazil.

23. For a thorough analysis of the new protectionist policies in MERCOSUR see MERCOSUR Reports 1998–99 and 1999–2000.

24. In this context, I only refer to the basic arguments. For a more detailed elaboration see Preusse (2001, 2004).

25. Still another prominent aspect of the expansion of intra-industrial structures of trade and production was that it would diminish the costs of adjustment from opening up. This point will be discussed separately later.

26. In a dynamic context, a specific competition effect may have to be considered, too. I shall come back to this point later.

27. Though MERCOSUR has been launched as an exercise in open regionalism, this sequencing of the opening-up process clearly resembles the infant industry argument of the import substitution era.

28. A frequent argument against this recommendation is protectionism in the advanced industrialized countries. In fact, protectionist tendencies in these countries (in agriculture in particular) hinder MERCOSUR export expansion significantly (Nowak-Lehmann D./Martínez-Zarzoso, 2003). Nevertheless, this situation should not lead to the wrong conclusion that opening up to world trade would not make sense. Rather, the adequate strategy would be to exploit the given scope for penetrating the world markets (which is still sufficiently high for an export expansion strategy to succeed) and insist on trade liberalization world-wide (and practice it by itself).

29. Inferring from the negotiations to the final result it is anything but certain that MERCOSUR car trade will really be freed in the foreseeable future.

30. To be sure, under the outdated import substitution regime, sluggish growth would have cut into wages permanently, while under the new approach, after the transition period, the growth dynamics are likely to recover.

31. In this context, the coalition against structural adjustment is a traditional one (capital and labor). In the case of NAFTA, a new coalition against open markets (including environmentalists) is operating.

32. For a detailed analysis of Latin American business groups and their particular interests in open markets see Fischer (1999, 195–218) and Chapter Six of this volume.

33. Traditional models of neo-classical and classic trade theory are based on the assumption of full employment thereby ruling out this important aspect.

6. The Free Trade Area of the Americas (FTAA)

6.1 THE FTAA AND THE AMERICAN SPAGHETTI BOWL REGIONALISM

Chapters Four and Five have discussed some of the major aspects of NAFTA and MERCOSUR. These regions dominate the American economic and political scenario. Politically, they include the most important players in the region, namely the USA, Canada, Brazil and Mexico. And economically, they account for more than 90 percent of the region's GDP. Focusing a study of the American regionalism on these two regions is a useful approach under these conditions, but it is not the whole story. The discussion of the North American (NAFTA) spaghetti bowl regionalism in Chapter Four, exemplified by the extended web of bilateral and plurilateral agreements that Mexico and Canada have superimposed on the continent (and beyond), has illuminated the complex structure of the American Regionalism, even in the limited NAFTA context. Extending this kind of investigation to Latin America reveals that the spaghetti bowl phenomenon is not restricted to NAFTA and its allies. Rather, the Latin American RIAs and their member countries have developed their own trade expansion strategies, thereby contributing to the establishment of a 'complex new matrix of interdependency' (Salazar-Xirinachs/Robert, 2001, 5) that stretches all over the Americas. The result of these activities is a highly discriminatory set of overlapping rules of trade and investment.

In order to understand this spaghetti bowl phenomenon more clearly three levels of integration might be distinguished. The first level contains the large multilateral agreements such as NAFTA, MERCOSUR, CACM and CARICOM, which form the backbone of the New American Regionalism. However, other than NAFTA, the Latin American RIAs have been planned to become common markets, and they are currently operating on quite different stages of implementation.

On the third level, purely bilateral agreements are located. Mexico and Canada have already been identified as major players in this camp of bilateralists (Chapter Four). In South America it is Chile in particular that ranges most prominently as a dedicated negotiator of bilateral agreements, keeping up FTAs with each single NAFTA country (an FTA with the USA was signed in December 2002 and will start in 2004), the European Union, Colombia, Venezuela and Peru.

Intermediately, on the second level, a number of heterogeneous arrangements can be classified. These agreements are located somewhere between categories one and two, keeping up special relations with varying intensity with one or more of the bigger regions. Frequently, these countries also employ purely bilateral FTAs separately. That way, they constitute a web of overlapping preferential schemes. Thus, Bolivia is a regular member of the Andean Community and an associate member of MERCOSUR. Chile is an associate member of MERCOSUR and at the same time forms the 'hub' of an extended system of bilateral FTAs with countries of the Western Hemisphere and beyond. The Dominican Republic has contracted an FTA with the CACM and another one with the CARICOM. Mexico, itself being a member of NAFTA, also participates in the Northern Triangle (a new regional formation in Central America, which overlaps with the CACM) and in the G3 together with Colombia and Venezuela. The latter, in turn, are members of the Andean Community.

Last but not least, the Andean Community and MERCOSUR are also engaged in year-long negotiations on the regional level in order to unify and form a South American FTA (SAFTA). Parallel to these talks, individual group members of both (emerging) common markets repeatedly tried to contract separately on the bilateral level (Brazil, in particular). SAFTA, if it comes to life, would largely substitute for the still existing ALADI (Latin American Integration Association established in 1980 as a successor of the Latin American Free Trade Association [LAFTA]), which still follows the traditional approach of gradual integration along a sequence of sector and bilateral agreements. While the ALADI has undoubtedly lost much of its former political impact, it still has an effect on the New Regionalism by means of the about 40 partial scope agreements that it has initiated since its foundation (IDB, 2002, 29).

Bringing together this multitude of overlapping preferential trading arrangements in one single graph is almost impossible without regress to a multicolor outline. An impressive presentation of this type can be found in the a.m. 2002 report of the Inter-American Development Bank, which tackles the New Regionalism in Latin America (IDB, 2002, 64). From this graph, one gets a visible impression of the chaotic structure of incentives that economic agents are exposed to in the region. Nevertheless, the true dimension of this program can only be understood when adequate attention is paid to the effects of incompleteness of the agreements. This point has already been stressed in Chapter Three and in the discussion on NAFTA.

Extending this approach to include Latin America certainly explains that the costs of coping with overlapping regulatory systems, varying expectations and intransparent rules of origin are mounting as the web of rules and exceptions from these rules becomes larger and more closely woven. In economic terms, these costs arise from decreasing transparency of the rules, from increasing costs of documentation and simply from waste of time. Performance requirements, for example, under the diverse rules of origin (ROO) regimes are raising the costs of information and documentation and at the same time cause a time consuming border administration (the IDB reports that 'close to half the time of international cargo transport by road in the Southern Cone is due to border delays' [IDB 2002, 5]). It is not surprising under these conditions that even enlightened advocates of the New Regionalism are becoming suspicious and warn against the pitfalls of the spaghetti bowl regionalism: 'The imperfect status of the regions customs unions has created precisely the type of costs that the system is supposed to eliminate' (IDB, 2002, 5).

Another fundamental point against the spaghetti bowl regionalism is that bilateralism per se is a potentially disruptive way to organize international transactions. The basic arguments against bilateralism are straightforward:

1. Given the intransparent situation of overlapping regulatory systems governments are tempted to look for means to circumvent uncomfortable international rules (such as the clear and public GATT provisions for emergency protection, anti-dumping procedures, dispute settlement etc.).
2. In bilateral negotiations on free trade the inclination to mutually beneficial agreements inherently works at the expense of outsiders. Thus, these 'special arrangements' are likely to be shaped in a way that takes care of the different structural properties of the partner countries. In as much as the partners differ in their economic and political structures, the structures of the FTAs (definition, scope, exceptions) will differ, too.

   In the Americas, the diversity of economies with quite different structural characteristics (population size, level of income, natural re-sources, degree of industrialization etc.) suggests that the bilateral FTAs are also following quite different strategies. Thus, Mexico and Chile have successfully exported a NAFTA-style FTA approach (not without considering own specific interests), while MERCOSUR and the Andean Community are proceeding along their respective approaches. Finally, the Caribbean Islands are more or less apart from the problems of the larger countries and will try to follow their own specific objectives.
3. Bilateral negotiations are usually biased by power political influences. The exceptional power political position of the USA in the Western Hemisphere is well known and it might even be welcomed at a first

glance, because it is hoped that the hegemon will exercise a 'benign' leadership based on mutually beneficial principles (what it in fact proclaims!). However, the mixed experience with this leadership during the last two decades on the multilateral level (neo-protectionism) warns against too much uncontrolled power even in the hands of a benevolent hegemon. Again, under the obscure conditions of the New American Regionalism the dangers from the asymmetry of power are particularly acute, and this is the more so as other subregional powers, too, may try to exploit the situation to their own advantage. One particular concern in this respect is about the US inclination to the 'hub-and-spokes' approach that might help to split the front of hemispheric countries and extract the rents of the power political approach country by country, thereby proceeding step by step on the path to a US tailored system.[1]

These inherent dangers of bilateralism are well known since the disastrous experience with the Great Depression 'and the rise of totalitarianism – the antithesis of globalization' (Dymond, 2001, 4), and led to the creation of the multilateral post World War II order that explicitly rejects bilateralism. In the discussion of the American spaghetti bowl these arguments are rarely heard, because the New Regionalism is firmly believed to be different from the old one. In fact, bilateralism is largely perceived as a negative but insignificant side-effect of the New Regionalism, which still promises to spur growth and development much better than multilateralism could do. As a consequence, under the cover of 'regional free trade', bilateralism has become a respected approach again in the Western Hemisphere.

However, taken together, the conditions under which economic agents have to operate in the spaghetti bowl environment suggest that efficiency is not a major concern of regional integration policy or, to come to the point, 'to hell with efficiency is what this preferential mismatch often signifies' (Weintraub, 2004). But when, in practice, efficiency is not a core preoccupation of the New Regionalism any more, its expected growth effects will certainly remain wishful thinking.

Following this reasoning, the precarious economic situation in the Americas (and Latin America in particular) in 2003 could well be an indication that the New Regionalism has come to its limits, even before it really started to prosper. While NAFTA still sticks to the principles of the open regionalism relatively clearly and the rhetoric of the New Regionalism is frequently nursed all over the continent, the reality in the Western Hemisphere after only a decade of political experimentation with this concept is that the region is deeply entangled in a highly opaque and inefficient web of bilateralisms and plurilateralisms and follows the worrisome route of a barely hidden mercantilism.[2]

Under these conditions, the idea to build an American Free Trade Area ranging from Alaska to Tierra de Fuego has taken on a tremendously important meaning. In fact, the FTAA may lead the region back to the principles of the New Regionalism under one single concept, thereby offering a solution to the spaghetti bowl phenomenon, or just superimpose another level of discrimination. In the latter case, the danger would become real, that the hemisphere (and Latin America in particular) falls back again into a fragmented system of old-fashioned protectionism that would most surely feed back on the global scene. In fact, as will be shown subsequently, the relationship between the Western Hemisphere and the global economy is not one-sided. On the contrary, the region neatly fulfills the large country condition of economics (in essence this assumption holds that the foreign supply curves are less than perfectly elastic), which, in political terms, means that the formation of the FTAA and the ongoing process of globalization (and the negotiations of the Doha Round of multilateral trade talks) are highly interdependent developments.

6.2   THE HISTORY OF THE FTAA

The official date of birth of the idea of the 'Free Trade Area of the Americas' initiative is the 1994 Miami Summit of the Organization of American States. From a broader perspective, however, the FTAA proposal is deeply rooted in American history and, as such, a new expression of an old 'US vision that had existed for almost 200 years' (Mace, 1999, 20). According to Molineu (1986, 13) this longstanding 'Western Hemisphere idea' is based on the political primacy of the USA, an American dispute settlement framework and a Free Trade Agreement. Thus, the FTAA is the outcome of a highly political concept in which free trade is a means to pave the way for a much broader political agenda including the promotion of democratic institutions, human rights, security issues (drugs traffic, international terrorism etc.) and, more recently, environmental and social policies.

The revival of these ideas in the 1990s is due to a profound change of internal and external conditions since the early 1980s. Externally, the globalization of the world economy (and the difficulties in promoting the GATT during the Uruguay Round) and the end of the Cold War have given rise to a reconsideration of the regional option (see Chapter Three). But, taken alone these events would hardly be a sufficient explanation for a venture such as the FTAA. In fact, it is true that external political changes have had an important impact on the Latin American governments to turn to new regional activities including North America. However, the dominant player in the field is unlikely to have been much influenced by these external events. Rather, from the US point of view, the profound changes within the region, such as the opening up strategies and the broad democratization movement in Latin America have opened up a 'window of opportunity' for the reconsideration of the hemispheric project based on a 'convergence of values' (Mace, 1999, 30).

From this point of view, the declaration of Miami can be seen as an offspring of the 'Enterprises of the Americas Initiative' (EAI) of 1990 (Schott/Hufbauer, 1999, 767), which in turn is a complement to the Brady Plan. The latter, then, has been the first part of a comprehensive concept to overcome the Latin American debt crisis and the EAI should become the offensive follow-up approach aimed at the economic revitalization of the region. CUSTA and NAFTA, in particular, are part of this strategy in that they function both as a gatekeeper and as a test case for a broader initiative in the hemisphere.[3]

In fact, the Miami declaration gave impetus to an intensive process of preparation talks that have helped to create credibility, mutual respect among the trade negotiators and, most certainly, it has greatly improved on the knowledge of the structures of trade and protection in the whole region. Politically, however, the FTAA initiative has found only weak support during the 1990s, and this may have been the consequence of both the absence of clear political motivation on the part of the US[4] and the negative reactions of US politics (and public perceptions) on NAFTA (Chapter Four). Thus, while the political will to create an FTAA was reiterated in the follow-up summit in Santiago de Chile (1998), to the public this declaration has been widely interpreted as a rhetorical exercise without much substance. In fact, during the following years, the FTAA process, though having been skillfully managed by the socalled Tripartite Committee (OAS, IDB, CEPAL), fell back again to the technical level. It was only in April 2001 at the Quebec Summit that the FTAA project reappeared on the political agenda. At that conference, a first 'bracketed draft' was published, which should become a firm basis for the ongoing process of the FTAA negotiations. Eighteen months later, in November 2002, the ministerial meeting in Quito noted 'with satisfaction that the process of building an FTAA ... had further advanced ... despite the deterioration in current global and hemispheric conditions and heightened international tensions' (Ministerial Declaration of Quito, 2002, 1) and agreed on the second bracketed draft that will become the basis for the ongoing negotiation process (Plan of Action).

With the Quito ministerial meeting the FTAA process has entered its final stage. The ministers not only agreed on the follow-up meetings in Miami (2003) and Brazil (2004) but, by passing the co-presidency to the USA and Brazil, the two most influential 'agenda setting countries', opened up the arena for the final countdown. This is scheduled to be concluded toward the end of 2005.

Should the scheduled dates be met and the diverse obstacles on the way to American free trade be overcome, the FTAA will become the world's largest regional venture unifying 34 nations with more than 800 million people and a combined GDP of nearly 13 trillion US$ in 2002. It will also be the first RIA to include countries of the whole spectrum of stages of economic development ranging from LLDCs such as Jamaica and Bolivia and the micro-island states of the Caribbean to the advanced economies of Canada and the USA. As such, the formation of the FTAA is a tremendous task even from the purely economic point of view. Reviewing the Miami Summit Plan of Action makes it clear, however, that trade and investment liberalization is just a vehicle used to transport a far reaching political agenda that fits neatly with the historical dimension of the project.

The FTAA Plan of Action identifies 23 cooperative initiatives under four headings (Figure 6.1). It is important to note that 'preserving and strengthening the Community of Democracies' ranges first on this agenda and explicitly goes beyond the general claim of democracy and human rights. Rather, it includes initiatives such as combatting corruption, illegal drugs and terrorism, which are among the standard issues of US security preoccupation in the region. The assertion to promote free trade ranges second, but is embedded in the broader context of deeper economic integration including such important issues as liberalizing the capital accounts, developing a hemispheric infrastructure, energy cooperation, and cooperation in science and technology. Clearly these issues recall the growth promoting qualities of the New Regionalism and link the FTAA to the long-run aspiration to eradicate poverty and discrimination in the region. Last but not least, the environmental agenda that still found itself restricted to a side agreement under the NAFTA treaty has graduated to become one of the four main targets of the FTAA program.

Based on this general agenda of political (democracy, human rights, peace) and economic (integration, growth, development) initiatives that has sometimes been called a laundry list (Weintraub, 2004) covering some purely national political aspirations rather than negotiable common objectives, the concrete structure of the FTAA negotiations meanwhile has centered around nine negotiation groups. These groups are complemented by a 'Technical Committee on Institutional Issues', a 'Consultative Group on smaller economies', the 'Electronic Commerce Committee', and the 'Civil Society Committee' (Figure 6.2). These committees and negotiation groups are coordinated by the 'Trade Negotiations Committee' that serves as a link between the technical and the political level. 'The goal is a balanced and comprehensive WTO consistent agreement by January 2005 that will be determined by consensus and be a single undertaking' (IDB, 2002, 45).

Preserving and Strengthening the Community of Democracies of the Americas

1. Strengthening democracy
2. Promoting and protecting human rights
3. Invigorating society/community participation
4. Promoting cultural values
5. Combatting corruption
6. Combatting the problem of illegal drugs and related crimes
7. Eliminating the threat of national and international terrorism
8. Building mutual confidence

Promoting Prosperity through Economic Integration and Free Trade

9. Free trade in the Americas
10. Capital markets development and liberalization
11. Hemispheric infrastructure
12. Energy cooperation
13. Telecommunications and information infrastructure
14. Cooperation in science and technology
15. Tourism

Eradicating Poverty and Discrimination in Our Hemisphere

16. Universal access to education
17. Equitable access to basic health services
18. Strengthening the role of women in society
19. Encouraging microenterprises and small businesses
20. White Helmers – emergency and development corps

Guaranteeing Sustainable Development and Conserving Our Natural Environment for Future Generations

21. Partnership for sustainable energy use
22. Partnership for biodiversity
23. Partnership for pollution prevention

Source: Salazar-Xirinachs/Robert (2001)

Figure 6.1   The Plan of Action of the FTAA (Miami Summit, 1994)

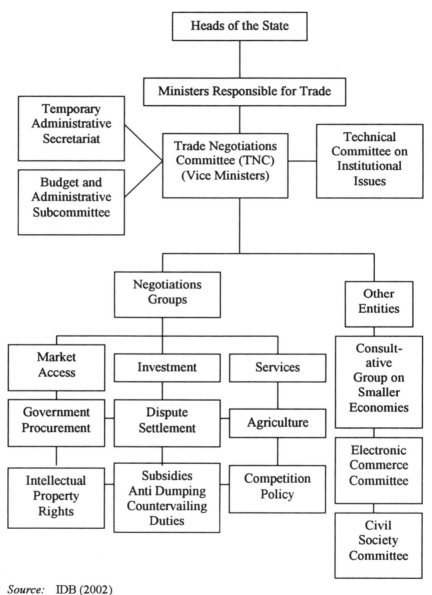

Source: IDB (2002)

Figure 6.2   The structure of the FTAA negotiations

The nine negotiating groups make it clear that the dominant elements of the FTAA agenda are economic. This is not to say that the political aspirations have already been downgraded. Rather, it reflects the fact that the overriding political objectives are long run by their very nature and not free from visionary elements. The economic issues, in turn, are both instrumental to the political ones and readily negotiable along well defined routes.

A closer look at the nine negotiating groups underlines this notion. In fact, these groups mirror the standard trade policy agenda of the WTO as it has emerged from the Tokyo Round, and they are also much in line with the NAFTA type FTAs. Market access, for example, used to be the traditional approach to trade liberalization on the multilateral and regional level. This topic has been complemented by the other areas of concern piece by piece as the world economy ventured into the era of globalization. International investment, for example, has already been identified as a core element of globalization and of the New Regionalism. Agriculture is an important traditional trade sector, too, which has been integrated into the GATT system with the foundation of the WTO, and it is of utmost importance for both the USA and Canada and most Latin American economies. Services and intellectual property rights, in turn, are the major new topics of the trade agenda and they have found a prominent place in the WTO and NAFTA, too. Their incorporation into the trade order is a central concern of the advanced economies, because new comparative (competitive) advantages are most often created in the modern service sectors and draw on sophisticated technologies and specific knowledge. Thus, as the successful emerging economies are proceeding along the stages of comparative advantage (Balassa, 1977), the advanced economies' escape window is exactly in modern services and high tech industries of this kind. Last but not least, dispute settlement and the interlinked 'subsidies–competition' complex are becoming the more important the more international transactions touch upon issues that initially were completely under the control of local governments. The FTAA process, so far, is firmly rooted in the modern international trade agenda. Electronic commerce may add to these topics as soon as the major new challenges of this innovative medium of exchange have been understood sufficiently well.

In order to investigate more deeply on the chances of the formation of the FTAA it is necessary to know more about the intentions of the more important players in the hemisphere with respect to the treaty. This investigation must again regress to the political background in which the economic agenda is embedded. Confronting these intentions with the critical issues of the liberalization of trade and investment on the hemispheric scale over the whole spectrum of issues will help to get a better understanding of the FTAA project. From this investigation one might proceed towards an evaluation of the chances that the project will mature in a way that really makes it a positive contributor to security and welfare in the region.

6.3   HOW SERIOUS IS THE PROJECTED FTAA?

The 1990s have shown that the political enthusiasm of the most important actors in the Western Hemisphere for the FTAA has not been impressive. But this relative discretion might have changed when the US–Brazil co-presidency began and the time for final decisions came closer. In order to shed some light on the question of the seriousness of the whole project, two different but interrelated aspects have to be taken into consideration. One is the relative importance of the FTAA (compared to the multilateral option) from the point of view of the more important actors. The other one is the web of specific interests that the potential partner countries unites (or separates). This second question will be considered first.

In view of the fact that the FTAA project is so much embedded in political and economic considerations, it is appropriate to elaborate on this problem by regressing on the basic model of Chapter One, and applying it to the US and the Latin American situation respectively. To make this analysis manageable the Latin American interests will, by and large, be approximated by the Brazilian position. This appears to be an acceptable restriction in so far as Brazil is the most important Latin American counterpart to the US political and economic aspirations. Some more important departures of the interests of individual Latin American countries from this sketch will then be treated separately.

Figure 6.3 applies the basic framework of Chapter One to the US (North American) and the Brazilian (Latin American) situation. According to this approach, the US and the Brazilian interests are both derived from foreign policy (security) and economic (growth and development) considerations. On this general level and from a longer-run perspective there is a high degree of harmony on both sides concerning the security and the growth objectives. Thus, the perception of these common interests could easily be translated into the FTAA negotiating agenda, which notes the promotion of democracy, the fostering of regional economic growth and development, and the liberalization of trade and investment as overriding common aspirations.

However, foreign policy is not restricted to the promotion of democracy but incorporates at least two additional objectives that are relevant in the FTAA context. One is hegemonic aspirations and the other one has been classified under the label 'generation of spillovers'. Spillovers from regional integration are expected in the fields of drug traffic, terrorist activities, and

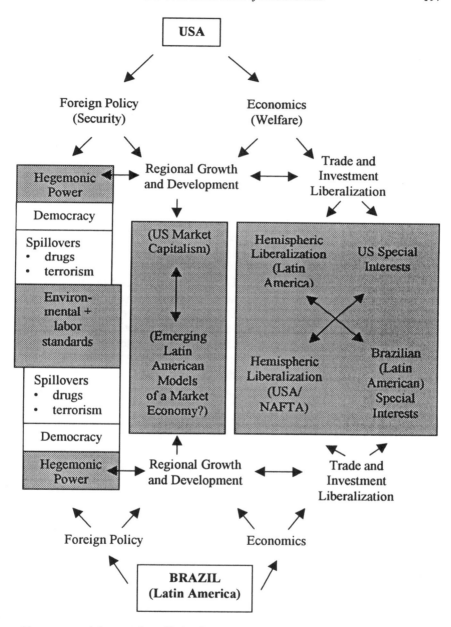

Note: potential areas of conflicting interests are shaded

Figure 6.3   The structure of interests of hemispheric integration

the setting of standards (this latter field of action is particularly important from the economic perspective, too).

Based on this outline of the general structure of interests, the specific positions of the USA and Brazil can be derived. Drawing on Schott and Hufbauer (1999) the US initiative concerning the FTAA was basically motivated by economic objectives. That is, stabilizing and developing Latin America after the debt crisis of the 1980s has been a major intuition of the USA. This approach has two interlinked aspects. One is the direct US economic interest in the region that can be realized by trade and investment liberalization. That way, the US producers are expected to penetrate Latin American markets more easily and without being discriminated against. Given market access, the Latin American economies will become the more attractive to US business the better the economic performance is in the partner countries. From the US perspective this means that supporting any kind of opening-up and institutional upgrading procedures based on market-oriented principles (e.g. along the lines of the so-called 'Washington Consensus') is important, and the FTAA initiative may foster this process.

Clearly, the US interest in a sustained economic growth process in the region also incorporates political aspects. In particular, 'the US benefits when its neighbors prosper and democratic processes take root' (Schott/Hufbauer 1999, 779)[5] and this will make it easier for the US to find cooperating partners regarding other non-economic issues (spillovers).

The US interest in the regionalization process is less clear, however, if a broader foreign policy perspective is taken. Most certainly, the US is interested in any development in the region that underscores its hegemonic position. The FTAA, by contributing to the stabilization of the region and making US political ideals better understood and more acceptable among the Latin American partner countries, is most likely to serve this objective. However, strengthening the hegemonic position in the region (and globally) by the means of regional integration does not come without cost. In fact, building regional institutions may limit the hegemon's 'room to maneuver' and burden it with a large part of the costs of cooperation (Bélanger, 1999, 99). It is not easy to quantify these costs. Nevertheless, their mere existence is used to question the rationale of the economic gains from integration. Bélanger, for example, argues that the US 'tentative and ambiguous policy' on hemispheric regionalism in the 1990s was due to the belief that building up of a hegemonic position and fostering harmonious economic relations by means of regional free trade are not a sufficient condition to launch a strategy of hemispheric integration (Bélanger, 1999, 100).

Implicit to this statement are a number of bold claims. First, a high priority is given to an independent position of foreign policy (autonomy), second, the FTAA must have a significant binding effect, and third, the economic gains from regional integration are low. This might in fact be a correct assessment. However, it lacks any serious empirical foundation so that changing priorities just marginally, an opposite result cannot be ruled out. This recognition documents the most serious deficiency of the political–economic decision-making model: it is usually fed by ad hoc explanations that are weighed according to individual preferences based on incomplete (selective) information and theoretical predisposition. Being unable to challenge this state of the art in this chapter I shall restrict myself to the sobering statement that we simply do not know what the relevant weights of politics and economics are in the decision-making calculus of those in charge of the FTAA process.[6] At this point it may be sufficient to note that, from the US perspective, the project of hemispheric integration has both economic and important political costs that must carefully be considered in order to find a positive overall balance for all its participants.

For Brazil, the gains from the political and economic benefits of the FTAA are even less obvious than for the USA. Looking at the prospective economic gains it is clear that more intensive trade relations with the USA would generate a potent market for Brazilian products and improve on the transfer of technology that is at the heart of economic upgrading. But, even though this approach has an intuitive appeal for Brazil and can in fact be expected to contribute positively to the economic development of the country, it would also be a viable Brazilian option on the multilateral level. Consequently, the multilateralism–regionalism puzzle is again at stake.

Things are even more difficult to evaluate from the political perspective. The point is that Brazil is a regional hegemon in South America and has even articulated its ambition to act as a global player, once it has substantiated on its economic and political power. Given this aspiration, the Brazilian foreign policy used to keep at distance from the USA by betting on the multilateral card while articulating its exceptional position as a regional hegemon in South America. An FTAA would surely challenge this constellation and reduce the potential influence of Brazil in the region. In Brazil, this aspect of the FTAA project is ranked highly and has led to considerable preoccupation with the whole venture. I shall come back to this point later.

Most other Latin American countries do not have a chance to articulate hegemonic aspirations on their own. But they may have sailed in the leeway of Brazil until recently. In fact, MERCOSUR has also been interpreted as a power bloc with Brazil as the agenda setter. Under the FTAA, a much larger power bloc would emerge, but under different leadership. It is not currently clear whether the power political upgrading that the participation in the FTAA would bring for the smaller countries would compensate the region for the change of Brazil from being a regional 'maker' within Latin America to being a 'taker' in the Americas (with the USA as the 'maker'). Last but not least, there are also some major exporters of mineral resources and resource-intensive goods which are heavily engaged on the global level and would not like to see their overseas connections being damaged by too much emphasis on the Western Hemisphere.

Even from such a crude sketch of interests it is clear that there are three classes of opposing interests that may give rise to difficulties in the FTAA negotiating process. Two of these follow directly from the discussion of Figure 6.3. One is political and the result of different interests concerning hegemonic pretensions. The other one is economic and derives from the existence of special interests concerning trade and investment liberalization within each country. The third field of potential dissent is not so obvious, but of fundamental importance from a neo-functionalist perspective. This is the different cultural backgrounds of the integrating countries.

Reducing these cultural differences to the most general level we have to consider the case of the smooth interrelationship between the (dominating) 'North American way of life' and the Latin American cultural system. In particular, the two subregions may interpret the meaning of 'Regional Growth and Development' so much differently that the correspondence of the objectives on the general level will be wiped out almost completely by disagreement on the operational level, and this dissent would most certainly feed back on other economic and political issues. Looking at the FTAA Plan of Action with due consideration of these potentially disruptive fields of disharmony reveals that the negotiating agenda concentrates very much on the economic aspects, while the political and the cultural dimensions of the Western Hemisphere integration project are given the status of benign neglect. In the following I will briefly discuss the cultural and the political dimension and then concentrate on the economic issue.

6.3.1   The Cultural Dimension

The FTAA aims at integrating 34 countries that cover almost the whole range of stages of economic development. It has long been recognized that this economic divide in the Americas goes hand in hand with a 'cultural divide' (Harrison, 1997, 11).This observation has given rise to a number of important studies on the impact of the political culture on economic development. One early influential study that analyzed the American situation is by Stein/Stein (1970). They stated that the different paths of economic development in North and South America are mainly to be attributed to the different cultural settings that prevailed in the region at the beginning of the era of modern industrial societies. More precisely, the former British Colonies were fortunate to inherit and build on the ideas of the philosophical underpinnings of the 'modern' British empire, which, at that time, had already developed the more important prerequisites of the so-called 'take-off' stage of development (in the sense of Rostow, 1960). In essence, this means that early on in the North, modern institutional structures were built up that permitted political, economic and scientific advancements to be incorporated in all fields of social life. Latin America, instead, was locked up in the Spanish cultural tradition that was in many respects still based on the stiff centralized organizational structures of the medieval colonial system and not much receptive to progress and change. From this insight it is but one step to bring in Max Weber's ideas about the impact of different religious perceptions of man on socioeconomic outcomes (Weber, 1950) and differentiate between the Anglo-Protestant and the Ibero-Catholic cultures (Harrison, 1997). Both cultural systems, according to this view, led to the formation of strictly different values and attitudes, which, in turn, translated into quite different institutional frameworks and economic outcomes. According to Harrison, the focal point of this divergent evolutionary path is that the Anglo-Protestant culture led to a progress-prone system of human organization, while the Ibero-Catholic system remained essentially progress-resisting. As a consequence, and contrary to claims of the influential Latin American 'dependencia' (dependency) school, the Catholic part of the Americas lost its initial lead position in the region (17th century), because it was unable to take advantage of the economic potential of the modern industrial societies. Namely, this was the case because the modern approach concedes an unprecedented surge of welfare on a broad front, but at the expense of the acceptance of rapidly and profoundly changing economic political and social structures. The progress-resistant Ibero-Catholic culture, instead, proved to be unable to give way to these challenges, stuck to its outdated institutional system and fell back to (remained at) the stage of an underdeveloped region.

Following this reasoning, two conclusions follow immediately. First, it is obvious that the idea of hemispheric integration could not succeed in the past, simply because there was no way to bridge the 'cultural divide' as long as the Latin American elites insisted on cultivating the notion of being victims of an external threat (the exploitative international system with the perceived US imperialism as a central feature) rather than realizing the endogenous nature of their misery, that is, the 'pre-industrial social model' (Mace/Bélanger, 1999b, 54) of the Ibero-Catholicism.

Second, and despite the fact that during the last decade and a half, substantial reform efforts have been undertaken in Latin America, the process of emancipation from the cultural chains of the progress-resistant Ibero-Catholic system of social organization is still underway and its outcome open. The core problem seems to be that under the cover of the technical (economic) reform activities the more fundamental changes in human attitudes and behavior are lagging behind and, after centuries of a formative influence, they are in fact far more difficult to alter.

This thesis cannot be proved easily but it gains plausibility from a number of casual observations. Most important in this context is the experience of MERCOSUR. It has been demonstrated in Chapter Five that a variety of most impressive reforms concerning trade, investment and other economic issues (e.g. privatization) have been brought underway in the Southern Cone at an astonishingly rapid rate of progress during the first stages of the reforms. Later, however, the reform efforts slowed down and, under increasing pressure of vested interests, they even had to be reversed in recent years. The Argentine tragedy, too, may be cited. In this case even the strict 'Currency Board' did not provide a sufficiently binding rule to discipline the traditional political forces to refrain from the largely discredited debt financing practices of the public sector. Neither did it succeed in overcoming the longstanding and so much paralyzing confrontation between capital and organized labor, that originates in the mental atmosphere of early capitalism.

The recent turbulences in MERCOSUR are not the only indications of a lamentable state of the affairs of the reform projects in Latin America after the era of import substitution, and most certainly they are not the most serious ones. Much more alarming for many observers of the region are some political developments that cast doubt on the reliability of the praised democratic reforms of the post-debt crisis era. Essentially, these events demonstrate a high degree of discontent in the population of many Latin American countries with the present political situation and with the political elites that are (believed to be) responsible for it. Given a diffuse perception of the complex reforms (including distinct technical failures) and their short-, medium- and long-run consequences on one side, and a definite experience of increased hardship under the new regimes (often measured with reference to a glorified history of import substitution) on the other, a firm basis for the ongoing reforms appears to be increasingly difficult to organize.

Even in the case that this pessimistic cultural–political analysis of the Latin American reform process is overdone, the consequences for the evaluation of the FTAA project are obvious and remain relevant.

Undoubtedly, the success of the FTAA project will depend crucially on the US willingness to engage in this matter. The diverse interests on the part of the USA have been outlined above. They are not unimportant, but they are also not vital. That is, the US may eventually push the FTAA, if it sees a real chance to shape it according to its own cultural and institutional conceptions. The FTAA, in other words, will become an RIA based on the Anglo-Protestant ideals or not venture at all.

Starting from this thesis, the future battlefields of bridging the 'cultural divide' are becoming clearly visible. The main burden of change will undoubtedly be on the Latin American economies and more importantly, their societies. Even if one concedes that this process is inevitable for Latin America in order to eventually get out of the underdevelopment trap, this transformation process will touch on fundamental areas of the way of 'Latin' life that are far beyond economics. In these 'beyond economics' areas of transition, changes of attitudes and patterns of behavior may prove to be the decisive but particularly sensitive issues that have to be mastered. Given the historically grown reservations in large parts of Latin America regarding the USA and their 'cultural dominance', and the frequently brusque way of the US management of its Latin American relations, a smooth functioning of this process of asymmetrical convergence does not appear to be a likely outcome. Rather, it is almost certain that this process will be accompanied by frequent irritations on both sides.

One important aspect of potential disharmony that may have an impact on the FTAA talks derives from the fact that, due to the Latin American lag of reforms in cultural matters, the negotiable concepts of growth and change on which the integration project will build, are limited. More precisely, there is a whole array of economic (political) models beyond import substitution but short of American-style capitalism that may find adherence in Latin America but is less likely to be admitted by the USA. Again, on a general level, there should be enough tolerance for diverse economic concepts to coexist. However, in reality the highly emotional dealing with the so-called 'Washington Consensus' teaches that the frontier between a purely economic rationale and fixed ideological positions is still a fundamental problem in the US/Latin American relationship. If this ideological component cannot be kept out of the political negotiations of the FTAA, the whole agenda may be overthrown in the end. This danger is certainly growing if the USA or NAFTA are coming to the conclusion that the cultural divide is still too large (or even growing again) so that the costs of hemispheric cooperation are becoming prohibitive.

From the present point of view (spring 2003) it appears to be too early to judge on the future of the FTAA project from the cultural perspective. In any case it is not unreasonable to assume that the prospective process of economic recovery in Latin America in the final years before the conclusion of the negotiations, as well as the development of the political situation in the crisis countries will have an important impact on the willingness of the USA to exercise political leadership and bring the project to a successful conclusion.[7]

6.3.2   The Political Dimension

According to the rough outline of the political interests of the major hemispheric actors concerning the FTAA in Figure 6.3, the principal area of dissent between the USA and Brazil arises from the regional hegemonic aspirations of Brazil, which are becoming challenged by the larger impact that the USA will exercise in the area under an RIA.

Starting from the security interest of the US, a stable South American region will undoubtedly exert a positive impact on the security position of the hegemon. The FTAA could help to foster such a development – but only if it becomes a success story! Drawing on the modern theory of integration, openness is indispensable for such a success, and in the case of the USA this is of an even greater importance because of the vital US global interests. Meanwhile, many Latin American countries share the US (Canadian) views on openness, because of their own global orientation and opening-up policies. Consequently, a broad front of agreement on this issue exists. Nevertheless, the Latin American countries are more reluctant as far as the implementation of the opening-up concept is concerned and this may in fact become a critical point in the FTAA negotiations (see below).

Another critical point is the expected impact of the FTAA on the US scope for maneuvering in the international arena. The discussion of this issue can be subsumed under two different headings, which both suggest that the FTAA does not come without a cost for the USA. The first point is that the hegemon may have to take care of the functioning of the regional integration scheme and must expect to have to bear the major monetary burden from exercising its responsibility. It is obvious that these operational costs will be the larger, the more obstacles to integration arise from the cultural divide and from a potential failure of the attempts to initiate a lasting process of convergence.

Second, the maneuvering scope of the hegemon will be the larger the less power the partner countries can exercise. The ongoing debate on the single package approach that gives the Latin American countries a better chance to articulate their specific interests in the negotiating process highlights the importance of this point for Latin America. The counter-position manifests itself in the repeated efforts on the part of the USA to undermine this approach by negotiating bilateral agreements separately.[8] The earlier discussion of the spaghetti bowl phenomenon points to the fact that the resolution of this power political dispute will also have important economic consequences.

As has been argued before, Brazil's regional ambitions are affected by the US position in various respects and will feed back on it. The crucial point is that Brazil will not be able to keep up with its undisputed hegemonic position in South America when the FTAA comes to life. Thus, the FTAA comes at a high political cost for Brazil.

In turn, Brazilians do not rank high the economic gains that might be expected from the FTAA. The US market and US technology are not unimportant for Brazil for sure. Yet, they may be available in an open multilateral environment as well and without the need to sacrifice its political position within the region.

There is one important caveat for this argument to hold, however. This is, the implicit claim that the global markets (and the US market in particular) remain open for Brazil. To put it differently, for Brazil, the risk of a global crisis may make a secure and institutionalized access to the US market attractive (this argument has had much impact on the Mexican decision to join NAFTA, too). Last but not least, taking the FTAA option will also become important for Brazil, when the USA fosters the 'hub-and-spokes' approach and isolates Brazil within its own the region.

Thus, from a power political perspective, Brazil finds itself in a dilemma situation. Agreeing on a US dominated FTAA will most likely threaten its hegemonic position in the region without adding too much to the economic benefits that it can realize from multilateral free trade. However, blocking the FTAA would probably make the USA turn to the hub-and-spokes strategy more rigorously and isolate Brazil within its own region. Eventually, Brazil might have damaged its economic position and, nevertheless, loses its power political impact in the region. An additional point is that Brazil's compatriot regional neighbors are following the evolution of the Brazilian stance on the FTAA closely. If they get the feeling that Brazil decides to defect and block the negotiations their incentive to contract with the US separately will increase.[9] Under this scenario bilateralism would probably spread, and the USA would not hesitate to exercise its power political impact to extract additional rents from the prospective partner countries. Eventually, the whole region would be worse off.

It is not surprising under these conditions, that Brazil is not enthusiastic about the FTAA project, but, nevertheless, unable to leave the arena. Until recently, the situation has led to a relatively passive Brazilian role in the FTAA process and an interpretation of the negotiating agenda that is as restrictive as possible (timetable, level of commitment etc.) (Soares de Lima, 1999, 140).

Under the opaque conditions that are governing the Brazilian position, the relative change in the perception of two critical parameters may easily turn the Brazilian calculus of the FTAA in favor of or against the treaty. One is political and may result from a major change in the Brazilian government. One such change took place in 1994 when Cardoso took office and opened up a period of a more sympathetic Brazilian FTAA policy (not without keeping up the generally hesitant position). Another change might be underway since the election of Luis Ignacio da Silva as the new Brazilian president in 2001 (having taken office in 2002). It is not possible at this time to give any serious statement about the political and economic priorities of the new government concerning the FTAA process.[10]

The second critical parameter is economic benefits. This parameter is shaped by the relative advantages that a prospective FTAA liberalization process may offer to Brazil (and the US, in turn). I will turn to this point in the next section.

6.3.3   The Economic Dimension

Traditional FTAs (CUs) are restricted to trade liberalization. The New Regionalism has extended the agenda of issues substantially. The negotiating agenda of the FTAA, too, is based on this extended approach and, with the definition of nine negotiating groups (Figure 6.2) covers the whole spectrum of issues that the modern international economic policy currently tackles.[11]

This agenda has evolved out of the need to find internationally binding rules for the new issues that the successful trade liberalization after World War II has brought about. In fact, it can be seen as a correlate of the changing international division of labor that has eventually led to the modern global economy (Chapter Two). In this 'new science based, globally integrated economy...trade, investment, and technology transfer have become complementary economic activities' (Dymond, 2001, 2) and must be treated jointly.

What this change of international economic policy issues really means can be discussed on the basis of the continuum of dynamic comparative advantages (Chapter Two, Figure 2.2). This model, being based on the theorem of comparative advantages, can easily be broadened to include some of the core elements of the present discussion. According to the continuum the trading nations are organized along a chain of comparative advantages and may upgrade on the continuum by accumulating capital (including human capital, scientific knowledge etc.) more rapidly than their competitors. In a typical North–South constellation with rates of growth converging towards a lower rate at higher levels of development (the steady state in the neo-classical terminology) this leads to increased pressure on the advanced economies. The basic reason is that successful developing countries are going to upgrade and enter more and more markets where the advanced economies used to dominate.

For the advanced economies to stand this increased competition 'from below' the continuum has to be opened up at its high end. That is, the producers in the developed countries must be able to 'create new comparative advantages' in order to defend their position on the world markets. A large part of what has changed the international division of labor during the last decades is indeed attributable to the creation of new comparative advantages. And it is the creation of new comparative advantages that enables the advanced developed countries to stand the competition with the emerging markets. In fact, one might say that they are very much depending on the functioning of this process of the formation of comparative advantages.[12] A crucial point in this context is that the creation of comparative advantages draws heavily on science and the use of specific knowledge,[13] and it takes place in an environment of innovational competition as outlined in Chapter Two. That is, the advanced economies are eager to develop new institutions that regulate international economic relations under the specific conditions of innovational competition, and they try to expand their firms' markets in segments that are responsive to the absorption of science based products (these are often found in the modern service and information sectors). For the international economic policy this opens up the need to extend the international economic order to incorporate exactly these new issues like services, intellectual property rights and foreign investment.

For many observers, such an extended economic order is an important precondition for the smooth functioning of global competition in the science based economy. First, by including the service sectors and the guarantee of intellectual property rights it enables the advanced economies to push forward production and trade at the frontier of economic development. Second, by opening up the continuum, it takes competitive pressure off the advanced economies (which results from emerging North–South competition) and thereby broadens the scope for the LDCs to upgrade production and trade.

The economic situation which is underlying the FTAA is an almost perfect illustration of this scenario. The Latin American developing countries, the more advanced emerging markets of Brazil, Argentina and Chile in particular, are the potential upgraders in the region. As such, they challenge the established high income countries with low skill, labor-intensive products and they are eager to increase the transfer of technology in order to advance their own competitive edge in 'higher segments' of the continuum of dynamic comparative advantages. An additional aspect of the Latin American situation is the region's relative abundance of natural resources, which, in the case of agriculture, leads to direct competition with North American products in the most sensitive US and Canadian agricultural sectors. Agricultural exports and the export of mineral resources are also particularly important for most of the less industrialized (poorer) LDCs in the region.

The USA and Canada, in turn, are operating on the frontier of the science based modern industries and services sectors. They both draw heavily on created comparative advantages in an environment of global (innovational) competition. For them, opening up the Americas for the new, high tech and service industries, the protection of intellectual property rights and the operation and the non-discriminatory treatment of US and Canadian firms in foreign markets is ranging high on the negotiating agenda.

This situation also defines the starting positions of the two subregions in the FTAA process. While the northern markets are relatively open on a broad front in the high tech industries, there are a number of severe limitations to imports in those sectors where comparative advantages have been lost to the LDCs (textiles and apparel, shoes, steel etc.), and which are particularly important from the point of view of Latin American exporters. The South, in turn, has its highest levels of protection in those industries that are perceived to be important for upgrading, that is, in the sectors in which the North hopes to gain an improved market access by means of the FTAA.

A second problem for the FTAA negotiations is the differing structure of protection in North and South America. The South is mainly operating its trade protection by means of tariffs that aim at two quite different objectives. One is infant industry protection (whereby 'infant' sometimes finds a very generous interpretation), the other one is 'the generation of government receipts' (which, economically, is a second or even third best practice, but still has a strong political appeal).

The North, in turn, has a virtually clean jacket as far as the overall level of tariffs is concerned (Chapter Four) but targets LDC (Latin American) exports by means of exceptions and the extensive use of hidden NTBs. In this context, the US anti-dumping practices, the so-called voluntary export restraints (VERs), and the quotas and subsidies in agriculture are of great concern.

This diverging structure of protection is a potential point of disharmony for the FTAA negotiations from two different but interrelated perspectives. *First*, the LAC (Latin America and the Caribbean) countries are preoccupied by the US efforts to concentrate the trade talks on tariffs and then proceed towards 'modern' issues such as services, intellectual property rights etc., but leave aside the NTB issue, which is vital for Latin American access to the USA, Canada and Mexico. One critical point, therefore, is the extension of the trade talks to include the case of US contingent protection in a meaningful way. Until today, the USA has remained so much reserved on this point that various high-ranked Brazilian officials have already stated that an FTAA under the present perspectives is rarely attractive for the country.

Second, the diverging structure of protection can be interpreted as the result of a strong divide on comparative advantages in the region that has brought about strong vested interests in the respective areas of comparative disadvantage. In the USA, these vested interests are basically the same as those discussed in the NAFTA chapter, but they are much more challenged by an FTAA. First, the FTAA brings in MERCOSUR with its relatively strong industrial corridor (Sao Paulo - Buenos Aires - Santiago de Chile). Giving MERCOSUR free access to the USA (NAFTA) would surely increase the pressure on the most sensitive US industrial areas substantially and cause the protectionist coalition against NAFTA (Chapter Four) to extend its activities and oppose the FTAA. Ironically, these activities would probably be applauded by the Mexican exporters of these same products to the USA, which will find it attractive now to fight for their preferential margin over the rest of Latin America. Second, South America disposes of some efficient agricultural producers that might bring in an array of agricultural products on the North American markets. These products, ranging from tropical fruit to cattle and grains, are going to compete with the most sensitive industries in the NAFTA states.

In Latin America (and in Brazil and Argentina in particular) one critical point is the outdated industrial structure that has been inherited from the era of import substitution. Until now, most Latin American governments have shied away from a firm restructuring strategy that would have repositioned these industries according to their competitive potential on the international markets. MERCOSUR in particular, employing the 'intra-industry' approach (Chapter Five) as a means to upgrade towards the world markets, largely avoided the necessary structural adjustments. The FTAA, which will include some of the leading industrial economies of the world, will bring about exactly the kind of global competition that has been carefully avoided so far.

In order to shed some light on the critical points of the Latin American political economic situation at the end of the import substitution era, a distinction made by Fischer of different segments of the Latin American business communities may be helpful (Fischer, 1999, 198 ff.).

Fischer classifies three entrepreneurial categories in Latin America. The first category comprises 'traditional exporters and merchants'. These are the exporters of primary commodities and the importers of industrial manufacturing goods for local consumption, and they constituted the traditional (North–South) backbone of Latin American international trade relations. The second group is constituted by the 'New Industrialists', which evolved out of the industrialization strategies under the import substitution regimes. Along with the change of the paradigm in the 1980s these industries came under increasing pressure to adjust. Some of them took the opportunity to upgrade and are competitive now in a number of low-level industries (transportation, processed food, steel and glass). They are now forming the emerging group of 'Third World Multinationals'. Many, however, from this category did not succeed and are still dependent on the 'exploitation of rents associated with barriers ... to trade' (Fischer, 1999, 202). They constitute a second subgroup in this category, which Fischer characterizes as 'political rent or market segmentation dependent national business' (ibid., 202). Finally, there is the third category, which embraces the multinational corporations.

This classification uncovers an important critical parameter of the reform strategies of many Latin American countries: the subgroup of 'political rent seekers', which has evolved under the import substitution regimes and which does have only scarce chances to survive in an open economy setting. Some others may simply lack the entrepreneurial capacities to survive in a competitive environment. In any case, these relicts of the import substitution era are fighting heavily against international competition, they are thought to be politically dominant in some countries[14] and have a considerable impact in countries like Brazil and Argentina. It is tempting, therefore, to suggest that this influential part of the business communities in the larger MERCOSUR countries is closely connected with the propagation of the 'intra-industry' strategy that tried to avoid any direct contact with global competition and instead provided local enterprises with an additional period of infant industry protection. Predictably, the FTAA would put an end to this special treatment and, consequently, is unlikely to meet much sympathy in these circles.

Given the state of affairs in both regions, it is clear that 'the most aggressive targets of many countries' FTAA trade agendas are often the most politically sensitive defensive sectors of others, and vice versa' (Blanco/ Zabludovsky, 2002). This makes the FTAA negotiations not only a particularly difficult undertaking that will have to solve quite a lot of serious conflicts between and within the participating countries. What might in fact become a precarious scenario is that the dynamics of the negotiation process will eventually enforce a treaty that defines 'free trade' on the lowest possible denominator and leaves the Western Hemisphere with just another piece of the spaghetti bowl puzzle.

A most concerning version of such an outcome would have to be expected, if the USA succeeds in dismantling tariffs (in Latin America) without moving in the field of its own contingent protection. In this scenario it would be most likely that the LAC countries, deprived from their tariffs, would follow the US path of anti-dumping and subsidization policies.[15] Eventually then, the Western Hemisphere would be able to formally dispose of a free trade agreement, but free trade would have essentially been damaged. It is worthwhile from this perspective to look separately on the contingent protection issue, which also has a link to the multilateral level.

6.4 ANTI-DUMPING POLICIES AND AGRICULTURAL PROTECTION – THE KEY TO FREE TRADE IN THE AMERICAS?

According to the declaration of San José the 34 Western Hemisphere states are planning to construct the FTAA to follow three basic criteria:

1. the substantial, mutual and equilibrated reduction of protection (in the broader sense in which it is outlined in the agenda);
2. the recognition of special treatment as a necessary precondition for the (small) least developed countries in the region;
3. WTO consistency.

In essence this means that the Plan of Action envisages a substantial reduction of tariffs *and* NTBs for all participating countries (in fact, the special treatment clause for poor countries even proposes an asymmetrical liberalization schedule). The major focus of the negotiation process will be on the discussion of the structure of protection between some more important South American emerging markets (with Brazil in a leading position) and the USA as the large counterpart in the North. Provided that these actors are taking the agenda seriously and remember that 'WTO consistency' implies 'reciprocity', a successful FTAA negotiation process should end up with both parties having agreed on moving towards a more liberal and transparent (regional) trade order. Drawing on the last section this means tariff reductions in the case of most Latin American countries and a return to a lower degree of contingent protection on the part of the USA.

After the discussion in this volume of the situation of trade policies in the region it is clear that the negotiations on the mutual dismantling of protection are not an easy task. And it also goes without saying that the principal actor in this game will have to be the USA. In particular, if the USA is ready to accept the principle of reciprocity in its original meaning and moves in the field of anti-dumping policies and agricultural protection, the LAC countries are likely to follow in due course by offering tariff reductions. The focus of this section will, therefore, be put on the US anti-dumping and agricultural policies.

6.4.1 The Anti-dumping Issue

Article VI of the GATT on dumping is one of the three principal routes for emergency protection that a member country may follow in order to get temporary relief from its obligations under the treaty, that is, when it suffers from overly strong import competition. The other ones are Article XII on balance of payments difficulties and Article XIX on market disruption. Article XIX concedes local producers a temporary relief when they have been hit by 'unexpected' changes of the international competitive situation and this has caused them to suffer a serious injury. Put differently, under this Article we have 'fairly' competing foreigners that meet a relatively inflexible local market. Drawing on Article XIX enables the government to concede the affected sectors a special treatment temporarily. Article VI in turn covers a quite different category of trade disruption. Here, the foreign competitor behaves 'unfairly' by charging 'dumping' prices on the import market. Thus, the response of local industries is to counteract 'unfair' competition from abroad.

Without going into a detailed discussion of the complex anti-dumping legislation of the GATT and the specific US provisions respectively, it is relatively easy to qualify the anti-dumping paragraph as one of the major loopholes of the present world trade order. In fact, what comes under the benign cover of preventing 'unfairness' has turned out to be a most easily accessible institutional path to plain protection, and, consequently, it has grown up to be one of the most frequently used instruments of the so-called contingent protection. The USA (and the EU) have been most active in using this instrument, and they did so with increasing intensity since the early 1980s.[16]

The basic point of concern with the anti-dumping paragraph is the GATT (US) dumping definition, which is aimed at the disclosure of 'predatory dumping', but essentially empowers national trade policy to discard any form of international price differentiation as 'unfair' trade practice. As a result, any customary form of pricing policy (that is, pricing policies that are legal on the national market and, in fact, are an essential instrument to keep markets open) may become the subject of a successful anti-dumping petition. In the past, these petitions, which in the USA may be filed by any industry association (and even by large single enterprises) have led to numerous anti-dumping cases with significantly negative welfare effects. Irwin (2002, 115), for example, reports that extremely large dumping margins of more than 50 percent have been found for the USA in the 1990s, which caused the respective imports to drop by more than 70 percent on average, while the prices rose by one-third.

Because anti-dumping cases are usually targeted on a small and exactly defined category of goods they are covering only a small fraction of total imports but their power to damage international trade and burden domestic consumers is enormous. Gallaway, Blonigen and Flynn (1999, 211 ff.), for example, have found that in 1993 the net welfare loss of US consumers from anti-dumping and countervailing duties was about 4 billion US$. However, this amount is likely to be only the tip of an iceberg since many anti-dumping practices end in bilateral 'voluntary agreements' between the parties involved. Messerlin has pointed to an important additional effect of these bilateral regulations, which bring together the local producer and its foreign competitor, giving them an incentive to talk about prices and costs. In essence, this means that anti-dumping policies act as a catalyst of cartelization among producers internationally, while nationally competition policies are targeted to prevent exactly this kind of collusion among local producers. Last but not least, it can be shown that the mere announcement of a petition can have significant trade restricting effects (Prusa, 2001, 594 ff.).

Knowing about this devastating record of the anti-dumping policies it is not easy to understand why the USA is so much fixed on this practice. A common explanation holds that the easiness of filing an anti-dumping case combined with the politically attractive expectation to blame the foreign producer for the need to intervene has made this instrument popular. Likewise, the decline of tariff protection has made it more attractive to invest in anti-dumping petitions and the lobbying groups have learned, meanwhile, to articulate their specific interests powerfully. Last but not least, it can be argued that the changing institutional structure of the US trade policy since the 1970s (Chapter Four) has opened up a more direct route for US business to influence the outcome of trade disputes to its own advantage. In any case, taking together these observations it becomes obvious that over the years strong vested interests have been nursed in the USA that are able now to quietly and perfectly handle the anti-dumping paragraphs to outpace foreign competition efficiently.

At this point it is worth remembering the coalition of labor and environmentalists, which has been discussed in the NAFTA chapter. Bringing both observations together uncovers that currently a broad coalition of protectionist forces is jointly operating in the US. While labor and the environmentalists are forming a coalition explicitly and publicly, in reality this interest group extends to the import competing capitalists. While the former act openly in favor of protection motivated on ethical grounds, the latter are working silently and justify protection as a means to prevent 'unfair' import competition. These motives have found benevolent recognition in the American public because spreading the feeling among people of being the victim of 'unfair' foreigners makes it easy to organize majorities against free trade.

For the US government it is not easy to consider the 'dumping issue' in international negotiations under these conditions. In fact, there are two important preconditions for a change of the US public perceptions on free trade. One precondition is leadership in the USA. This leadership would first have to name clearly the advantages of open markets for the USA, which go far beyond popular mercantilist perceptions on trade. Second, it would have to list frankly the adjustment deficits within the country itself (including the macroeconomic issues) that prevent US export companies from being more successful internationally and import substituting producers from adjusting more courageously to the changing international competitive situation – a notorious claim of the USA against its own trading partners.

The second pre-condition touches upon the international situation, that is, America's global competitors. They are apparently plagued by quite similar problems (EU, Japan), and they too would have to remember the virtues of open markets. In this case, the USA would not stand alone as the one in charge of free trade, being surrounded by a hostile army of free riders. Being able to avoid this impression would greatly improve the scope for the US administration to sell a more stringent free trade policy to the American public.

There was a certain euphoria among many observers of the international economic situation that, after the conclusion of the Uruguay Round, such a trade policy rebound would take place with the foundation of the WTO, and the road to freer trade would be reopened. However, the experience with the first WTO decade is mixed at best. This is particularly so with respect to the expectations of the many LDCs, which are 'bitterly disappointed over the meager benefits of the Uruguay Round' (Dymond, 2001, 9).

Under these conditions it is the new Doha Round of multilateral trade negotiations that may open up a new and more promising perspective for freer world trade. The USA has now accepted putting the dumping issue on the negotiating agenda after a long period of hesitation. That way, the multilateral trade talks are intimately linked now to the FTAA process. Progress on the anti-dumping issue on the multilateral level would presumably have a positive effect on the US willingness to negotiate on dumping in the regional talks. Ironically, this argument implies that the fate of the New Regionalism in the Americas is closely linked to progress on the multilateral level. Or, to put it differently, it is the acceptance of the need to actively promote the WTO framework that is likely to condition the success of the FTAA and not vice versa.

6.4.2   The Agricultural Issue

Many Latin American countries dispose of a comparative advantage in agricultural products. The Southern Cone, for example, produces large amounts of grains and cattle at competitive prices and qualities. Brazil and the members of the Andean Community are rich in tropical fruit, and others, being located in temperate climates, have important fruit and vegetable sectors including wine. Most of these agricultural products are promising candidates for export, provided the prospective target markets are accessible.

In reality, the most important of these markets are not. The EU, for example, has grown into a permanent troubleshooter on the world markets for agricultural products because of its highly protectionist 'common agricultural policy' (CAP). This policy could freely unfold after World War II because the agricultural sector had not been included in the GATT. In fact, the EU (the former EWG) made agricultural protection one of its foundation principles.[17] It was only during the Uruguay Round that the agricultural sector could be brought back into the GATT after very difficult negotiations between the so-called 'Cairnes' group plus the USA and the European Union (and Japan). Nevertheless, agricultural protection is still not under control in the EU and Japan, and it remains an important negotiation point on the Doha agenda.

What is irritating under these conditions is that the USA and Canada, too, both among the most efficient producers of agricultural products in the temperate climate zone, are far from free in protecting their local markets. A country from the Western Hemisphere that suffers most seriously from the US agricultural protection is, again, Brazil, which faces strong NTBs for exports of sugar and citrus products on the North American markets, for example.[18] Argentine grain producers, in turn, are hurt from US policies to subsidize local farmers. The US farm bill of 2002, which has raised farm subsidies substantially, has made the situation even more difficult.

Quite similar to anti-dumping policies (steel), the US protection in agriculture is a key area of dispute between the US and Brazil (Latin America) in the FTAA negotiations. Agricultural exports, in fact, are vital for many Latin American economies. Many of them are disposing of strong comparative advantages in the world and relative to the USA. Most certainly, these countries are unlikely to accept an FTAA under which the USA succeeds in getting market access in the southern industrial markets while keeping closed its own borders in the areas in which Latin American producers are about to exploit their competitive edge.

Once again the issue has an important international dimension, because the USA sees its scope of action limited by the agricultural protection in other regions of the world. The EU and Japan in particular are important players in this field. A common argument holds that, in as much as Europe, for example, opens up its agricultural markets, pressure is taken away from the US agricultural producers and this would enable the administration to respond to LAC demands in the FTAA negotiations. Thus, in the agricultural sector, too, the fate of the FTAA might be closely tied to the multilateral trade talks in the Doha Round.

It is worth noting, however, that the FTAA dispute over agricultural products is not identical structurally with the global dispute. This is particularly so in the case of tropical fruits where neither the EU nor Japan have to control strong producer lobbies (except, perhaps, in bananas in the EU), but the USA apparently has. In the sugar sector, too, more openness on the EU market is unlikely to give US producers a much better stance. Thus, even though the Doha Round might give US agricultural exporters a stimulus, the need for the USA to go beyond simply passing this advantage onto the LAC countries under the FTAA will still remain. That is to say that the readiness of the US administration to concede the LAC countries a better access to the North American market cannot be just linked to the results of the Doha Round, but must go beyond the multilateral talks. This is, by the way, the claim that is implicit to any FTAA concept.

Following this reasoning it is obvious that the fate of the FTAA as an equilibrated venture to cut market entry barriers across industries and countries is intimately tied to the US readiness to go ahead in resolving its own internal problems of structural adjustment and exercise discipline in the agricultural sector and regarding the anti-dumping issue. As it has been argued above, a potent phalanx of protectionists is presently blocking any such attempt on part of the administration. The arguments in favor of free trade are in the defensive, and bringing them back on track may turn out to be a Herculean task. This is particularly so because the case for protectionism appears to be deeply rooted now in ethical concerns about the ecology and human rights (labor standards), and the deep conviction of the average American to be the victim of 'unfair' foreign trade practices.

6.5   SUMMARY

The formation of the FTAA is a most ambitious regional integration project from different perspectives. It is a very complicated project, because of the 34 countries at extremely different stages of economic development, which are going to participate. And, though formally proclaimed to become a 'simple' FTA, it is in fact a highly ambitious political experiment that resumes important aspects of the concept of the New Regionalism. As such it has to reconcile important cultural, political and economic differences in the region.

Culturally, the Anglo-Protestant North meets the Ibero-Catholic South in a renewed effort to find a better way of coexistence. The issues raised by the cultural aspects of hemispheric integration do not have a place on the open agenda, but in the obscure areas of mental dissent and clandestine distrust they appear to be omnipresent. It is most important to see whether these 'background' obstacles will be overcome and the FTAA will eventually lead to a well-functioning 'All American' society.

Politically, the world hegemon (USA) meets the regional hegemon (Brazil) and it is not clear today how the future integration area will be arranged with both of them being satisfied with their distinct international aspirations. This potential area of dissent will be all the more difficult to reconcile after the political change in Brazil.

Economically, an FTA between the North and the South has a lot to offer but it also faces strongly opposing interests. The North is apparently interested in market access in the industries and services sectors of the South and pushes for tariff liberalization and the inclusion of the modern trade agenda (investment, international property rights etc.) into the negotiation process. Accepting these demands implies that the South would have to comply with open markets in its most sensitive areas. The South, in turn, is eager to break down the sophisticated US (NAFTA) fence of contingent protection and agricultural subsidies, which hinders it from exercising its own comparative advantages. Though the USA has agreed recently to talk about these issues on both the WTO and the FTAA level, it is not clear how far it is going to move.

By linking the cases of agricultural and contingent protection to the multilateral trade talks the global dimension of the FTAA project becomes openly visible. Apparently, the USA is considering a deal in the Doha Round trade talks in order to get room for maneuvering on the FTAA level. That is, it pushes for open agricultural markets in Europe and Japan, in particular. If this strategy succeeds, new opportunities for US exporters will emerge. In turn, Latin American exporters of agricultural products may find the US team in the FTAA negotiations more willing to make concessions to the Latin American claims. In the area of contingent protection (dumping) a similar situation exists. Here the US anti-dumping policies are a major stumbling bloc in the global and regional talks alike. In this case, too, the USA might be willing to accept a more disciplined anti-dumping regime in exchange for progress in its other fields of interest.

As the end of both the FTAA process and the Doha Round are scheduled for the end of 2005, it is clear that the fate of the FTAA is intimately linked to progress on the global level. This time schedule may be helpful for the FTAA talks and foster its creation as an offspring of the multilateral talks.

Currently it is not clear, however, how strong the commitment of the world's large trading nations is to agree on a generous improvement of the WTO system. Neither the EU, being heavily engaged in a complicated process of enlargement (in 2004, ten new Eastern European members are joining the Union), nor Japan, being in the midst of an oppressive deflationary spiral, appear to be especially interested in a serious program of multilateral trade liberalization. And, as far as the USA is concerned, the discussion of the national perceptions of the globalization process presented in this volume does not lend support to much optimism.

In the USA, more optimistic statements have been articulated recently. They argue that:

1. the trade policy stalemate of the late 1990s has been ended now by the new trade promotion authority given to president George W. Bush in 2001,
2. the USA has put all critical issues on the table of the Doha Round (and the FTAA).

These events are believed to be an indication that the USA is willing now to collaborate seriously on these critical issues. A positive spillover of this readiness to go ahead on the FTAA process would, therefore, be most likely. The 2002 farm bill and the recent resurgence of steel protection are played down from this perspective as tactical maneuvers by the administration with little impact on the general strategy. This strategy, more than ever, would be on free open markets.

These signs of hope notwithstanding, it may turn out that the main obstacles remaining to a substantial progress in the WTO as well as in the FTAA process may be US public opinions. On this battlefield, the future of free trade (and the FTAA) does not shine so bright as long as the present coalition against open markets does not find a courageous and persuasive response from within the country.

Under these conditions the different structures of interests on the multilateral level and in North and South America are forming substantial barriers for the successful conclusion of the FTAA negotiations in 2005. Successful, in this context, means that the future FTAA will have to be constructed in a way that resembles the basic principles of the New Regionalism (deepness, comprehensiveness and openness) thereby helping to overcome the present spaghetti bowl situation.

There is a real danger that the political dynamics of the FTAA process have grown strong enough to force the conclusion of an agreement, even if a consensus on vital elements of a sound integration framework has not been achieved. Such an 'alibi-agreement' rather than being a catalyst for regional integration, would probably do no more than obscure a still unbridgeable North–South dissent and establish an inherently ambiguous framework of action that adds to the prevailing spaghetti bowl regionalism.

In order to prevent such an outcome both sides will have to move substantially during the final negotiating rounds. But it will be up the USA to exercise prudent political leadership. That is, the USA would have to deploy its exceptional power political position carefully and with due consideration of its own obligations in the fields of contingent and agricultural protection, in particular.

At the time of finishing this book, the fate of the New American Regionalism appears to be open. Neither NAFTA nor MERCOSUR are particularly good examples of the smooth functioning of the concept of the New Regionalism along the ideas of its adherents. While NAFTA had a most promising start as far as the internal reallocation is concerned, Mexico and to some extent Canada, sailing in the lee winds of the US trade policy deadlock of the 1990s, have built up a complex web of separate regional agreements. These activities run counter to basic principles of multilateralism and GATT conform regionalism, namely the principle of non-discrimination. As many Latin American countries, too, have regressed to this strategy meanwhile, the whole region is now affected by a system of highly discriminatory and overlapping trade rules.

MERCOSUR, after having shown a good integration performance during the start-up period, fell back again to old-fashioned nationalist policies since the late 1990s. That way, the integration process became ever more undermined by protectionism and unilateral actions. Today, and despite repeated revitalization efforts, the future of MERCOSUR is in doubt.

Altogether these findings suggest that the present record of the New Regionalism in the Americas is rather ambiguous and does not support the notion of regionalism being a source of prosperity. Nevertheless, regionalism is likely to remain an important part of the world economy because it is not just economic but, to a certain extent, the response of politics to globalization. If this claim holds, the world will have to cope with it – for better or worse.

With the creation of the FTAA the idea of the New Regionalism may have another chance. It will be important not only for the Americas to use this chance, but also because the New American Regionalism will shape the global system.

NOTES

1. The US–Jordan FTA for example contains environmental and labor provisions in the main text for the first time and this approach may now serve as a blueprint for new treaties.
2. This danger has been recognized relatively early by Wyatt-Walter, who claimed that 'the proliferation of national and regional rules of origin and local content will lead to a competitive scramble' (Wyatt-Walter, 1997, 119).
3. Interpreting these US initiatives as part of a comprehensive long-term strategy is not without problems. From the preparation of the Miami Summit it is known that the FTA initiative was put on the agenda only at a very late stage and came as a surprise for most observers.
4. This point has been raised by Bélanger (1999, 99 ff.), for example, who argues that neither the hegemonic interest nor the promise of welfare effects from free trade in the region alone

could persuade Washington to follow a regional strategy that implies 'a firm commitment to a regionalist policy'. In order to make this happen, a clear strategic objective would have to exist.

5. Note that this argument was already developed after World War II, when the USA turned to Europe and Japan in order to help create strong economies (as by the Marshall plan, for example). Strong partners and open markets were supposed to be indispensable for sustained economic growth in America itself.

6. What should at least be noted is the fact that the political decision-making mechanism on weighing the political and economic arguments (which inevitably governs the FTAA process – implicitly or explicitly) is not independent from the global situation and from the kind of regional regime that will eventually be established.

7. For an analysis of the critical situation in Latin America in early 2003, and the particular impact of 11 September on the US position regarding the region, see Castañeda (2003, 67 ff.). Hufbauer/Vega-Canovas (2003) report on the US reactions with respect to NAFTA.

8. The declaration of San José and the Santiago Summit (1998) have documented the declared will of all participants to foster a single package approach. At that time the result has been celebrated in Latin America as a great success that would demonstrate the relative political strength that Latin America can exercise even in the face of the US superpower. Since then, the US (as well as many Latin American countries) went on negotiating bilateral agreements that principally run counter to the single package approach. For a critical statement see IDB, 2002, 12 ff.

9. Brazil, in turn, is anxious about 'Argentina's opportunistic behavior each time the US makes positive gestures towards hemispheric integration' (Soares de Lima, 1999, 137).

10. During the election campaign 'Lula' adhered to his long time cultivated anti-American position (and rejected the FTAA explicitly). However, the tone became more and more moderate the closer he came to power (Williamson, 2003). This observation and the experience with the new government after the first hundred days in office suggest that Lula is not going for outright confrontation. However, this observation should not be mis-interpreted. It is still likely that Brazil, under the new president, will try particularly hard to defend its specific interests in the region and internationally. The role that Brazil played at the WTO conference in Cancun in September 2003 may be a first indication of a new self-confident Brazilian strategy. The successful organization of a powerful Third World coalition against agricultural protectionism of the industrialized world and the 'new trade issues' on behalf of the Brazilian government has not only uncovered the unwillingness of the latter to agree on substantial reforms, but certainly it has encouraged the Latin American coalition in the FTAA talks.

11. It is important to note that these issues are almost identical with the multilateral agenda that has evolved out of the Tokyo and the Uruguay Rounds of multilateral trade talks and is presently negotiated in the Doha Round.

12. Note that the LDCs, too, depend on the functioning of this mechanism in the advanced economies.

13. An early and particularly useful interpretation of this process can be found in Bhagwati's model of the formation of created comparative advantages as an eco-biological process (Bhagwati, 1982).

14. According to Fischer the political dominance of this coalition in Colombia and Venezuela largely explains the limited success of the G3 initiative (Fischer, 1999, 204).

15. Experience has shown that the LDCs are eager to learn from the practices of the leading economies and are using anti-dumping procedures much more frequently now than a decade ago.

16. There are numerous investigations on the dumping issue. (For important contributions with varying emphasis on theoretical, political and empirical aspects see Finger, 1993; Hoekman/Kostecki, 2001; Messerlin, 2001; Prusa, 2001; Irwin, 2002.)

17. The Treaty of Rome (1957) has been made possible because of a deal between France and Germany on the treatment of agriculture and industry. Germany agreed to the French desire to raise permanent barriers to agricultural trade at the price of open industrial markets. The

USA at that time accepted the deal. However, during the 1980s it began to oppose the ever more rampant EU protectionism when extremely subsidized European exports began to penetrate the world markets.

18. According to Brazilian sources US NTBs cover about 60 percent of its exports, mainly in steel, textiles, frozen orange juice and sugar (Horlick/Palmer, 2001, 9).

Bibliography

Ames, Barry (2001), *The Deadlock of Democracy in Brazil*, Ann Arbor: University of Michigan Press.

Anderson, K. and H. Norheim (1993), 'From Imperial to Regional Trade Preferences: Its Effects on Europe's Intra- and Extra-Regional Trade', *Weltwirtschaftliches Archiv*, **129** (1), 78–102.

Arndt, S. (2000), 'The USA in the World Trading System', in Thomas L. Brewer and Gavin Boyd, *Globalizing America: The USA in World Integration*, Cheltenham, UK and Northampton, MA, USA: Edward Elgar, 63–82.

Averbug, A. (2002), 'The Brazilian Economy in 1994–1999: From the Real Plan to Inflation Targets', *The World Economy*, **25** (7), 925–944.

Baer, W., T. Cavalcanti and P. Silva (2001), 'Economic Integration without Policy Coordination: The Case of Mercosur', *Emerging Markets Review*, **3** (3), 269–291.

Baer, W., P. Elosegui and A. Gallo (2002), 'The Achievements and Failures of Argentina's Neo-liberal Economic Policies', *Oxford Development Studies*, **30** (1), 63-85.

Balassa, B. (1977), 'A "Stages" Approach to Comparative Advantage', *World Bank Staff Working Paper 256*, May.

Baldwin, R. E. (1995), 'A Domino Theory of Regionalism', in Richard E. Baldwin, P. Haaparanta and J. Kiander (eds), *Expanding Membership in the European Union*, Cambridge: University Press, 25–48.

Baldwin, R. E. (1997), 'The Causes of Regionalism', *The World Economy*, **20** (7), 865–888.

Baldwin, Richard E. and Christopher S. Magee (2000), *Congressional Trade Votes: From NAFTA Approval to Fast-Track Defeat*, Policy Analyses in International Economics 59, Washington DC: Institute for International Economics.

Baldwin, Richard. E., Daniel Cohen, André Sapir and Anthony Venables (eds) (1999), *Market Integration, Regionalism and the Global Economy*, Cambridge: University Press.

Banco de Mexico (2002), Economic and Financial Indicators, Balance of Payments, www.banxico.org.

Barry, T. (1995), *Zapata's Revenge, Free Trade and the Farm Crisis in Mexico*, Boston: South End Press.

Baucus, Max (2002), 'The Trade Act of 2002', Keynote speech at a conference on Trade Policy in 2002, Institute for International Economics, www.iie.com/papers.

Bayard, T. O. and K. A. Elliot (1992), 'Aggressive Unilateralism and Section 301: Market Opening or Market Closing?' *The World Economy*, **15**, 685–706.

Bayer, S. and D. Cansier (1998), 'Methodisch abgesicherte inter-generationelle Diskontierung am Beispiel des Klimaschutzes', *Zeitschrift für Umweltpolitik und Umweltrecht (Journal of Environmental Law and Policy)*, **1**, 113–132.

Beaulieu, E. (2000), 'The Canada – U.S. Free Trade Agreement and Labour's Market Adjustment in Canada', *Canadian Journal of Economics*, **33** (2), 540–563.

Beckman, Steve (1998), *Statement on the US and its Trade Deficit*, Subcommittee on International Economic Policy and Trade, Committee on International Relations, United States House of Representatives, 22 July.

Bélanger, L. (1999), 'U.S. Foreign Policy and the Regionalist Option in the Americas', in Gordon Mace, Louis Bélanger and Contributors, *The Americas in Transition, The Contours of Regionalism*, Boulder and London: Lynne Rienner Publishers, 95–109.

Ben-David, D., H. Nordström and A. L. Winters (1999), 'Trade, Income Disparity and Poverty', *WTO, Special Studies 5*, Geneva.

Bende-Nabende, Antony (1999), *FDI, Regionalism, Government Policy and Endogenous Growth*, Aldershot: Ashgate.

Bergoeing, R., P. J. Kehoe and R. Soto (2002), 'Policy-Driven Productivity Growth in Chile and Mexico in the 1980s and 1990s', *The American Economic Review*, **92** (2), 16–21.

Bergsten, C. F. (1997), 'Open Regionalism', *Working Paper 97-3*, Institute for International Economics.

Bergsten, C. F. (2002), 'A Renaissance for United States Trade Policy?' *Foreign Affairs*, **81** (6), 86–98.

Berthold, N. (1996), 'Regionalismus, Multilateralismus und GATT', in Michael Frenkel and Dieter Bender (Hrsg.), *GATT und neue Welthandelsordnung*, Wiesbaden: Gabler.

Bhagwati, J. N. (1982), 'Shifting Comparative Advantage, Protectionist Demands and Policy Response', in Jagdish N. Bhagwati (ed.), *Import Competition and Response*, Chicago and London: University of Chicago Press, 153–195.

Bhagwati, J. N. (1999), 'Regionalism and Multilateralism: An Overview', in Jagdish N. Bhagwati, Pravin Krishna and Arvind Panagariya (eds) (1999), *Trading Blocs, Alternative Approaches to Analyzing Preferential Trade Agreements*, Cambridge and London: The MIT Press.

Bhagwati, J. N. and A. Panagariya (1999), 'Preferential Trading Areas and Multilateralism – Strangers, Friends, or Foes', in Jagdish N. Bhagwati, Pravin Krishna and Arvind Panagariya (eds), *Trading Blocs, Alternative Approaches to Analyzing Preferential Trade Agreements*, Cambridge and London: The MIT Press, 33–100.

Blanco, H. and J. Zabludovsky (2002), *Alcances y límites de la negociación del ALCA y escenarios de su interacción con las negociaciones multilaterales*, Integration and Regional Programs Department, Inter-American Development Bank, Washington, DC.

Blanes, J. V. and C. Martín (2000), 'The Nature and Causes of Intra-Industry Trade: Back to the Comparative Advantage Explanation? The Case of Spain', *Weltwirtschaftliches Archiv*, **136** (3), 423–441.

Borner, Silvio (1986), *Internationalization of Industry. An Assessment in the Light of a Small Open Economy (Switzerland)*, Berlin: Springer.

Bresser-Pereira, L. C. (2002), 'Latin America's quasi-stagnation', in Paul Davidson (ed.), *A Post Keynesian Perspective on 21st Century Economic Problems*, Cheltenham, UK and Northampton, MA, USA: Edward Elgar, 1–28.

Brewer, Thomas L. and Gavin Boyd (eds) (2000), *Globalizing America, The USA in World Integration*, Cheltenham, UK and Northampton, MA, USA: Edward Elgar.

Brown, D. K., A. V. Deardorff and R. M. Stern (1992), 'A North American Free Trade Agreement: Analytical Issues and a Computational Assessment', *The World Economy*, **15** (1), 11–29.

Brown, D. K., A. V. Deardorff and R. M. Stern (2003), 'The Effects of Multinational Production on Wages and Working Conditions in Developing Countries', *NBER Working Paper 9669*, www.nber.org.

Buckley, Peter J. and Marc Casson (1976), *The Future of the Multinational Enterprises*, London and Basingstoke: Macmillan.

Burfisher, M. E., S. Robinson and K. Thierfelder (2001), 'The Impact of NAFTA on the United States', *Journal of Economic Perspectives*, **15** (1), 125–144.

Casson, Marc and Associates (1986), *Multinationals and World Trade. Vertical Integration and the Division of World Labor in World Industries*, London: Allen & Unwin.

Castañeda, J. G. (2003), 'The Forgotten Relationship', *Foreign Affairs*, **82** (3), 67–81.

Caves, Richard E. (1982), *Multinational Enterprises and Economic Analysis*, Cambridge: Cambridge University Press (second edition 1996).

CEPAL, UN (2001a), *Panorama de la Inserción Internacional de América Latina y el Caribe, 1999–2000*, Santiago de Chile.

CEPAL, UN (2001b), *Estudio Económico de America Latina y el Caribe, 2000–2001*, Santiago de Chile.

CEPAL, UN (2002a), *Panorama de la Inserción Internacional de America Latina y el Caribe, 2001–2002*, Santiago de Chile.

CEPAL, UN (2002b), *Globalización y Desarollo*, Santiago de Chile.

CEPAL, UN (2003a), *Panorama de la Inserción Internacional de América Latina y el Caribe, 2001–2002*, Santiago de Chile.

CEPAL, UN (2003b), *La Inversión Extranjera en América Latina y el Caribe – in 2002*, Santiago de Chile.

Chambers, Edward J. and Peter H. Smith (eds) (2002), *NAFTA in the New Millenium*, Center for U.S.–Mexican Studies, University of California, San Diego: The University of Alberta Press.

Chenery, Hollis B., Sherman Robinson and Moshe Syrquin (1986), *Industrialization and Growth. A Comparative Study*, Oxford University Press.

Child, Jack (1985), *Geopolitics and Conflict in South America: Quarrels among Neighbors*, New York: Praeger.

Clausing, K. A. (2001), 'Trade Creation and Trade Diversion in the Canada–United States Free Trade Agreement', *Canadian Journal of Economics*, **34** (3), 677–696.

Chudnovsky, D. and A. López (2002), *Integración Regional e Inversión Extranjera Directa: El Caso del MERCOSUR*, BID-INTAL.

Clark, Colin (1940), *The Conditions of Economic Progress*, London: Macmillan.

Cohen, R. (1994), 'Pacific Unions: A Reappraisal of the Theory that Democracies do not go to War with Each Other', *Review of International Studies*, **20** (3), July.

Comisión Nacional de Inversiones Extranjeras (2002), *Informe Estadístico sobre el Comportamiento de la Inversión Extranjera Directa en Mejico* (Enero–Marzo de 2002), Mexico.

Connolly, M. and J. Gunther (1999), 'Mercosur: Implications for Growth in Member Countries', *Current Issues in Economics and Finance*, **5** (7), 1–6.

Cooper, R. E. and B. F. Massell (1965), 'A New Look at Customs Union Theory', *Economic Journal*, **75**, 742–747.

Cooper, Richard N. (1968), *The Economics of Interdependence*, New York: Columbia University Press.

Cooper, Richard N. (1980), *The Economics of Interdependence: Economic Policy in the Atlantic Community*, New York: Columbia University Press.

Cooper, R. N. (1986), 'Economic Interdependence and Foreign Policy in the Seventies', in Richard N. Cooper (ed.), *Economic Policy in an Interdependent World Economy: Essays in World Economics*, Cambridge, MA: Cambridge University Press, 1–22.

Crabb, C. V. and P. M. Holt (1992), *Invitation to Struggle. Congress, the President, and Foreign Policy*, 4th ed., Washington, DC: CQ Press.

Deardorff, A.V. (1982), 'The General Validity of the Heckscher–Ohlin Theorem', *The American Economic Review*, 72, September, 683–694.

Deardorff, Alan V. and Robert M. Stern (1991), *Computational Analysis of Global Trading Arrangements*, New York, Studies in International Trade Policy, Ann Arbor: University of Michigan Press.

De Luna-Martinez, J. (2000), 'Management and Resolution of Banking Crisis: Lessons from the Republic of Korea and Mexico', *World Bank, Discussion Paper 413*, March.

Devlin, R. and A. Estevadeordal (2001a), 'What's New in the New Regionalism in the Americas?', *INTAL-ITD-STA*, Working Paper 6.

Devlin, R. and A. Estevadeordal (2001b), 'Growth is good for the Poor', *Policy Research Working Paper 2587*, Washington, DC: World Bank.

Devlin, R. and R. French-Davis (1998), 'Towards an Evaluation of Regional Integration in Latin America in the 1990s', *The World Economy*, 21 (2), 261–290.

Dillinger, W. R. and S. B. Webb (1999), 'Fiscal Management in Federal Democracies: Argentina and Brazil', *World Bank Working Paper 2121*, Washington, DC.

Dinopoulos, E. and M. E. Kreinin (1988), 'Effects of the U.S.–Japan Auto VER on European Prices and U.S. Welfare', *The Review of Economics and Statistics*, 70 (August), 484–491.

Dollar, D. and A. Kraay (2002), 'Spreading the Wealth', *Foreign Affairs*, 81 (1), 120–133.

Dunning, John H. (1981), *International Production and the Multinational Enterprise*, London et al.: Allen & Unwin.

Dussel Peters, Enrique (2000), *Polarizing Mexico, The Impact of Liberalization Strategy*, Boulder and London: Lynne Rienner Publishers.

Dymond, W. A. (2001), 'The Regional Dynamics of FTAA Negotiations', *IDB Regional Policy Dialogue*, Base Documents, www.iadb.org.

ECLAC, UN (2001), *Latin America and the Caribbean in the World Economy 1999–2000*, Santiago de Chile.

Edwards, Sebastian (1995), *Crisis and Reform in Latin America, From Despair to Hope*, Washington, DC: The World Bank.

Egner, Erich (1935), *Blüte und Verfall der Wirtschaft: Eine Theorie der wirtschaftlichen Entwicklung,* Leipzig: Meiner.

Eichengreen, B. and A. M. Taylor (2003), 'The Monetary Consequences of a Free Trade Area of the Americas', *NBER Working Paper Series,* Working Paper 9666.

Estevadeordal, A. (1999), 'Negotiating Preferential Market Access: The Case of NAFTA', *INTAL Working Paper 3,* June.

Estevadeordal, A., J. Goto and R. Saez (2000), 'The New Regionalism in the Americas: The Case of MERCOSUR', *Working Paper 5,* INTAL-ITD, April.

Esty, Daniel C. (1994), *Greening the GATT. Trade, Environment and the Future,* Washington, DC: Institute for International Economics.

Esty, D. C. (2001), 'Bridging the Trade–Environment Divide', *The Journal of Economic Perspectives,* **15** (3), 113–130.

Ethier, W. J. (1998), 'The New Regionalism', *The Economic Journal,* **108,** July, 1149–1161.

Faust, J. (2003), 'Brazil: Resisting Globalization Through Federalism?' in: Barrios, Harald, Martin Beck, Andreas Boekh, Klaus Segbers (eds), *Resistance to Globalization: Political Struggle and Cultural Resilience in the Middle East, Russia, and Latin America,* Münster et al.: LIT Verlag, 158-177.

Fawcett, L. (1997), 'Regionalism in Historical Perspective', in Louise Fawcett and Andrew Hurrell (eds), *Regionalism in World Politics: Regional Organization and International Order,* Oxford: University Press, 9–36.

Feenstra, R. C. (1988), 'Quality Change under Trade Restraints on Japanese Autos', *Quarterly Journal of Economics,* **103** (1), 131–146.

Ferrantino, M. J. (2001), 'Evidence of Trade, Income, and Employment Effects of NAFTA', *Industry Trade and Technology Review,* USITC, December, 1–8.

Finger, Michael J. (ed.) (1993), *Antidumping: How it Works and Who Gets Hurt,* Ann Arbor: University of Michigan Press.

Fischer, K. P. (1999), 'Business and Integration in the Americas: Competing Points of View', in Gordon Mace, Louis Bélanger and Contributors, *The Americas in Transition, The Contours of Regionalism,* Boulder and London: Lynne Rienner Publishers, 195–218.

Fischer, Stanley, Rudiger Dornbusch and Richard Schmalensee (1988), *Economics,* New York: McGraw-Hill.

Fishlow, Albert (ed.) (1994), *Miracle or Design? Lessons from the East Asian Experience,* Policy Essay 11, Washington, DC: Overseas Development Council,

Francois, J. F., B. McDonald and H. Nordström (1994), 'The Uruguay Round: A Global General Equilibrium Assessment', *GATT Working Paper*, Geneva.

Frey, Bruno S. (1985), *Internationale Politische Ökonomie*, München: Vahlen.

Fritsch, B. (1995), 'On the Way to Ecologically Sustainable Economic Growth', *International Political Science Review*, **16** (4), 361–374.

Gallaway, M. P., B. Blonigen and J. E. Flynn (1999), 'Welfare Costs of U.S. Anti-Dumping and Countervailing Duty Laws', *Journal of International Economics*, **49** (12), 211–244.

Gilpin, Robert (2000), *The Challenge of Global Capitalism, The World Economy in the 21st Century*, Princeton: Princeton University Press.

Greenaway, D. and R. C. Hine (1991), 'Intra-Industry Specialization, Trade Expansion and Adjustment in the European Economic Space', *The Journal of Common Market Studies*, **24** (6), 603–622.

Greenaway, David and Chris Milner (1986), *The Economics of Intra-industry Trade*, Oxford: Basil Blackwell.

Gresser, E. (2002) 'Toughest on the Poor, America's Flawed Tariff System', *Foreign Affairs*, **81** (6), 9–14.

Grimwade, Nigel (1996), *International Trade Policy*, London and New York: Routledge.

Grossman, G. and E. Helpman (1995), 'The Politics of Free Trade Agreements', *The American Economic Review*, **105** (9), 667–690.

Grossman, Gene M. and Elhanan Helpman (2002), *Interest Groups and Trade Policy*, Princeton and Oxford: Princeton University Press.

Grossman, G. and A. B. Krueger (1995), 'Economic Growth and the Environment', *Quarterly Journal of Economics*, **110** (2), 353–377.

Hakim, Peter and Robert E. Litan (eds) (2002), *The Future of North American Integration, Beyond NAFTA*, Washington, DC: Brookings Institution Press.

Hanson, G. H., R. J. Mataloni Jr. and M. J Slaughter (2001), 'Expansion Strategies of US Multinational Firms', *BEA Working Paper*, April.

Harris, Richard G. (2001), 'North American Economic Integration: Issues and Research Agenda', *Discussion Paper 10*, Industry Canada Research Publications Program, April.

Harrison, A. and G. Hanson (1999), 'Who Gains from Trade? Some Remaining Puzzles', *Journal of Development Economics*, **59** (1), 125–154.

Harrison, Lawrence D. (1997), *The Pan-American Dream*, Boulder: Westview Press.

Hauser, H. and T. Zimmermann (2001), 'Regionalismus oder Multilateralismus', *Die Volkswirtschaft*, **74** (5), 4–8.

Helpman, Elhanan and Paul R. Krugman (1989), *Trade Policy and Market Structure*, Cambridge, MA: MIT Press.

Hesse, Helmut (1967), *Strukturwandlungen im Welthandel*, Tübingen: Mohr.

Hesse, H. (1974), 'Hypotheses for the Explanation of Trade between Industrial Countries, 1953–1970, in, Herbert Giersch (ed.), *The International Division of Labour: Problems and Perspectives*, Tübingen, 39–59.

Hesse, H. (1984), 'Aussenwirtschaft und zukünftiges Wirtschaftswachstum', in Erich Helmstädter (Hrsg.), *Die Bedingungen des Wirtschaftswachstums in Vergangenheit und Zukunft*, Tübingen: Mohr, 153–166.

Hesse, Helmut, Horst Keppler and Heinz G. Preusse (1985), *Internationale Interdependenzen im weltwirtschaftlichen Entwicklungsprozess*, Reports of the Ibero-America Institute for Economic Research, 22, Georg-August-University Göttingen, Göttingen: Schwartz & Co.

Hettne, B. (1999), 'Globalization and the New Regionalism: The Second Great Transformation', in Björn Hettne, Andras Inotai and Osvaldo Sunkel (eds), *Globalism and the New Regionalism*, London and New York: Macmillan, 1–24.

Hillberry, R. and C. McDaniel (2002), 'A Decomposition of North American Trade Growth since NAFTA', *International Economic Review, USITC Publication* 3527, May/June, 1–5.

Hillman, A. L. (1982), 'Declining Industries and Political-support Protectionist Motives', *The American Economic Review*, 72 (5), 1180–1187.

Hirsch, Seev (1977), *Rich Man's, Poor Man's, and Every Man's Goods: Aspects of Industrialization*, Tübingen: Mohr.

Hiscox, Michael J. (2002), *International Trade and Political Conflict: Commerce, Coalitions and Mobility*, Princeton and Oxford: Princeton University Press.

Hoekman, Bernhard M. and Michael M. Kostecki (2001), *The Political Economy of the World Trading System, The WTO and Beyond*, 2nd ed., Oxford: University Press.

Hoffmann, Walter G. (1931), *Stadien und Typen der Industrialisierung*, Jena.

Horlick, G. N. and C. R. Palmer (2001), 'The Negotiation of a Free Trade Area of the Americas', *IDB Regional Policy Dialogue*, www.iadb.org.

Hufbauer, G. C. (1999), 'World Trade after Seattle: Implications for the United States', *International Economics Policy Briefs*, No. 99-10, Washington, DC: Institute for International Economics.

Hufbauer, Gary C. and Jeffrey J. Schott (1994), *Western Hemisphere Economic Integration*, Washington, DC: Institute for International Economics, July.

Hufbauer, G. C. and G. Vega-Canóvas (2003), 'Whither NAFTA: A Common Frontier?' in Peter Andreas and Thomas J. Biersteker (eds), *Inte-*

gration and Exclusion in a New Security Context, Routledge, forthcoming.

Hurrell, A. (1997), 'Regionalism in Theoretical Perspective', in Louise Fawcett and Andrew. Hurrell (eds), *Regionalism in World Politics*, Oxford: University Press, 37–73.

Hurrell, A. and L. Fawcett (1997), 'Conclusion: Regionalism and International Order?' in Louise Fawcett and Andrew. Hurrell (eds), *Regionalism in World Politics*, Oxford: University Press, 309–327.

Hymer, Stephen H. (1960), *The International Operations of National Firms: A Study of Direct Foreign Investment*, Ph.D. Diss., MIT (published 1976).

Ibarra-Yunez, A. (2003), 'Spaghetti Regionalism or Strategic Foreign Trade: Some Evidence for Mexico', *NBER Working Paper Series*, Working Paper 9692.

IDB (Inter-American Development Bank) (1998), 'Integration and Trade in the Americas', *Department of Integration and Regional Programs, Periodic Note*, Washington, DC, August.

IDB (1999), 'Integration and Trade in the Americas, Special Report', *Department of Integration and Regional Programs, Periodic Note*, Washington, DC, February.

IDB (2001), *The Business of Growth, Economic and Social Progress in Latin America*, 2001 Report, Washington, DC: John Hopkins University Press.

IDB (2002), *Beyond Borders, The New Regionalism in Latin America, Economic and Social Progress in Latin America*, 2002 Report, Washington, DC: John Hopkins University Press.

IDB – INTAL (1999), *MERCOSUR Report No. 5*, 1998–1999, Buenos Aires.

IDB – INTAL (2000), *MERCOSUR Report No. 6*, 1999–2000, Buenos Aires.

IDB – INTAL (2001), *MERCOSUR Report No. 7*, 2000–2001, Buenos Aires

Instituto Nacional de Estadística Geografica e Informatica (INEGI) (1999), 'Industria Maquiladora de Exportación', *Estadísticas economicas INEGI*, Mexico D.F., Julio.

Irwin, Douglas A. (2002), *Free Trade under Fire*, Princeton: Princeton University Press.

Janovichina, E., A. Nicita and J. Soloaga (2002), 'Trade Reform and Poverty: The Case of Mexico', *The World Economy*, 25 (6), 945-972.

Johnson, H. G. (1965), 'An Economic Theory of Protectionism, Tariff Bargaining and the Formation of Customs Unions', *Journal of Political Economy*, 73 (3), 256–283.

Kaltenthaler, Karl and Frank O. Mora, (2002), 'Explaining Latin American Economic Integration: The Case of Mercosur', *Review of International Political Economy*, 9 (1), 72–97.

Keohane, Robert O. (1984), *After Hegemony*, Princeton: University Press.

Keohane, Robert O. and Joseph S. Nye (1977), *Power and Interdependence: World Politics in Transition*, Boston: Little, Brown and Company.

Kerremans, B. (2000a), 'The Links between Domestic Political Forces, Inter-Bloc Dynamics and the Multilateral Trading System', in Bart Kerremans and Bob Switky (eds), *The Political Importance of Regional Trading Blocs*, Barlington: Ashgate, 119–167.

Kerremans, B. (2000b), 'Competition and Cooperation Between Blocs: The Case of North America and Europe', in Bart Kerremans and Bob Switky (eds), *The Political Importance of Regional Trading Blocs*, Barlington: Ashgate, 169–212.

Kornis, M. (2000), 'Delayed Implementation of NAFTA Provision to Open US Roads to Mexican Trucks', *International Economic Review*, USITC, February/March, 5–6.

Kornis, M. (2002), 'Mexican Trucks Gain Access to U.S. Highways', *International Economic Review*, USITC, March/April, 1–5.

Krasner, Stephen D. (ed.) (1983), *International Regimes*, Ithaca, NY: Cornell University Press.

Kravis, J. B. (1970), 'Trade as a Handmaiden of Growth', *Economic Journal*, **80** (320), 850–872.

Krueger, A. O. (1974), 'The Political Economy of Rent-Seeking', *The American Economic Review*, **64** (3), 291–303.

Krueger, Anne O. (1977), *Growth, Distortions, and Patterns of Trade among Many Countries*, Princeton Studies in International Finance 40, Princeton University Press.

Krueger, A. O. (1985), 'Import Substitution versus Export Promotion: Why Outward-oriented Policies are Better', *Finance and Development*, **72** (6), 20–23.

Krueger, Anne O. (1995), *American Trade Policy: A Tragedy in the Making*, Washington, DC: AEI Press.

Krueger, A. O. (1997), 'Free Trade Areas Versus Customs Unions', *Journal of Development Economics*, **54** (1), 169–187.

Krueger, A. O. (1999), 'Are Preferential Trade Agreements Trade-Liberalizing or Protectionist?', *Journal of Economic Perspectives*, **13** (4), 105–124.

Krueger, A. O. and A. Tornell (1999), 'The Role of Bank Restructuring in Recovering from Crisis: Mexico 1995–98', *NBER Working Paper* 7042, March.

Langhammer, R. (1992), 'The Developing Countries and Regionalism', *Journal of Common Market Studies*, **30** (2), 211–231.

Langhammer, R. (2003), 'Alternative Integrationskonzepte: theoretische Begründung, empirische Befunde und pragmatische Implikationen', in: Dieter Cassel and Paul J. J. Welfens (eds), *Regionale Integration und*

Osterweiterung der Europäischen Union, Schriften zu Ordnungsfragen der Wirtschaft, Band 72, Stuttgart, 249-266.

Langhammer, R., D. Piazolo and H. Siebert (2002), 'Assessing Proposals for a Transatlantic Free Trade Area', *Aussenwirtschaft*, **57** (2), 161–185.

Lash III, William H. (1998), *U.S. International Trade Regulation. A Primer*, Washington, DC: The AEI Press.

Lawrence, Robert Z. (1996), *Regionalism, Multilateralism, and Deeper Integration*, Washington, DC: Institute for International Economics.

Lewis, A. W. (1954), 'Economic Development with Unlimited Supplies of Labour', *Manchester School of Economic and Social Studies*, **22**, 139–191.

Lin, J. Y. and J. B. Nugent (1995), 'Institutions and Economic Development, in Jere Behrman and T. N. Srinivasan (eds), *Handbook of Development Economics*, Amsterdam: North Holland.

Lindbeck, A. (1982), 'Emerging Arteriosclerosis of the Western Economies: Consequencies for the LDCs', *India International Centre Quarterly*, **1**, 37–52.

Lindert, P. and J. Williamson (2001), 'Does Globalization Make the World More Unequal?' *National Bureau of Economic Research Working Paper*, 8228.

Lloyd, P. (1992), 'Regionalism and World Trade', *OECD Economic Studies*, 18, Spring.

López-Córdova, J. E. (2001), 'NAFTA and the Mexican Economy: Analytical Issues and Lessons for the FTAA', *INTAL, ITD-STA Occasional Paper* 9, July.

Lübbe, H. (1986), 'Ursprung und Folgen der Wohlfahrt', *Frankfurter Allgemeine Zeitung*, 12 December.

Mace, G. (1999), 'The Origins, Nature, and Scope of the Hemispheric Project', in Gordon Mace, Louis Bélanger and Contributors, *The Americas in Transition, The Contours of Regionalism*, Boulder and London: Lynne Rienner Publishers, 19–36.

Mace, G. and L. Bélanger (1999a), ''Hemispheric Regionalism in Perspective', in Gordon Mace, Louis Bélanger and Contributors, *The Americas in Transition, The Contours of Regionalism*, Boulder and London: Lynne Rienner Publishers, 1–16.

Mace, G. and L. Bélanger (1999b), The Structural Contexts of Hemispheric Regionalism: Power, Trade, Political Culture, and Economic Development', in Gordon Mace, Louis Bélanger and Contributors, *The Americas in Transition, The Contours of Regionalism*, Boulder and London, Lynne Rienner Publishers, 37–67.

McNay, D. and L. Polly (2000), 'Mexico's Emergence as a Global Automotive Production Center Drives Trade and Investment', *Industry Trade and Technology Review*, USITC, October, 19–23.

Meade, James E. (1955), *The Theory of Customs Unions*, Amsterdam: North Holland.

Mena, R. (1999), 'Weak Public Support for NAFTA even During Boom', *The News*, 10 February.

Messerlin, Patrick A. (2001), *Measuring the Costs for Protection in Europe*, Washington, DC: Institute for International Economics.

Michaely, M. (1981), 'Income Levels and the Structure of Trade', in Sven Grassman and Eric Lindberg (eds), *The World Economic Order. Past and Prospects*, London and Basingstoke: Macmillan, 121–161.

Miller, E. (2002), 'The Outlier Sectors: Areas of Non-Free Trade in the North American Free Trade Agreement', *IDB, INTAL-ITD-STA Working Paper* 10.

Ministerial Declaration of Quito (2002), *Seventh Meeting of Ministers of Trade of the Hemisphere*, Quito, Ecuador, November, www.ftaa-alca.org.

Mistry, P. S. (1999), 'The New Regionalism: Impediment or Spur to Future Multilateralism?, in Björn Hettne, Andras Inotai and Osvaldo Sunkel (eds), *Globalism and the New Regionalism*, London and New York: Macmillan, 116–154.

Mittleman, J. H. (1996), 'Rethinking the "New Regionalism" in the Context of Globalization', *Global Governance*, **2** (May–August), 189–213.

Mohs, Ralf-M. (1983), *Exporte, komparative Vorteile und wirtschaftliche Entwicklung in den Schwellenländern*, Reports of the Ibero-America Institute for Economic Research, 21, Georg-August-University Göttingen, Göttingen: Schwartz & Co.

Molineu, Harold (1986), *U.S. Policy toward Latin America: From Regionalism to Globalism*, Boulder: Westview Press.

Moran, T. H. (1985), 'Multinational Corporations and the Developing Countries: An Analytical Overview', in Theodore H. Moran (ed.), *Multinational Corporations, The Political Economy of Foreign Direct Investment*, Lexington, MA: Lexington Books.

Morley, Samuel, Roberto Machado and Stefano Pettinato (1999), *Indexes of Structural Reforms in Latin America*, Series Reformas Economicas 12, ECLAC.

Morse, Edward L. (1976), *Modernization and the Transformation of International Relations*, New York: The Free Press.

Mortimore, M. (1998), 'Corporate Strategies and Regional Integration Schemes in Developing Countries: The Case of NAFTA and MERCOSUR Automobile Industries', *Science, Technology, and Development*, **16** (August), 1–31.

Mosley, P. (2000), 'Globalization, Economic Policy and Convergence', *The World Economy*, **23** (5), 613–634.

Mundell, R. (1957), 'International Trade and Factor Mobility', *The American Economic Review*, **67** (3), 321–335.

Mussa, Michael (2002), *Argentina and the Fund: From Triumph to Tragedy*, Washington, DC: Institute for International Economics

Myint, H. (1958), 'The Classical Theory of International Trade and the Underdeveloped Countries', *The Economic Journal*, **68** (June), 318–319.

Nau, Henry R. (1995), *Trade and Security, U.S. Policies at Cross-Purposes*, Washington, DC: The AEI Press.

Nguyen, T., C. Perroni and R. Wigle (1993), 'An Evaluation of the Draft Final Act of the Uruguay Round', *The Economic Journal*, **103**, 1540–1549.

Nicolini, Juan Pablo, Josefina Posadas, Juan Sanguinetti, and Mariano Tommasi (2002), *Decentralization, Fiscal Discipline in Sub-National Governments and the Bailout Problem: The Case of Argentina*, Washington, DC: Inter-American Development Bank.

Nowak-Lehmann D., Felicitas and Inmaculada Martínez-Zarzoso (2003), 'Would MERCOSUR's Exports to the EU Profit from Trade Liberalization? Some General Insights and a Simulation Study for Argentina', Ibero-America Institute for Economic Research, Georg-August-University Göttingen, *Discussion Paper* 92, May.

Nunnenkamp, P. (1997), 'Winners and Losers in the Global Economy: Recent Trends in the International Division of Labor, Major Implications and Critical Policy Challenges', *German Yearbook of International Law*, **39**, 42–81.

Nunnenkamp, P. (2000), 'Globalisierung der Autoindustrie: Neue Standorte auf dem Vormarsch, traditionelle Anbieter unter Druck?' *Kieler Arbeitspapier* 1002, September.

Nunnenkamp, P. (2002), 'Wie gut gerüstet ist Mexiko für die wirtschaftliche Globalisierung?', *Lateinamerika Analysen*, **2** (June), 29–54.

Nunnenkamp, Peter, Erich Gundlach and Jamuna P. Agarwal (1994), *Globalisation of Production and Markets*, Kieler Studien 262, Tübingen: Mohr.

Nye Jr., Joseph S. (2002), *The Paradox of American Power. Why the World's only Superpower can't go it Alone*, Oxford: University Press.

OECD (1997), *Review of Agricultural Policies in Mexico*, Paris.

OECD (2002), *Economic Outlook*, 72, Paris.

O'Keefe, T. A. (2001), 'Estados Unidos de América y su posición frente al ALCA', *Cuaderno de Negocios Internacionales e Integración*, **33-34-35**, Universidad Catolica de Montevideo, 8–14.

O'Keefe, Thomas A. (2002), *Latin American Trade Agreements*, Ardsley: Transnational Publishers.

Olson, M. (1982), *The Rise and Decline of Nations*, New Haven and London: Yale University Press.

Padoan, P. C. (2001), 'Political Economy of New Regionalism and World Governance', in Mario Teló (ed.), *European Union and New Regionalism. Regional Actors and Global Governance in a Post Hegemonic Era*, Aldershot: Ashgate, 39–58.

Panagariya, A. (1999), 'The Regionalism Debate: An Overview', *The World Economy*, **22** (1), 477–511.

Pastor, Robert A. (2001), *Toward a North American Community, Lessons from the Old World for the New*, Washington, DC: Institute for International Economics.

Pastor, M. and C. Wise (2001), 'From Poster Child to Basket Case', *Foreign Affairs*, **80** (6), 60–72.

Paunovic, Igor (2000), *Growth and Reforms in Latin America and the Caribbean in the 1990s*, Serie Reformas Económicas 70, ECLAC.

Peña, F. (1998), 'MERCOSUR – un projecto estrategico viable?' (unpublished).

Peña, F. (1999), 'Broadening and Deepening: Striking the Right Balance', in Riordan Roett (ed.), *MERCOSUR: Regional Integration, World Markets*, Boulder and London: Lynne Rienner Publishers, 49–61.

Perkins, Dwight H., Steven Radelet, Donald R. Snodgrass, Malcolm Gillis and Michael Roemer (2001), *Economics of Development*, 5th ed., New York and London: Norton.

Perroni, C. and J. Walley (2000), 'The New Regionalism: Trade Liberalization or Insurance?' *Canadian Journal of Economics*, **33** (1), February, 1–24.

Piazolo, D. (1996), 'Die Pläne für eine Transatlantische Freihandelszone: Chancen, Risiken und Alternativen', *Die Weltwirtschaft*, 1, 103–116.

Porter, Michael, E. (1991), *The Competitive Advantage of Nations*, New York: Free Press.

Presidencia de la Republica (1999), *5. Informe del Gobierno*, Mexico DF.

Preusse, Heinz G. (1991), *Handelspessimismus – alt und neu*, Tübingen: Mohr.

Preusse, H. G. (1994), 'Regional Integration in the Nineties. Stimulation or Threat to the Multilateral Trading System?' *Journal of World Trade*, **28** (4), 147–164.

Preusse, H. G. (1996a), 'Die Welthandelsorganisation (WTO) und die geistigen Eigentumsrechte', *Aussenwirtschaft*, **51** (1), 27–50.

Preusse, H. G. (1996b), 'Change in Development Strategies in Latin America – Another Transitory Move Towards an Open Market System?' in Franz

Peter Lang and Renate Ohr (Hrsg.), *Openness and Development*, Heidelberg: Physika, 133–164.

Preusse, H. G. (2000), 'Sechs Jahre Nordamerikanisches Freihandelsabkommen (NAFTA) – eine Bestandsaufnahme', *Aussenwirtschaft*, **55** (3), 333–370.

Preusse, H. G. (2001), 'Mercosur – Another Failed Move Towards Regional Integration?' *The World Economy*, **24** (7), 911–931.

Preusse, H. G. (2004), 'The Future of MERCOSUR', in Sidney Weintraub, Alan M. Rugman and Gavin Boyd (eds), *Free Trade in the Americas*, Cheltenham, UK and Northampton, MA, USA: Edward Elgar, Chapter 6, forthcoming.

Prusa, Thomas J. (2001), 'On the Spread and Impact of Anti-dumping', *Canadian Journal of Economics*, **34** (3), 591–611.

Reuvany, R. and W. R. Thompson (2000), 'Trade, Regionalization, and Tariffs: The Correlation of Openness in the American Long Run', in Bart Kerremans and Bob Switky (eds), *The Political Importance of Regional Trading Blocks*, Aldershot: Ashgate, 55–83.

Reynolds, C. W. (1997), 'Open Regionalism, Lessons from America for East Asia', *Kellogg Institute, Working Paper* 247, August.

Riley, R. (1999), 'NAFTA: The U.S. Perspective', in Peter Coffey, J. Colin Dodds, Enrique Lazcano and Robert Riley (eds), *NAFTA – Past, Present and Future*, Boston, Dordrecht and London: Kluwer Academic Publishers, 113–168.

Robertson, R. (2000), 'Trade Liberalization and Wage Inequality: Lessons from the Mexican Experience', *The World Economy*, **23** (6), 827–849.

Robson, Peter (1998), *The Economics of International Integration*, 4th ed., London and New York: Routledge.

Rodrik, D. (2000), 'Trade Policy Reform as Institutional Reform', *IDB Regional Policy Dialogue*, Base Documents, www.iadb.org.

Roett, Riordan (ed.) (1999), *MERCOSUR: Regional Integration, World Markets*, Boulder and London: Lynne Rienner Publishers.

Romalis, J. (2002), 'NAFTA's Impact on North American Trade', *University of Chicago GSB*, July.

Rosenberg, Nathan and L. E. Birdzell (1986), *How the West Grew Rich, The Economic Transformation of the Industrial World*, London: I. B. Tauris Publishers.

Rostow, Walt W. (1960), *Stages of Economic Growth*, New York: Cambridge University Press.

Ruggie, J. G. (1975), 'International Responses to Technology: Concepts and Trends', *International Organization*, **29** (3), 557–584.

Rugman, Alan M. (ed.) (1982), *New Theories of the Multinational Enterprise*, London and New York: Croom Helm.

Salazar-Xirinachs, José M. and Maryse Robert (eds) (2001), *Toward Free Trade in the Americas*, Washington, DC: Brookings Institution Press.

Santos, L. E. (1995), 'Trade Politics of the American Congress', *Journal of World Trade*, **29** (6), 73–78.

Sapir, A. (1998), 'The Political Economy of EC Regionalism', *European Economic Review*, **42** (3-5), 717–732.

Schiff, M. (2002), 'Chile's Trade and Regional Integration Policy: An Assessment', *The World Economy*, **25** (7), 973–990.

Schirm, Stefan (1999), *Globale Märkte, nationale Politik und regionale Kooperation*, Baden-Baden: Nomos.

Schott, Jeffrey J. (2001a), *Prospects for Free Trade in the Americas*, Washington, DC: Institute for International Economics.

Schott, J. J. (2001b), 'Understanding US Trade Policy: Circa 2001', *Institute for International Economics*, www.iie.com/papers.

Schott, J. J. (2002), 'US Trade Policy: Method to the Madness', *Institute for International Economics*, http://www.iie/papers.

Schott, J. J. and G. C. Hufbauer (1999), 'Whither the Free Trade Area of the Americas?', *Institute for International Economics*, Washington, DC, www.iie.com/papers.

Scott, Allen J. (1998), *Regions and the World Economy*, Oxford University Press.

Selcher, W. A. (1999), 'The Politics of Decentralized Federalism, National Diversification, and Regionalism in Brazil', *Journal of Interamerican Studies and World Affairs*, 40 (4), 25-50.

Siebert, H. (1998), 'Disziplinierung der nationalen Wirtschaftspolitik durch internationale Kapitalmobilität', in Dieter Duwendag (Hrsg.), *Finanzmärkte im Spannungsfeld von Globalisierung, Regulierung und Geldpolitik, Schriften des Vereins für Sozialpolitik*, Bd. 261, Berlin: Duncker & Humblodt, 41–67.

Smith, Clint E. (2000), *Inevitable Partnership, Understanding Mexico–U.S. Relations*, Boulder: Lynne Rienner Publishers.

Smith, Peter H. (1993), *The Challenge of Integration: Europe and the Americas*, New Brunswick, NJ: Transaction Publishers.

Soares de Lima, M. R. (1999), 'Brazil's Alternative Vision', in Gordon Mace, Louis Bélanger and Contributors, *The Americas in Transition, The Contours of Regionalism*, Boulder and London, Lynne Rienner Publishers, 133–151.

Solimano, A. (2001), 'International Migration and the Global Economic Order: An Overview', *The World Bank, Globalization Working Papers 2720*, November.

Stalker, P. (2000), 'Workers Without Frontiers: The Impact of Globalization on International Migration', *International Labour Organisation*, Geneva.

Stein, Stanley and Barbara Stein (1970), *The Colonial Heritage of Latin America: Essays on Economic Dependence in Perspective*, New York: Oxford University Press.

Summers, L. H. (1999), 'Reflections on Managing Global Integration', Distinguished Lecture on Economics in Government, *Journal of Economic Perspectives*, **13** (2), Spring, 3–18.

Syrquin, Moshe and Hollis B. Chenery (1989), *Patterns of Development 1950–83*, Washington, DC: The World Bank.

Taccone, Juan J. and Uziel Nogueira, (2001), *Mercosur Report 2000–2001*, INTAL, Buenos Aires.

Tavares de Aranjo jr., J., C. Macario and K. Steinfelt (2001), 'Antidumping in the Americas', *Serie comercio internacional, Division of Integration and International Trade*, ECLAC, Santiago de Chile, March.

Ten Kate, A. (1992), 'Trade Liberalization and Economic Stabilization in Mexico: Lessons of Experience', *World Development*, **20**, May, 659–672.

The World Bank (1993), *The East Asian Miracle, Economic Growth and Public Policy*, Washington, DC: Oxford University Press.

The World Bank (2002a), *Globalization, Growth, and Poverty*, A World Bank Policy Research Report, Washington, DC: Oxford University Press.

The World Bank (2002b), *Trade Blocks*, Washington, DC: Oxford University Press.

Thorbecke, W. (2000), 'A Public Choice Perspective on the Globalizing of America', in Thomas L. Brewer and Gavin Boyd, *Globalizing America, The USA in World Integration*, Cheltenham, UK and Northampton, MA, USA, 83–97.

Tuchlin, Joseph S. and Ralph H. Espach (eds), *Latin America in the New International System*, Boulder and London: Lynne Rienner Publishers.

Tuong, H. D. and A. Yeats (1980), 'On the Relation Between Income Levels, Industrialization and the Future Composition of Developing Countries Exports', *Development and Change*, **11**, 531–544.

United Nations Centre on Transnational Corporations (UNCTC) (1988), *Transnational Corporations in World Development*, New York.

United Nations Conference on Trade and Development (UNCTAD) (2000), *World Investment Report 2000*, New York and Geneva.

UNCTAD (2000), *World Investment Report 2000*, New York and Geneva.

UNCTAD (2001), *World Investment Report 2001*, New York and Geneva.

UNCTAD (2002a), *World Investment Report 2002*, New York and Geneva.

UNCTAD (2002b), *UNCTAD Handbook of Statistics*, New York and Geneva.

United States Department of Commerce, *Economic Indicators*, www. EconomicIndicators.gov.

United States International Trade Commission (USITC) (1999), *Industry & Trade Summary, Apparel,* Publication 3169, Washington, DC, March.

USITC (2001), *Industry Trade and Technology Review,* July.

USITC (2002), *Industry & Trade Summary, Motor Vehicles,* Publication 3545, Washington, DC, September.

United States Trade Representative (USTR) (1999a), *1999 Trade Policy Agenda and 1998 Annual Report of the President of the United States on the Trade Agreements Program,* www.ustr.gov

USTR (1999b), *Fifth Annual Report to Congress Regarding the Impact of the North American Free Trade Agreement upon U.S. Automotive Trade with Mexico,* www.ustr.gov/reports.

USTR (2000), 'Argentina', *Foreign Trade Barriers Report,* www.ustr.gov.

USTR (2001a), *The President's 2000 Annual Report on the Trade Agreements Program,* www.ustr.gov.

USTR (2001b), *Fourth Report to Congress on the Operation of the Caribbean Basin Economic Recovery Act,* December, www.ustr.gov.

USTR (2002a), *2002 Trade Policy Agenda and 2001 Annual Report of the President of the United States on the Trade Agreements Program,* www.ustr.gov/reports.

USTR (2002b), 'The Economic Effects of Significant U.S. Import Restraints', Third Update 2002, *Investigation No. 332–325, Publication 3519,* June, www.ustr.gov.

USTR (2002c), 'The Year in Trade 2001, Operation of the Trade Agreements Program', *53rd Report, Publication 3510,* May, www.ustr.gov.

USTR (2002d), 'NAFTA at Eight, A Foundation for Economic Growth', www.ustr.gov.

USTR (2003), *2003 Trade Policy Agenda and 2002 Annual Report of the President of the United States on the Trade Agreements Program,* www.ustr.gov/reports.

Ursprung, H. (2000), 'Die Modellierung endogener Handelspolitik: The Rake's Progress', *Aussenwirtschaft,* **55** (1), 85–119.

Venables, A. J. (1999), 'Regional Integration Agreements. A Force for Convergence or Divergence?', *Policy Research Working Paper 2260,* Washington, DC: World Bank.

Venables, A. J. and A. Smith (1986), 'Trade and Industrial Policy under Imperfect Competition', *Economic Policy,* **2** (3), 622–672.

Vernon, R. E. (1966), 'International Investment and International Trade in the Product Cycle', *The Quarterly Journal of Economics,* **80** (2), 190–207.

Vernon, Raymond E. (1971), *Sovereignty at Bay: The Multinational Spread of U.S. Enterprises,* London: Pelican.

Viner, J. (1948), 'Power Versus Plenty as Objectives of Foreign Policy in the Seventeenth and Eighteenth Centuries', *World Politics*, **1** (1), 1–29.

Viner, J. (1950), *The Customs Union Issue*, New York: Carnegie Endowment for International Peace.

Wallace, William (1990), *The Transformation of Western Europe*, London: Pinter.

Watkins, R. (2001), 'Production-Sharing Update: Developments in 2000', *Industry Trade and Technology Review*, USITC, July, 11–23.

Weber, Max (1950), *The Protestant Ethic and the Spirit of Capitalism*, New York: Scribner's.

Weintraub, Sidney (1994), *NAFTA. What Comes Next?*, The Washington Papers, The Center for Strategic and International Studies, Washington, DC, Westport and London: Praeger.

Weintraub, S. (1997), 'U.S.–Latin American Economic Relations', *Journal of Interamerican Studies and World Affairs*, **39** (1), 59–69.

Weintraub, S. (2004), 'Potential for Hemispheric Regional Integration', in Sidney Weintraub, Alan M. Rugman and Gavin Boyd (eds), *Free Trade in the Americas*, Cheltenham, UK and Northampton, MA, USA: Edward Elgar, forthcoming.

Wellisz, S. and J. Wilson (1998), 'Lobbying and Tariff Formation: A Deadweight Loss Consideration', *Journal of International Economics*, **20**, 367–375.

Williamson, John (2003), 'Lula's Brazil', *Foreign Affairs*, **82** (1), 105–113.

Winters, A. (2000), 'Regionalism and Multilateralism in the Twenty-First Century', *IDB Regional Policy Dialogue*, Base Documents, www.iadb.org.

Won, C. and A. L. Winters (2002), 'How Regional Blocks Affect Excluded Countries: The Price Effects of Mercosur', *The American Economic Review*, **92** (4), 889–904.

Wonnecott, R. J. (2000), 'Regional Trade Agreements', in Thomas L. Brewer and Gavin Boyd (eds), *Globalizing America, The USA in World Integration*, Cheltenham, UK and Northampton, MA, USA: Edward Elgar, 211–241.

Wonnecott, P. and R. Wonnecott (1992), 'The Customs Union Issue Reopened', *The World Economy*, **60** (2), 119–135.

World Trade Organization (WTO) (1998), *Annual Report*, Geneva.

WTO (1999), *Trade and the Environment*, Special Studies 4, Geneva.

Wyatt-Walter, A. (1997), 'Regionalism, Globalization, and World Economic Order', in Louise Fawcett and Andrew Hurrell (eds), *Regionalism in World Politics*, Oxford: University Press, 74–121.

Yeats, A. (1989), 'Developing Countries' Exports of Manufactures: Past and Future Implications of Shifting Patterns of Comparative Advantages', *The Developing Economies*, **27** (2), 109–145.

Yeats, A. (1998), 'Does Mercosur's Trade Performance Raise Concerns about the Effects of Regional Trade Arrangements?', *The World Bank Economic Review*, **12** (1), 1–28.

Index